Music Online

ALTERNATIVE

MUSIC

blues

Easy Listening

LATIN

Pop & Rock

Country

Frank Lenk

Online

electronic

CLASSICAL

and more . . .

Macmillan Canada
Toronto

First published in Canada in 2000 by
Macmillan Canada, an imprint of CDG Books Canada

Canadian Cataloguing in Publication Data

Lenk, Frank, 1954–
    Music online

ISBN 0-7715-7700-1

1. Music – Computer network resources.   I. Title.

ML74.7.L56 2000   O25.06'78   C00-930654-4

This book is available at special discounts for bulk purchases by your group or organization for sales promotions, premiums, fundraising and seminars. For details, contact: CDG Books Canada Inc., 99 Yorkville Avenue, Suite 400, Toronto, ON, M5R 3K5.

1 2 3 4 5 TRANS–B–G 04 03 02 01 00

Cover and text design by Gord Robertson

Macmillan Canada
An imprint of CDG Books Canada Inc.
Toronto

Printed in Canada

Acknowledgements

A number of people helped make this book happen.

Above all, I'd like to express my gratitude to everyone at CDG Books Canada, especially to President and Publisher Robert Harris, for getting behind this concept so whole-heartedly. Thanks are also due to Senior Editor Jill Lambert and to Vice-President of Sales Jennifer Smith, for helping to move the book forward, and to Jamie Broadhurst for getting out there and promoting the heck out of it.

Special thanks must go to Andrew Winton, Associate Editor, whose tolerant good-nature encouraged me through the grueling deadlines (and beyond!), and whose understanding of the subject matter constantly challenged me to dig deeper.

Thanks also to the people who worked behind the scenes: Rebecca Conolly, Production Editor, who ensured that things stayed on track and came out right in the end; Liba Berry, whose lucid and consistent copyedits have been a major factor in the ultimate readability of this book; and Amber Wallace, proofreader, for cleaning up what the rest of us missed.

My appreciation also goes to three lawyers who did their very generous best to help me understand the inner mysteries of copyright: Robert S. Schwartz, with McDermott, Will & Emery, in Washington, DC, Howard P. Knopf, with Shapiro, Cohen, in Ottawa, and Michael A. Geist, Professor at University of Ottawa Law School.

Massive personal thanks go to Beverley Slopen, the kind of agent every writer hopes to work with, but despairs of finding. You not only made this project happen, but made it happen smoothly, efficiently and gracefully.

A very special word of gratitude to Gordon Brockhouse, editor, journalist and true professional, from whom I've learned a lot about this business over the years, and who provided the original nudge that turned Music Online from a personal pastime into a marketable concept.

Most important of all, thanks to my wife Sú Allison-Lenk, who shared equally in the burden of creating this book, and without whom it wouldn't have been worth doing.

And finally, a quick but very grateful tip of the hat to Tzuriel, Bongripper, redbeard, Skankweed and the rest, whose unstinting uploads made sure that the music never stopped.

Contents

1   **What is Music Online?**   1

What's Going On?   3
What is the Internet?   5
What is Digital Music?   8
What is MP3?   14
What are the Alternatives to MP3?   28
What is Desktop Audio?   37

2   **Getting It**   39

Types of Transfers   40
Clients and Servers   41
World Wide Web: Downloads   43
World Wide Web: Purchases   47
Streaming Music   56
Usenet   70
Other Internet Protocols   95
Home Recording   99
Conclusion   107

3   **Playing It**   109

Hardware   110
Software   121

Accessories   132
Conclusion   138

4   Processing It   139

A Bit of History   140
Types of Processing   142
Sound-Editing Basics   145
Representing Sound   147
Sound Editors   150
Basic Editing Tasks   157
Cleaning Up Your Sound   168
Conclusion   180

5   Storing It   183

Compressed Audio Encoders   184
CD Recordable Hardware   204
CD Recordable Software   209
How CD-Rs Fail   214
Tracking Your Collection   220
Conclusion   230

6   Commercializing It   231

You and Your Rights   231
The Music Industry   241
What Happens Next?   248
Intellectual Property Revisited   249
The Business of Music   252
The Best Is Yet to Come!   254

Appendix:
A Music Online Internet Directory   255

Index   275

1
———

What is Music Online?

This chapter introduces some of the key concepts that you'll need to know about to understand what's going on with digital music:

- How music is converted from analog to digital form.
- What compression is all about, and MP3, the most popular way of compressing music.
- The alternatives to MP3, which may be less well known at the moment, but could be very significant in the future.

A RE YOU A MUSIC FAN? If you've picked up this book, I'm assuming you must be. Great! So am I. This is an exciting time for us. The music we love, whatever genre it may fall into, is becoming dramatically more accessible. We're going to hear more of our favourite performers, and hear them more clearly than we ever thought possible.

We're also going to discover new musical artists, and communicate with them in a whole new way—or maybe in a very old way that we've all but forgotten since the invention of the phonograph.

We've become convinced, over the last hundred years or so, that music is something that comes from a factory. It's a product, and as such, needs to be packaged, promoted and, ultimately, mass-produced. But there was a simpler time, when everyone made at least a little music. Music was a form of communication, not just between performer and audience, but also back again. *Interactive.* Ironically, in today's age of interactivity, that element has been largely forgotten.

Today, we get our music from factories, just like our beer and our hamburgers. Maybe that's okay. Factories can do some amazing things, and there's certainly something to be said for standardization and commercial polish. But that doesn't mean we have to give up the homemade burger, and the microbrewed beer—nor our homegrown, face-to-face, all-natural, no-preservatives-or-artificial-colourants . . . *music.*

Commercial music has achieved great things, and if you're enjoying it (or making money from it!), fear not, it's not going away. As technology moves ahead, experience teaches us that nothing is lost. TV didn't wipe out radio—it opened up an entirely new mode of entertainment and communication. Cars didn't make horses extinct—they freed them from routine drudgery, to be loved and appreciated and enjoyed by those individuals who felt that particular calling.

Mass-produced recordings didn't wipe out "genuine" music, either, even though at times it may have seemed so. Music is an incredibly diverse art form. In its essence, it's just *sound*—vibrations in the air that stimulate our inner ear and tickle the pleasure centres in our brain. It's also *rhythm*—the fundamental time-keeping pulse beat of the world around us. Music is in *us*—all of us, in one way or another.

It's inevitable then that any new development in communication technology would be exploited to spread music a little farther and a little faster than before. The only real surprise is that we are surprised at all—it's so inevitable, and it's happened so often before.

So as our weird and wired world rolls forward into the 21st century, music is going *online.*

What's Going On?

Music online. That's a nice glib thing to say, but what does it mean?

It means a lot of different things. It means so many things, that the word *revolution* is hardly strong enough to describe the scope and magnitude of the changes that are taking place. Music online is going to transform the world of music, the performing arts, the entertainment industry, our economic models, and even such fundamentals as the ideas of profit and property.

On top of all that, music online is only the first phase of a larger change—a precursor to video online, virtual reality, telepresence (the next best thing to being there), video telephones, and a bunch of other things that previously existed only in fantasy.

Music online will mean something to all of us, but different things to each of us. This book has been written as a primer for the average, moderately computer-literate consumer—a beginner's guide to the entertainment revolution.

You may already have an idea what you want from music online, and this book will help you find it. But this field is so large—already!—and so fast-moving, that you're inevitably going to discover more than you ever bargained for. That's why the approach has been to lay a foundation, to introduce all the basic tools that you'll need to keep pace with the whirlwind and extract whatever benefits most appeal to you.

Those benefits are going to fall into a number of categories (although it wouldn't be too surprising if the number of categories itself continued to grow). Here are a few we can identify today, roughly in order from the simplest and most mundane to the most exotic and exciting:

- **Easier shopping.** There's a lot of talk about "e-commerce," or electronic retailing, and it's much more than just hype. It's going to get dramatically easier to shop for music in its established, manufactured guises—CDs, tapes, and even LPs. Whatever music you most enjoy, you're going to be able to hear more of it and spend less time and effort tracking it down and buying it.

- **Downloadable purchases.** Electronic retailing is going to have the most remarkable impact in fields such as music, where the product itself consists of information, and hence can be delivered electronically. Major companies are already putting the machinery in place to let you buy your music electronically, doing away with the plastic media we've almost come to think of as some solid form of music.

- **Digital radio.** Don't like the top radio stations in your hometown? No problem. Music "broadcasting" just went global. Tune in Internet "stations" that play what *you* like, and that even allow you to customize the playlist!

- **Flexible storage.** Buy an album once, play it anywhere in your house, once you've got it on your home network. Digital storage of music allows you more control over how and where you play your music. There are still some copyright issues to be worked out, but the technology is ready.

- **Reference information.** Database sites offer enormous resources of background information. Want to know how many operas Beethoven wrote? (The answer is one, *Fidelio*, but he wrote four overtures for it.)

- **Performer interaction.** Most musicians already have Web sites, where you can get information about their music and their upcoming projects. These sites will become more and more interactive, allowing fans to get closer to musicians, who have lately been forced to hide behind bodyguards and barbed wire.

- **Fan communities.** Similarly, fans are already using the Internet to get in touch with each other, for exchange of opinion, information and, yes, even music. (Many bands allow free trading of their music, and are being rewarded by a fanatically devoted fan community.)

This book will give you the information you need to get involved in this fast-moving new world of digital audio—digital *desktop* audio. Just as desktop publishing brought typography and page layout within reach of any computer user, desktop audio is going to make you your own recording engineer. It's not as hard as it sounds, and it's lots of fun.

What is the Internet?

(. . . or Who Needs a Superhighway when You're Already There?)

If you're a seasoned Net surfer, skip to the next section. Otherwise, press on. A bit of background will definitely make the whole techno-logical explosion a lot easier to understand.

Of course, this book is *not* a basic manual on how to surf the In-ternet, or hook up a modem, or troubleshoot your network settings. There are lots of those already. But even if you've been cruising around the Net for years, many parts of it may still be a mystery to you. The Internet is a very big place, and some of the parts we'll be visiting are not all that well known yet.

Despite its being such a hot topic of conversation these days, most people probably don't have a clear idea of just exactly what the Internet *is*, and how it works. These are not mere academic ques-tions—they're key issues in the distribution of digital music and the ongoing development of music online in general.

First, a tiny bit of history.

As most everybody has heard by now, the Internet was born in the early 1970s as a project of the U.S. military. The idea was to build a communications system that could survive nuclear attack. The designers felt, quite wisely, that the surest way to achieve maximum reliability would be through *redundancy*—ensuring that every signal has as many ways as possible of getting from source to destination. As a result, the Internet really was spun like a web—a complex network of interconnections that has now literally enveloped the globe.

Communication across this net was based on a concept known as *packet switching*, which is in marked contrast to the civilian telephone system and its *circuit switching*. This may sound mysterious, but it's very easy to explain. When you call up Aunt Millie in Medicine Hat, the phone company (or companies) throw a bunch of switches that join long wires into a direct path—a *circuit*—between you and her. It's very much like the old two-cans-and-a-string communications system you tried when you were a kid. (Some of the links may be via satellite rather than by actual wire, but the principle is the same.)

On the Internet, this kind of one-to-one connection never happens. The Internet really is a net, and all points (*nodes*) are always connected to each other in many ways. If you send a long e-mail to Aunt Millie over the Internet, it's free to bounce around like the ball in a Pachinko machine. At each node, where connections cross, a *router* examines the address information on the electronic "envelope" and decides where to send it. The beauty of this is that no matter how much of the web you wipe out, there's almost certainly going to be some roundabout way for that message to get to Aunt Millie. As you can see, this approach provides superb *reliability*. The downside is that there's no guarantee of *performance* whatsoever.

Longer messages are broken into parts (*packets)* and each packet is likely to travel via a different route. Again, this virtually guarantees that the information is going to get through. However, each piece may take a different length of time to arrive. With a text message, such as an e-mail, this hardly matters; all the pieces get reassembled before the message is delivered. If any pieces are a few seconds, or even a few hours, late, the rest can wait at the electronic post office (*mail server*) until they catch up.

But when it comes to music, things go wrong in several ways. Most obviously, if you try to play a song over the Internet, you may hear the end before the beginning, which would probably not sound quite right.

Of course, you can do the same thing as with the e-mail message—hold the first parts to arrive until they're joined by the last parts, and then play the whole thing. That approach is actually being taken currently by real commercial music-broadcasting systems; the Real Networks system, for example. The software accumulates (*buffers*) up to about a minute's worth of audio, then starts to play. But why just one minute and not the whole song?

This brings us to the second problem. *Bulk.* As data goes, music is vastly bulkier than text e-mail. If not correctly managed, it tends to choke up Internet connections and clog up your computer. Internet-based music software is forced to make a tricky trade-off, hoping that the incoming music will never get more than about a minute behind what you're hearing. Unfortunately, it often does get behind, and you end up hearing a pause, or hiccup (*glitch*).

Then there's a third problem, which has to do not with moving data, but storing data. The Internet is essentially a *distributed* system, a network of connections with various kinds of hardware resources scattered all over it, like dewdrops on a cobweb at sunrise. While nobody owns the network as a whole, each piece of it is owned by *somebody*. When it comes to huge quantities of music data, one question becomes quite pressing. Where do you *put* all those gigabytes? Better yet, once you've put them there, *who owns them?*

The fact is that information on the Net exists in a sort of jurisdictional limbo. As we saw earlier, it may be spread all over the place—a packet here, a packet there, a few more en route, and a bunch of packets stored in Aunt Millie's mailbox waiting for the others to arrive. If my data is on your wire, or passing through your router, or stored on your mail server, is it okay for you to look at it? Enjoy it? *Copy* it? Give copies to all your friends?

There was a case written up a few years ago, of someone who mailed a camera across Canada. When the film it contained was processed, it had photos of strangers on it. Turns out some rambunctious postal employees had, at some point along the route, taken snaps of each other clowning around. Nobody doubted that this was a naughty thing to do, since, as we all know, the mail is sacred. But how sacred is e-mail? How sacred is stuff that can be read by anybody and copied—a million million times—without making a mark on the original?

That's just the bare beginning of a very long and controversial story, which we'll deal with in some detail in Chapter 6. As a consumer, you need to know your rights. What can you copy, what can't you copy, and when can't you copy it? Who decides, and on what basis?

There's been a lot of publicity around the idea that music "piracy" is rife on the Internet. But what's the reality? If everybody's doing it, does that mean it's *okay* or even *safe*? Or is letting your kids have free run of your computer and Internet connection eventually going to land you in the pokey?

There are lots of other issues that arise out of the technological phenomenon we've dubbed the Internet. Some are beyond the scope of this book, and, indeed, have yet to be properly explored in any book. But the more practical issues will be dealt with, in order as they come up. So will the many other technical details you'll need to have at least a working knowledge of. Don't worry—there's nothing in this book that requires a Ph.D. But if you're the sort of person who enjoys having at least an inkling of how the world around you works, you may find that a lot of the information contained here is quite interesting, not to mention useful, when it comes to accessing, playing, storing and manipulating digital music.

Which, as it happens, is the subject of the next section.

What is Digital Music?

There are a lot of misconceptions about just what digital music actually is. For example, many people who should know better still cling to the notion that "digitized" music is somehow robbed of its life and soul, or sounds worse than "genuine" (*analog*) music.

We'll see that, while there are definite limitations on digital reproduction of music, they are a lot less severe than the equally real limitations on the reproduction of music using more traditional methods.

Since the human ear is not infinitely accurate, all audio reproduction is a matter of carefully chosen compromises. A lot of this book deals with how to choose those compromises to suit your own ear and your own musical tastes.

> **Digital.** Information represented by discrete numeric values. The opposite of *analog*. For example, a paint-by-numbers picture describes colour digitally by assigning a different number to each of its colours. The drawback is that you can only have as many colours as you have numbers.

Analog. Composed of smoothly varying values. The opposite of *digital*. For example, we think of a rainbow as being
composed of certain specific colours—red, orange, yellow,
green, blue, indigo, and violet. Actually, there are a virtually in-
finite number of shades of orange in between red and yellow.

One of the most important factors, often left out of the reckoning
by serious audiophiles, is *money*. Digital recording technology can
deliver an amazing bang for bare-minimum bucks. And the bang-to-
buck ratio continues to become more and more advantageous as personal computers enter the mix.

Most of the technology we'll be concerned with in this book de-
rives from the development of the audio CD, or compact disc. This
was the first form of digital audio recording that became widely
available to consumers, and it established the basic principles that
now define the field of music online.

The CD as we know it today was developed by Sony and Philips
in the early 1980s as a way of delivering music. However, by a combination of good luck and good planning, a corresponding standard—
CD-ROM—was almost immediately created, taking advantage of
the same technology to store computer data. Even more remarkable,
this new data standard was made compatible with the audio standard, so that computers could read CD-audio discs, and CD-audio
information could be combined with computer data for what
quickly became known as "multimedia" applications.

Ironically, computers originally borrowed CD technology from
the consumer electronics business. Now, with the advent of music
online and desktop audio, they've come full circle, bringing a revolution in audio back to consumer electronics.

CD. Short for Compact Disc. A standard format for
recorded music that stores digitized information as a
series of tiny pits on a metallic foil, protected by a layer of
laminated plastic. Like an LP record, an audio CD has a single spiral track, which winds around the surface. However,
unlike records, CDs are recorded from the center *outward*.

CD-ROM. Short for Compact Disc Read-Only Memory. A standard format for storing computer data, physically identical to an audio CD and capable of being manufactured on the same equipment. However, where an audio CD stores information as a continuous stream of *bits*, CD-ROMs contain a directory catalogue that allows specific pieces of information—such as data files—to be quickly retrieved from any part of the disc.

The principle behind the CD is simple. It's also fundamental to everything else in this book, so if you're not entirely clear on this point, read on.

Music—in fact, all sound—consists of waves. This is *analog* information—a signal that varies smoothly and continuously in volume and pitch (*amplitude* and *frequency*).

A traditional vinyl record directly captures sound waves as ripples in a piece of plastic. The waves are re-created by running a sensitive stylus over those plastic ripples, converting the resulting vibrations into electricity, then amplifying the electricity and using it to vibrate the cone of a speaker. The speaker pushes the air inside it in such a way as to reproduce the original sound wave, more or less.

Digital music converts sound waves into numbers, which can then be stored in several ways. To play the music, a relatively simple processor called a D/A (Digital to Analog) converter interprets the numbers and rebuilds the original waveform. This is passed to an amplifier, and then to speakers, just as with a vinyl record.

The beauty of the digital approach is that the numbers can be in *binary* (base-two) form, represented entirely by combinations of the two values 0 and 1. That means that to read back one bit (*bi*nary dig*it*) of information, you need only recognize whether it's 0 or 1—on or off, black or white. The reading mechanism can be simple and the potential for error is tiny, compared to the enormous complexity of the needle following a finely etched plastic surface and generating a minute current of electricity.

That's why we store the music digitally. Now here's how. It's a simple trick, about on an intellectual par with using a Captain Midnight decoder ring. Picture a graph that shows a sound wave (see Figure 1.1). The vertical axis is volume (more accurately, *amplitude*). The horizontal axis is time. You can see that the wave gets louder and softer over time. To convert this smoothly curved line into numbers, we *sample* it, that is, we store the specific height value of the curve wherever it crosses one of the time divisions on our graph.

How often we sample is defined as the *sample rate*. In the case of the audio CD, the sample rate is arbitrarily set to 44.1 Kilohertz—44,100 times per second.

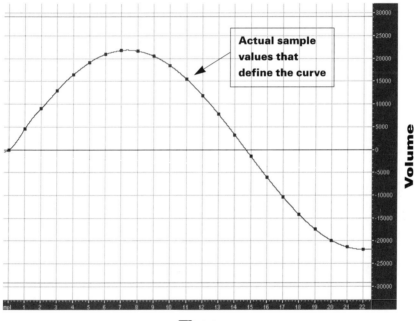

Figure 1.1 How music is converted to numbers

Each time we sample the wave, we record its vertical distance from the horizontal axis of our graph. This measurement is obviously just a number. We save the number, then check the next sample. Over and over and over.

Obviously, what results is a stream of numbers. That stream of numbers can later be used to rebuild the original sound wave, much like a connect-the-dots picture. We read all the numbers and plot them as dots on the graph. Then we use some fairly simple electronics to draw the curve through those points.

There's only one problem. No matter how often you sample the height of the curve, you are left wondering what the height actually was in between those times. It's tempting to suppose that if one sample was 4 and the next was 6, the height halfway in between must have been 5—but that's just a guess. The curve could have jumped up to 236 and back down again, for all we know.

The more samples you take, the less doubt there is. It's exactly like setting the resolution on your scanner, or digital camera. If a picture has a million individual dots (*pixels*), it's going to capture a lot more of the original detail than a similar picture with only half a million pixels.

The sampling rate used on audio CDs is based on the responsiveness of the human ear. The highest pitched sounds we can hear are just over 20 kilohertz—that is, sounds produced by a wave that has about 20,000 peaks in each second. CDs sample that worst-case wave 44,100 times per second, which is enough to record the height once for each peak and valley, but not to get any further information about the *shape* of the curve.

When the tone is played back, the best we can do is assume it's a pure *sine wave* of that particular frequency—any further detail is lost. (Any deviation from a sine wave can actually be interpreted as the presence of higher frequencies within the wave, and as we've shown, nothing above about 20 Kilohertz is captured on CD.) It turns out that for most purposes, that's good enough. Most people can barely hear a sound of this frequency at all, so who cares whether it's being reproduced all that accurately? Especially if all those big middle tones and rumbling bass notes are being reproduced with superb accuracy.

Sine wave. The simplest form of sound wave, representing a clear, pure tone of one specific frequency. So called because the shape of the curve corresponds to a graph of the sine function from trigonometry. The sine wave is the building block of sounds, the "atom" that all sound is composed of. All sound can be represented as a

combination of sine waves; the more complex or noisy the sound, the more sine waves it contains.

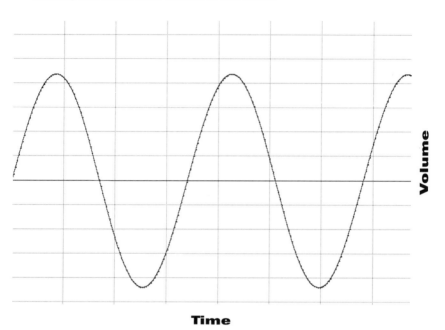

Time

Figure 1.2 A sine wave

Well, there is a minor problem. Although we can't actually distinguish those really high-pitched sounds, we do perceive them at a less conscious level. They carry a lot of what we would call the *ambience* of the sound—that feeling of *space* produced by subtle echoes off the walls or around obstacles that may block part of the sound from reaching us.

So the quest for really perfect audio goes on. Meanwhile, the CD digital format is awfully good. It reproduces high-pitched sounds better than any analog audio tape, and low, low bass sounds far better than vinyl records. Because it's recorded digitally, as a series of binary numbers, digital audio is not subject to interference, or noise, or distortion in the process of being stored. And it's resistant to damage. It takes a really major scratch on your CD to make the laser jump off the data track, and unless that happens, the loss in sound quality is virtually nil.

What Is MP3?

So we've established that digital recording, in the form of the audio CD, is a great thing. But that revolution occurred more than a dozen years ago. The current digital audio revolution was touched off when CD audio in turn came together with two other digital technologies—the Internet and digital compression.

We talked about the Internet earlier in this chapter. Now let's talk about compression. Then we'll be ready to get down to specifics.

The key form of compression that really unleashed the current wave of digital music distribution is known as *MP3*. Just understanding this name takes a bit of study. However, it's rather an interesting story, going back almost a hundred years.

First, let's look at what MP3 *is* and what it *does*.

MP3. Short for MPEG-1 Layer III (a designation explained later in the chapter). MP3 is an international standard for compressing audio data. It defines both the software techniques used to discard unneeded information in order to make the data smaller, as well as the format in which the data is stored, so that any MP3 player can play any MP3 file.

Image Compression

Ten years ago, the Internet was all about text. If you were lucky enough to be online at all, you used a selection of text-based programs. With the advent of "fast" 28.8 kbps (kilobits of data per second) modems, the Internet went graphical. The World Wide Web displaced Gopher and other information publishing tools, and lured users with pages that lavishly mixed text and images.

Graphic images use storage much more voraciously than text, and over a modem connection, this difference really matters. For example, look at this page. To cover the page completely requires just one or two kilobytes' worth of text. But a full-page graphic is likely to bulk a thousand times larger, up to dozens of *mega*bytes. The reason for this difference is that most of the information defining text characters is not stored in the text itself, but elsewhere, in font files or layout files. A lot of this information can be reused by many pages, for a considerable savings.

Kilobyte. 1,024 bytes.

Megabyte. 1,024 kilobytes.

Gigabyte. 1,024 megabytes.

A graphic image is stored more simply, as an array, or grid, of tiny dots (*pixels*). For a black-and-white image, each dot takes exactly one bit, no more, no less. No space saving is possible; it takes millions of dots to fill a typeset page.

Enter compression: a way of squashing data to make it use less storage space. Most data has a lot of "air" in it that can be squeezed out. For example, it's quicker to write the word *googol* than the number it names: 1 followed by 100 zeros, or 10^{100}. (Note that the same number is represented three different ways in this sentence, each taking up a different amount of space on the page.)

There are as many ways of compressing data as there are types of data. We've just seen one, in the case of text—by removing repetitive information. In the case of graphic images, it's not quite so obvious, but the same basic principle can be applied. We can't break the image into previously defined pieces, as we can an English-language word, since we have no idea what kind of image it might be. Instead, we search through the image data and see if we can find some bits that turn up over and over. We can replace all of these pieces with a single, much shorter code.

It's like a digital IOU. Suppose we search the image data and find 1,000 zeros in a row. We can insert a code, any code we like, as long as we remember that it means "IOU 1,000 zeros." You can get as clever as you like with this kind of thing. For example, you can be very sneaky about what codes you use. If an image contains lots of ones, for example, you might assign codes to those combinations first, and not worry so much about the zeros.

This is the origin of the widely used GIF and JPG image files that today litter the World Wide Web. These images are compressed by being coded internally, so that repetitive information is stored only once. The size reduction can be astounding. JPG images are routinely compressed by a factor of 100 to 1—say, from 5 megabytes down to 50 kilobytes. This means they'll load 100 times faster when your Web browser tries to display the page.

Audio Compression

Now we come to music. Even with the latest 56 kbps modems, music is just too huge to contemplate moving around over the Internet. A single three-minute pop song takes up more storage than the text of a small encyclopedia, and takes hours to transfer using the fastest telephone (modem) connection. The text of this book was only about 1 megabyte in size, but a tape of me reading it would run into many *giga*bytes.

Again, the reason is that digitally recorded sound is very much like a graphic image. It's stored as an array of data points, and it takes 44,100 points, no more, no less, to represent one second of sound.

And again, the solution is compression. But in this case, it's even more difficult to decide what can be compressed. Digitized sound data doesn't have the obvious patterns that you find in image data.

Sound obviously does have patterns. They're just harder to find. It turns out, however, that even by hunting very carefully for patterns, music won't compress by much more than about one-third. Increasingly clever processing techniques may eventually improve on this, but not dramatically. And music files are so bulky to begin with that this just isn't enough savings.

Enter *lossy* compression. In this case, the compression routine not only looks for duplicated information that can be eliminated, it actually looks for unnecessary data and discards it entirely. Again, we can see the parallel with images. Suppose you have a photo of a horse standing in a bright, sunlit field. In the foreground, there's a barn, with its doors standing open. What you can see of the inside of the barn is very dark by comparison with the rest of the scene. You can make out a few vague outlines of objects within, but only barely.

An image compressor might look at that scene and find that most of the detail within the barn doors can be removed. Dazzled by the bright, sunny landscape, our eyes really don't expect to see anything inside the barn. What's more, the camera that recorded the scene probably didn't see much in there either, and recorded a bunch of spurious false detail, or misleading partial detail, in there. Discarding this rubbish may actually make the image look better. It certainly won't detract from the usefulness of the image, which, after all, is a picture of a horse.

This is roughly how JPG images work. Examine one closely sometime, and magnify it if you have the software to do it. The compression *algorithm* is really very wily about what to keep and what to throw away. If you have a program that can do JPG compression, such as Corel PhotoPaint, Adobe PhotoShop, or ACD Systems' ACDSee, try compressing an image more and more, until you can see it start to break up. This is a good way to get a feel for how this type of compression works.

> **Algorithm.** A set of instructions for doing a particular job, like a recipe, or the exercises in this book. In software, an algorithm is the series of steps a program takes to accomplish a particular task.

Number Crunching

MP3 is just a standardized format used for storing audio data, just as TIF, JPG and GIF are used for storing images, and DOC and TXT for storing text. The idea of any standard data format is that once it's defined and accepted, you can count on many different hardware and software products being compatible with it. Thus, almost any graphics product will be happy to deal with a JPG image, and any word processor can open a TXT file.

What makes MP3 files more interesting than other audio formats is that they're compressed with amazing efficiency. As we saw in the previous section, it's not easy to compress audio information, compared to, say, text or graphics. With the advent of MP3, however, computer users had access to a technology that could compress audio files to as little as one one-hundredth of their original size—and do so in a standardized way that quickly came to be recognized by most audio-related software and devices.

> MP3 files on the PC are distinguished by the *extension* .MP3. That is, the very last part of the file name is ".mp3." (Capitalization doesn't matter.) The icon you see for these files in Windows will depend on the software that's currently associated with them. Since there are many programs that play MP3 files, the icon you see corresponds to any of these. If you use the WinAmp player, for example, you'll see a diamond with a yellow lightning bolt.

Like JPG image compression, MP3 works on a sliding scale. You can make a sound file just about as small as you like, but it will sound pretty horrible. MP3 is designed to give the best trade-off of file size versus audio quality at a compression ratio of about 10 to 1. That doesn't mean they won't sound better at a lower compression ratio, just that this ratio gives the nicest balance of size versus quality.

In practice, MP3 is generally restricted to a certain range of compression ratios, if not by the underlying technology, then by the available encoding software. However, most popular encoding software will compress files all the way down to about 2 percent of their original size. (Actually 1 percent, since the same software will be glad to reduce a stereo file to mono, further cutting the size by half.)

When it comes to audio, compression is usually measured in terms of *bitrate*—the number of bits of data it takes to play back a second of music. Table 1.1 should make this much clearer. You can see that the optimum compression rate of 10 to 1 corresponds to a bitrate of 128 kilobits of data per second (kbps).

Calculating the CD bitrate

All these compression rates are relative to uncompressed CD audio, which requires 1378 kbps. That number is easily worked out from the digital sampling rate, which, as you may recall, has been arbitrarily fixed at 44,100 samples per second. Equally arbitrarily, each sample point is stored using 16 bits of data (allowing sample values from 0 to 65,536).

Multiplying it out, you get:

16 bits/sample x 44,100 samples/second x 2
   (because the music is in stereo!)
/ 1024 (for kilo) = 1378 kilobits/second
/ 1024 (for mega) = 1.346 megabits/second

This number, and the way we arrived at it, will both be helpful later on, when you start thinking about how much space you can save by compressing music data files, or how much speed you can gain by compressing audio that's broadcast directly over the Internet.

The *Shrunk By* column in the Table 1.1 shows the ratio of the compressed file's size to that of the CD audio file at the bottom. The *Size* column gives the percentage of the original size to which the file has been shrunk. The shaded rows indicate the most popular bitrates favoured by the online community.

Table 1.1: Standard MP3 Compression Rates

Bitrate Kbps	Shrunk By (X)	Size %	Typical Uses	Notes
32	43	2	voice: comedy, radio	usually mono, adequate quality
64	22	5	Voice, radio; old 78 rpm recordings	usually mono; good enough for old material (Note that mono 64 is same quality as stereo 128.)
96	14	7	streaming	moderate quality for undemanding users; relatively little use (Also: the highest bitrate offered by RealAudio codec.)
128	11	9	most music	best balance of compression vs quality; the usual default
160	9	12	higher-quality music; classical	sharper treble sounds, much better clarity, rapidly becoming the default where quality counts
192	7	14	audiophiles	even closer to CD-quality; occasionally used when 160 doesn't seem good enough
256	5	19	audiophiles	excellent quality; increasing use on fast connections (cable, ADSL, etc.); becoming the standard for audiophiles
320	4	23	audio fanatics	slightly better quality than 256, but little used (potential users would rather switch to lossless compression, e.g. SHN)
~1400	1	100	CD audio	most commercial recordings

(Shading indicates the most popular encoding rates.)

The table shows dramatically why MP3 has been so important. Although other types of compressed formats are now available, MP3 was the first widely available compression technology that allowed music files to be shrunk to sizes that are manageable on 56 kbps modems.

Compare the speeds—you'd expect that on a 56 kbps modem you should be able to listen continuously to music compressed at the 32 kbps bitrate. In fact, the results aren't quite so favourable, but MP3 puts you in the ballpark at least.

Lossy versus Lossless Compression

Note that GIF images are compressed using a *lossless* technique, while JPG images are *lossy*. GIF compression retains absolutely all the original detail, while JPG compression discards the least useful detail. Not surprisingly, JPG files can be compressed much, much more tightly than GIF files.

With music, lossless compression can't cut file sizes by all that much; so far, about a 30 percent to 50 percent reduction. As with images, it turned out that to get audio files down to a size that makes sense on today's Internet connections, lossy compression is the only way to go.

The first technology to accomplish this was MP3. Today there are a number of others, but all are based on the same underlying principle: the ability to identify audio data that "doesn't matter." MP3 does this using a technique known as *perceptual coding*.

Perceptual coding tries to discard parts of the signal that are *masked*—essentially inaudible because they're obscured by other parts of the signal. In practices, this means breaking the audio wave into components by frequency, then comparing these against a mathematical "model" of the human auditory system. The encoder then allocates the available data space to those parts of the frequency spectrum that are most necessary to retain the original sound quality.

Encoder. Hardware or software that performs compression on an audio *stream*, or file.

Decoder. Hardware or software that performs decompression on an audio stream, or file.

Codec. Short for (en)*coder-dec*oder, usually used when referring to the entire technology that defines a matched set of encoder and decoder. For example, many discussions will refer to "the MP3 codec."

One of the tricks in making MP3 really useful was to make the encoder much more complex than the decoder. All the hard work is done by the creator, who presumably has both time and computing power to spare, and only has to do the job once for an unlimited number of users to benefit. This approach allows the decoding software or hardware to be simple, compact and inexpensive.

Several newer formats boast "better than MP3" quality. There's no magic involved. Mostly, the compression step has been made even more complex, using much more computer horsepower (or running much more slowly on the same hardware). The compression algorithm scrutinizes the data more exhaustively, and hence does a better job of identifying what can reasonably be discarded. The decompressor may get more complex as well, but as computers get faster, this is increasingly irrelevant.

Another neat thing about MP3 is that it's capable of *streaming*. Imagine a piece of music encoded in MP3 format as it downloads to your computer. After a few seconds, you may have 500KB of data, but there's still 4MB to come. With MP3, you can start to decode, and listen to, the part you've got.

Now you can see why MP3 technology was such a bombshell, catalyzing an overnight transformation of the Internet. Just as GIF and JPG opened up the visual dimension, MP3 made the Internet an auditory experience as well. It's an amazing transformation, and it's still under way, all over the world, at all levels of technology, business and creativity. But what's almost more remarkable is that it all started by accident.

A Bit of History

It's important to understand the origin of MP3, since this has a bearing on a number of very practical issues, not least of which is who "owns" MP3, the subject of the next section.

MP3 compression unleashed the potential of music online, but nobody planned it that way. As with so many things in the computer world, in hindsight it seems almost an act of fate. Digital music was sitting around on CDs in great quantities. The Internet was moving masses of text and even starting to handle graphics with aplomb. Meanwhile, an organization usually referred to as the Moving Picture Experts Group (MPEG, pronounced "em-peg") was working on compression technologies, chiefly to do with video, as you might guess from the name. These developments collided and combined, as technologies so often do in the computer world. The result was like a fusion explosion—a tremendous release of market energy that the corporate world is only beginning to harness, and an explosion of creative possibilities that even the most avant-garde artists have only begun to explore.

What we now casually refer to as "MP3" is a standard that was promulgated by MPEG in about 1992. MPEG itself is actually a committee bearing the ungainly official name ISO/IEC JTC/SC29 WG11. This isn't gibberish; reading from right to left, it stands for "working group 11, subcommittee 29 of Joint Technical Committee 1, of the ISO/IEC." This MPEG working group was established in 1988 by a combination of larger organizations—ISO/IEC being a combination of the International Organization for Standardization (ISO) and the International Electrotechnical Commission. These standards bodies have a wide range of tasks, and have a long history. ISO, for example, has its roots in several organizations dating back to the early 1900s, but was actually founded just after World War II to coordinate industrial standards.

ISO. Interestingly, the letters ISO are *not* an acronym for anything. Rather, ISO is derived from the Greek word *isos*, meaning "equal," and is seen as a prefix in many English words, such as "isometric."

Today, ISO, according to its own Web pages, "is a worldwide federation of national standards bodies from some 130 countries." The ISO standards you've probably bumped into without knowing it include the ISO film-speed code, symbols used to mark automobile controls, and metric screw threads. ISO comprises thousands of committees and working groups. According to its home page, MPEG was created to develop "international standards for compression, decompression, processing and coded representation of moving pictures, audio and their combination." It is a busy group, and has so far produced several standards, or *phases*, each including various versions, and is actively working on several more. These include:

- **MPEG-1** is a standard for compressed storage of audio and video.
- **MPEG-2** is a more advanced standard for digital television.
- **MPEG-4** deals with integration of production and distribution of content for digital television, interactive graphics applications, and interactive World Wide Web applications.
- **MPEG-7** (due to be approved in 2001) deals with specs for integrating video and multimedia applications.
- **MPEG-21** is a "multimedia framework" that aims to further harmonize all electronic media.

Note that these standards deal mostly with video, not audio, as you might expect, having been generated by a group with a "Moving Picture" in its name. However, since compression that worked only on silent movies would be of limited popularity, the standards also include detailed work on audio.

What is now widely known as MP3 is actually defined under MPEG-1, Part 3 (ISO/IEC 11172-3), developed in 1992 and first published in 1993. This spec deals with the compression of audio, and defines three classes of compression, dubbed Layers I, II, and III. MP3 is actually short for MPEG-1, Layer III. The three layers offer a choice of trade-offs, going from the least complexity and lowest compression in Layer 1, to the greatest complexity and highest compression in Layer III.

Layer I was designed mainly for the now-defunct Digital Compact Cassette (DCC), and is similar to the compression scheme used by Sony for its MiniDisc products. Layer II is used in satellite television.

If you've hung on this far, you're obviously fascinated by this background material. If you want more, start with some of the links provided in the directory at the back of this book. For example, MPEG's own home page (drogo.cselt.stet.it/mpeg) offers lots of technical detail.

Who Owns MP3?

A lot of people have been tempted to assume that because the ISO specification is public, MP3 is essentially public property. Nothing could be further from the truth. In fact, while the ISO *specification* that defines MP3 is public, various technologies used in creating MP3 files are covered by patents. The patent holders have no doubts about the value of this intellectual property, and no reluctance to capitalize on that value, or to pursue those who might deprive them of it. Bottom line: if you want to use the genuine MP3 compression technology, you'll be paying a healthy royalty to the developers.

However, as with most things in the crazy world of online music, that's not the end of the story. It turns out that there are a number of free compression tools that do not include a royalty, and they're not likely to go away. Which do you use? Well, we're coming to that.

Most of the fundamental work on the MP3 technology was done by two organizations: Fraunhofer-Gesellschaft in Germany, and Thomson Multimedia, based in France. Thomson is better known as the current owner of the RCA brand name. It's mostly owned by Thomson SA, but companies such as Microsoft and NEC hold smaller chunks. Fraunhofer is a sprawling government-backed, not-for-profit research organization, which does basic research for German (and recently for other) companies.

Partly because Fraunhofer is a pure-research establishment, Thomson handles licensing of the patents for both organizations. The individual to talk to is Henri Linde, vice-president, New Business and Intellectual Asset Management, in San Diego, California.

(You can also hit the Web site: mp3licensing.com.) According to Linde, within Fraunhofer, Dr. Karlheinz Brandenburg was head of the multimedia department, and led the most important work on perceptual audio coding. So, if there's one man who might be considered the "father" of MP3, it would be Brandenburg.

Brandenburg's work dates back to the early and mid 1980s, while Thomson's patents are mostly dated in the late 1980s or early 1990s. "There are at least 18 patents used by the MP3 standard," says Linde. Based on these patents, Thomson currently offers several licensing plans:

1. **Software players.** Publishers are allowed to distribute these for free. "We don't ask a licence for that," says Linde.

2. **Hardware players.** Manufacturers pay US$0.50 per unit sold. Alternatively, they can buy MP3 decoder chips from a licensed manufacturer. As of January 2000 there were two of these, both based in Switzerland (make of it what you will): STMicroelectronics, in Geneva, and MICRONAS INTERMETALL GmbH, in Zurich. (The former was created when Thomson Semiconducteurs was spun off and merged with SGS Microelettronica of Italy.) Linde reports that Thomson has been talking with another half-dozen chip makers, and expects to have more licensees this year.

3. **Encoders.** Makers of hardware or software encoders pay US$2.50 per unit. An upfront payment of $15,000 per year is required, applied against per-unit royalties. This helps keep out companies that aren't really serious.

   "There are many, many small companies that are active in this field," notes Linde. In January 2000, he reported that more than 60 companies had taken out encoder licenses, and that at least double that number were in active discussion. He expected that there would be more than 100 licensees by spring, and as many as 200 by the end of 2000.

4. Music distribution. This, Linde admits, is the most controversial requirement. The other licences cover encoding and decoding for internal use only. "As soon as you start distributing music, you would need a licence from us," says Linde. When you sell a song encoded in MP3 format, you owe the greater of US$0.01 or 1 percent of the retail price. Thus, if you sell a song for $2, Thomson and Fraunhofer split two cents.

Linde explains that Thomson expects the encoder-decoder market to erode quickly. "There's a tendency to give away the software to generate traffic on Web sites," say Linde. Hence the need to hitch the fee structure to the music itself.

5. Software royalties. This covers copyright royalties for use of the specific Fraunhofer encoder software, as opposed to patent licence fees on the underlying technology. The rate is typically US$5 per unit. This includes both use of the actual software and licensing of the underlying patented technology.

"I have to do a daily explanation on why there is a difference between patents and copyrights," laments Linde. Actually, the distinction is simple enough, and has to do with the fact that Fraunhofer not only developed much of the technology, but has also built what virtually everyone acknowledges is the best implementation of that technology, a software encoder that is both fast and produces high-quality results.

Many encoders, especially the freeware variety, are based on a quick perusal of the programming examples published by the ISO. Linde points out that this typically produces an encoder that probably creates good-quality audio, but isn't likely to work at more than real-time speed—taking about a minute to encode a one-minute song. (And, as far as Thomson and Fraunhofer are concerned, it still requires licensing of their patents.)

Freeware. Software licensed by the creators for free, non-commercial distribution. You can download it for free, use it for free and give it to your friends. Most freeware authors do retain copyright control of their products, but chiefly to prevent them from being modified or distributed for profit by unscrupulous third parties.

Fraunhofer has done a lot of work to optimize its own programming so that its encoder runs very quickly, an important consideration for commercial use. It's not an easy thing to do well. Linde reports that as of January 2000 there were only three commercial MP3 encoding "engines"—Fraunhofer's, plus ones from Xing Technology Corporation (based in San Luis Obispo, CA), and Qdesign Corporation (based in Vancouver). The Fraunhofer encoder has the best reputation, and the widest market acceptance, with a total of about 28 licensees.

Probably the biggest single user of the software is none other than Microsoft, which has incorporated it in various components of its online multimedia offering. Other well-known users include Music-Match, Ahead, Apple, Macromedia, Syntrillium, Sonic Foundry, Nullsoft (which uses the decoder only, in the popular WinAmp player), Adaptec, and Cakewalk. We'll bump into many of these companies later on.

What Are the Alternatives to MP3?

MP3 was at the right place at the right time, and has become ubiquitous on the Internet—yet another of the endless *de facto* standards that pepper the computing world. But MP3 is certainly not the end of the line for audio compression.

A number of companies are doing serious work on new compression technologies. These in turn will be incorporated in the next generation of audio data formats. However, these compression schemes may no longer be the focus, as they were in establishing MP3. The next generation of audio standards will be almost equally concerned with practicalities such as delivery, the ability to include promotional information such as album-cover graphics and text lyrics, and, perhaps most important, the ability to lock the data against unlimited copying.

"MP4" and AAC

It might seem natural that MP3 would over time be replaced by something called MP4. In fact, that's unlikely. For one thing, there is no MP4. For that matter, as we've seen earlier in this chapter, there is no "MP3" either; this is just a loose abbreviation of the official term MPEG-1 Layer III.

Your next guess might be that MP3 would therefore be replaced by MPEG-1 Layer IV. That's close. In fact, the likeliest successor is MPEG-2 AAC (Advanced Audio Coding), as defined by the spec ISO/IEC 13818-4, 5.

Even AAC isn't really a true successor to MP3. It does incorporate more advanced audio compression, but it also includes a lot of other stuff that's of little or no concern for audio applications. For example, AAC includes support for multiple channels of data, for applications such as video or surround sound. Liquid Audio Inc. (based in Redwood City, CA) is already using AAC as the preferred compression technology in its technology for streaming and downloading music over the Internet. Sound quality is excellent, and the advanced codec (for definition, see page 22) is definitely more efficient than MP3, allowing either equivalent sound at the same bitrate, or equivalent bitrate with improved sound.

This might seem to be a strong endorsement for AAC, but the Liquid Track format also allows use of several other popular coding techniques, including MP3 and Dolby AC3. The decision is up to the creator, and the user will never be aware which technology is being employed for a particular piece of music.

Just to confuse things totally, there's also an MPEG-4 (*not* MP4!) standard that pertains to the next generation of audio. Again, however, this is *not* simply an extension of the MPEG-1 Layer III standard, but an entirely new type of specification—a sort of Grand Unifying Standard for Everything. MPEG-4 defines the concept of audio *objects*, which can be bundled together in a single complex data stream.

If the standard succeeds in the real world (always a matter of doubt), it would allow things like multilingual broadcasts, or narration that could be turned on or off by the user. This is exciting stuff, but for our purposes, it's enough to note that the AAC standard is essentially included within MPEG-4. This would indicate that the big revolution in audio is over, and that future steps will be evolutionary, more concerned with applications that exploit audio in new ways, or combine audio with video, than with any fundamental change in the audio technology itself.

Windows Media Audio (WMA)

While AAC, MP3, and MPEG-4 are being developed by standards bodies, their main challenge will come from proprietary schemes now being promoted by various large corporations. The battle really focuses on the next generation of commercial applications, since everyone seems to realize that MP3 is now so ubiquitous—and hence uncontrollable—that it's never going to go away. In fact, from a commercial point of view, it's actually highly desirable to come up with a format that's not *quite* as open and accessible as MP3.

The most serious of these challengers is Microsoft's Windows Media Technologies initiative, which includes Windows Media Audio (WMA). Microsoft claims that this format can provide sound quality equivalent to MP3 at half the file size (or bitrate). Put another way, the system is said to offer "near FM-radio quality" over a 28.8 kbps modem, and "near CD-quality" over 64 kbps or faster connections (which would include technologies such as ISDN, ADSL, or cable). Microsoft's WMA encoder supports bitrates from 5 to 160 kbps. According to Microsoft, higher rates are possible, but unnecessary, offering minimal improvement in audible quality.

Ahead of sound quality, or technological superiority in general, however, Microsoft's main edge with Windows Media is its business case. First, in marked contrast to Thomson/Fraunhofer, Microsoft charges absolutely no royalties on the encoder, decoder, or on encoded music. Companies can freely download Microsoft's development tools simply by signing a licence agreement. Presumably, the software giant expects its profits to come from increased sales of Windows to end-users, and of the Windows 2000 Server to content providers.

Second, Windows Media offers what is probably the most secure Digital Rights Management (DRM) solution on the market. It's difficult to make something as widespread as MP3 secure. By starting over and controlling all aspects of the technology and marketing, Microsoft is able to promise a secure pipe, from creator to user. This may have been a strong factor behind the early endorsement of Windows Media by Liquid Audio, which early in 2000 announced that it would support Windows Media within its distribution system. Of course, Liquid is hedging its bets, since it continues to support the other popular formats as well, and declares itself to be format-neutral.

A third advantage that Microsoft brings to the party is its ability to construct complete end-to-end business-ready systems. Already, Windows Media is probably ahead of most competitors in this regard, including a complete suite of authoring tools for creating content, and server packages, and support, for deploying the technology on a large-scale commercial basis. The Windows Media server is included in the Windows 2000 Server package, along with Microsoft's IIS Web server and other components. So, for about US$1,200, anyone (with the necessary skills) can be a content provider.

For users, its worth noting that Microsoft currently gives away both its Media Player and full encoding tools. Both can be obtained from the Windows Media Web site (www.microsoft.com/windows/windowsmedia). Other popular players and tools are also supporting the Windows Media WMA format. This is powerful stuff, as previous formats have failed for lack of this grassroots support.

Since the technology encompasses both audio and video (based on the MPEG-4 codec), one can just imagine businesses salivating at the opportunity to become leaders in online media in one fell swoop.

Another format that seemed at one time on the verge of a break-through is TwinVQ (Transform-domain Weighted Interleave Vector Quantization), developed by Nippon Telegraph and Telephone (NTT), and licensed to Yamaha for its SoundVQ player. There's no question that the VQF files created by this technology sound better than MP3 at a given size or bitrate. This fact was discovered by amateurs, and for a while the Internet was littered with VQF files as users discovered their superior sound quality.

However, some issues blew up with Yamaha objecting to freeware authors distributing portions of its own software decoder. The complaint was certainly not unreasonable, but it cast a bit of a chill on the VQF community. As of early 2000, VQF activity had declined to almost nothing. The last entry on Yamaha's SoundVQ Web page dated back to September 1999, and related to release of the latest encoder software, with a note stipulating that it can be used for only 90 days after installation. Nonetheless, VQ could be back. Yamaha is obviously a highly respected player in the audio community, and the technology was good.

Another interesting technology is PAC (Perceptual Audio Coder) marketed by Lucent Digital Radio Inc. and based on patented technology developed at Bell Labs in the late 1980s. This system is already being used by Digital Audio Broadcast (DAB) systems, which provide a higher-quality alternative to traditional AM and FM broadcast radio.

According to studies cited by Lucent, PAC gives superior audio quality at a bitrate of 96 kbps, which is, coincidentally, a common rate for streaming content and digital broadcasting. Whether PAC will ever go head-to-head with MP3 seems doubtful at this point, but the prospect certainly can't be ruled out.

Lossless Compression Revisited

As Internet connections get faster, giving users more *bandwidth* to play with, the pressure for efficient data compression is starting to relax. Early fans of MP3 have upgraded to cable modems, *ADSL* connections, or other technologies, and are now hungry not just for more music, but higher-quality music. One result has been a trend toward using less tightly compressed MP3 files. (See Chapter 5.) Another trend has been the increasing use of *lossless compression* schemes. Music files transmitted in this way are equivalent in quality to *WAV* files—that is, *truly* CD-quality.

Bandwidth. A term borrowed from broadcasting, denoting the data-carrying capacity of a connection, be it a physical wire, a specified set of broadcast frequencies, or a satellite link.

ADSL. Short for Asynchronous Digital Subscriber Line. The current favourite technology for delivery of high-speed digital service using existing telephone lines. Uses the same copper wire in your home, but requires installation of newer switching equipment by the phone company. A number of ADSL systems are in operation across Canada, although the regional phone companies don't always use this technical designation. Also often written as xDSL, indicating a wider range of similar technologies.

Lossless compression. Any technique that compresses data and allows it to be uncompressed with absolutely no degradation in the content. For example, JPG images are compressed by discarding some of the details of the original image. TIF images typically use a scheme that compress without losing any image detail at all.

WAV. On the PC, this is the file type used for files that store audio data in the same raw format that's used on audio CDs. This format is more generally referred to as Pulse Code Modulation (PCM). A WAV file is essentially just a continuous series of 16-bit binary numbers, one for the 44,100 sample points in each second of digitized audio.

Lossless compression has two main drawbacks. First, it can't compress by nearly as much as MP3. Typically, lossless files are only about 30 to 50 percent smaller than the equivalent WAV files. Second, they can't be played as is, or streamed over the Internet. Instead, they must be downloaded in full, then uncompressed. If even a single bit is missing, uncompression is likely to fail.

Despite these problems, audiophiles are drifting toward lossless compression. Lossless files are typically expanded into WAV files and then immediately recorded on CD-recordable discs, for play in a traditional audio CD player. Now *that's* "CD quality."

Although no lossless format can claim to be a standard as yet, the one being most widely used is Shorten, developed by SoftSound Ltd., in England. Files in this format are distinguished by the extension .SHN. Shorten actually does support both lossy and lossless compression, but it's the latter that's drawing the greatest interest among amateur users. In fact, entire Usenet newsgroups (see Chapter 2) are being devoted to lossless files. SHN files are often so huge that they are split into multiple parts for posting. As you can imagine, it takes some dedication to capture all the pieces and reassemble them, but the reward is absolutely crystalline sound quality.

Another lossless format that's being put forward is WaveZIP, from Gadget Labs LLC. Others are in the wings, and may yet make an appearance. The main thing to realize is that this area is evolving quickly, as more users acquire fast Internet connections.

Ultimately, it seems likely that lossless compression could be used for commercial sale of music, the first applications possibly for kiosks that manufacture CDs while you wait. Since this type of retail product has to compete with the audio quality of today's factory-made audio CDs, it could be that the losses inherent in MP3 or other lossy formats will be unacceptable to consumers.

However, for many applications, it also seems very probable that the efficiency of MP3 and similar formats will continue to make them very desirable, even on Internet connections faster than any we've seen so far. After all, moving and storing ten files as easily as one will always be a good deal, when the loss in sound quality is small enough not to matter to most users.

MID Files

Occasionally, you'll encounter music stored in files that have the .MID extension. These aren't actually audio recordings. They're more like programs written in MIDI format, which will create music when run on any MIDI-compatible device. This can be lots of fun, and it's worth having a quick look at before we proceed to weightier matters.

Of course, if you're a musician, all this is probably second nature to you already. It's been well over a decade since MIDI revolutionized music *creation* the way MP3 is currently revolutionizing music distribution. It's not possible to include a comprehensive discussion of MIDI here, but it's definitely worthwhile running through some of the basics.

MIDI. Short for Musical Instrument Digital Interface. Defines a standard for digital data communication between musical instruments and various types of recording devices. MIDI data consists of messages that tell an instrument when to start playing a note and when to stop, how hard to play the note, and what instrument sound (*voice*) to use when playing it. A compatible synthesizer can turn these into music.

General MIDI

A MIDI file is like the paper roll in a player piano, only much more sophisticated. Like sheet music, it contains the general specifications of a piece of music, but not the nuances that come from an individual performance. Like sheet music, MIDI files include the notes to be played, plus a few suggestions on how to play them, loud or soft, fast or slow, and so on. But just as each musician will interpret the music differently, and produce a very different performance, each MIDI instrument will produce somewhat different sounds.

General MIDI (GM). A standard developed by the MIDI Manufacturers Association, specifying a basic set of 128 instrument and percussion voices, as well as minimum capability for compatible devices, such as the ability to play at least 24 notes at once. Both Yamaha (XG) and Roland (GS) offer proprietary "enhanced" versions of GM, but they are backward-compatible, so GM remains the fundamental standard. Most good sound cards support GM, as does Apple's QuickTime streaming format, widely used by Web sites.

One very positive thing about MIDI files is that they're tremendously compact compared to digital audio recordings. In our earlier publishing example, MIDI files would be equivalent to text files, where most of the information is implicit, and stored elsewhere rather than in the file. When the MIDI file calls for, say, a C-sharp, that's like a text file calling for a capital H. If the MIDI file specifies that the note is to be played with a certain quality, that might be like the text file saying it wants the H to be in the Times Roman font.

MIDI files can be a lot of fun to play around with, even if you're not a musician. The neat thing about them is that they'll play very nicely on most any recent PC sound card, since these cards usually include MIDI synthesizers that would shame the outrageously expensive professional MIDI instruments of just a few years ago.

It's rather interesting, listening to MIDI files. Before MP3 really exploded, I went through a huge number of them. I discovered a whole new appreciation for musical composition. Something like Saint-Saëns's *Danse Macabre* done entirely for MIDI by some amateur in his spare time lets you focus on the cleverness of the music. When you know that the instrument sounds are entirely arbitrary, the relationships between the notes become more important.

MIDI files are also a great aid in learning to create music. You can use a simple MIDI editor, such as the "lite" version of Cakewalk Express Gold included with Creative Labs' Sound Blaster cards, to pick a piece of music apart. You can eliminate the melody, and sing along, or try to create your own rhythm track. You have total control over tempo, pitch, and instrumentation, so you can focus on music theory, and, of course, creativity.

When you're done, upload your efforts so they can be enjoyed and critiqued by other MIDI buffs. Check the directory at the back of this book for a listing of MIDI groups on Usenet to get started. Or just load up your Usenet software (see Chapter 2) and search for groups with "midi" in their names.

MOD Files

A MOD file is essentially a MIDI file with all of the voices embedded in it—the audio equivalent of the increasingly common Adobe PDF (Portable Document Format) files, which combine text with all the fonts and formatting information they need to look good.

One problem with MODs is that they come in a disturbingly large number of flavours, each identified by its own file extension. These include .MOD, .S3M, .XM, .IT, .MDL, .MTM, .669, .DBM, and .UMX. The best way to keep up with them is to get a player like MODPlug (see Chapter 3) that will handle pretty much everything out there.

MOD-file trading is a fairly big deal on the Internet, in a small way. This little backwater category of online music isn't going to replace MP3 or your CD player, but it has a certain charming simplicity. The fact that it's not really mainstream gives it an atmosphere of pure fun that the mad scramble over MP3 audio has lost.

What is Desktop Audio?

Desktop Audio is what you get when you bring all these technologies together . . . and the whole is definitely greater than the sum of its parts.

As with each successive revolution in digital technology, this one has caught everyone by surprise, including those who've been working to bring it about. "We always kind of thought it would happen," says Bob Ellison, president and co-founder of Syntrillium Software Corporation, publishers of Cool Edit Pro professional sound-editing software (see Chapter 4). The success of the company's recently introduced consumer product, Cool Edit 2000, has surprised even Ellison himself.

Henri Linde, of Thomson Multimedia, similarly recalls the serendipitous origins of MP3. "Our interest at that point was not really Internet, but other digital standards that were under discussion." These included Digital Audio Broadcasting (DAB) and Digital Versatile Disc (DVD). "We failed to make MP3 part of those standards—and then the Internet came along. . . We would like to rewrite history, and claim we saw the Internet coming," he laughs, adding slyly: "We'll have to wait another ten years for that!"

As Ellison points out, it's easy to see (especially in hindsight) that a lot of elements have had to come together to make this revolution reach critical mass. PC sound cards had to be ubiquitous, and sufficiently powerful to handle reasonably good sound quality. Hard drives needed to be big enough to store a useful amount of music data. Modems had to be fast enough to transmit music at a manageable speed—or the music had to be compressed enough to become manageable at available modem speeds.

"The main thing is to get the power of recording and editing into people's hands," says Ellison. "We're saying this kind of processing is not for audio pros exclusively."

You said a mouthful, Bob! In fact, that's what the rest of this book is about.

2
_____

Getting It

This chapter tells you everything you need to know to start hunting for music online:

- The World Wide Web, and two ways you can use it to download music directly to your computer.
- Buying music online for delivery by conventional mail or courier.
- *Streaming* music, which works like online radio, allowing you to listen to music directly from "broadcast" sites on the Net.
- The wild-and-woolly world of Usenet newsgroups, how music is posted, and how you can download it.
- Other protocols used for transferring music, including *ftp* (file transfer protocol) and Napster.
- Creating your own digital recordings on your PC, either from analog sources such as your old vinyl LPs and cassette tapes, or by *ripping* it from digital audio CDs.

S o, EXACTLY WHERE *is* all this music we've been talking about? It's out there on the Internet somewhere, but where? How do you find the good stuff? And having found it, how do you get it into your computer so you can listen to it? These questions are all closely related, because of the way the Internet works.

Before we begin, you do need to realize that no book can find the music *for* you, because a) there's so much of it out there, b) the online landscape keeps shifting and changing much too quickly for anyone to keep track of, and, finally c) a lot of the best stuff is deliberately hidden. This may sound intimidating, but a bit of basic information is all it takes to get started in the right direction, after which your problem won't be finding music and acquiring it, but deciding how to filter the enormous volume of available material down to something you can listen to in a human lifetime.

Types of Transfers

The first thing to consider is how the Internet can be used to transfer music. In fact, there are two fundamentally different ways of accessing music online. You'll almost certainly want to alternate between the two, depending on your mood of the moment. Basically, digital music data can be provided as a single *download*, or in a continuously *streaming* format.

> **Download.** To obtain a specific quantity of data, such as a file, from a remote server. Music files that you download end up on your own computer, where you can play them over and over, at your leisure.

> **Streaming.** To obtain data from a server in a continuous stream, rather than in chunks such as files. As music data arrives on your computer, it is played back immediately, and typically not stored for later replay. (The term *Internet radio* is also used in this book for streaming audio applications. Note, however, that video can also be streamed.)

The difference is very much like the difference between listening to the radio and buying a CD. You'll find yourself tuning in a streaming site while you're sitting at the computer, to provide a bit of background music, and maybe to surprise yourself by exploring performers and musical genres you haven't tried before. Downloads are more permanent, so you'll use those to acquire music you want to listen to more than once. Music that you download can be stored on disk, transferred to one of the new portable music players (see page 132), or even recorded onto audio CDs that you can play on your home stereo.

Clients and Servers

So how do you download music, or listen to a music stream? In fact, there are lots of ways, some that are based on relatively familiar environments such as the World Wide Web, others that rely on more obscure Internet conventions, and still others that create their own unique worlds.

It's easy to see how this works, when you recall how the Internet works (see Chapter 1). The power of the Internet is that it's simply a network of interconnected resources, of any type. Compare it to the telephone. The telephone network is relatively simple and limited; you always access it using a telephone, and transfer just one kind of information, your voice. With the Internet, you can pass absolutely any information that can be represented digitally, and there's no one handset you use to access that information. Instead, you can attach any software handset you need at the moment.

Some of those handsets have become almost as familiar as the telephone. The World Wide Web is one. The Web is just a specified way of arranging text and graphics (HTML, Hypertext Markup Language) so that your handset (your Web browser) can hook up to it. E-mail is another type of handset. Your e-mail program connects you to another whole world of messages, completely separate from the World Wide Web, yet running over the same Internet connections.

Other standard Internet handsets are less well known: Usenet, ftp (see page 95), ICQ, IRC, Telnet, and many more. Each represents a slightly different way of transferring information, which may suit specific applications. New handset *protocols* are always appearing, created by anyone who has a clever idea for a new way of transferring information for a particular purpose. An excellent example is Napster (see page 98), a data-transfer scheme designed specifically to let users exchange music files.

> **Protocol.** As in diplomacy, a set of rules that define relationships—in this case, the relationship between a client program running on your computer and a data server program running on a computer somewhere on the Internet. As long as both sides follow the same protocol, everyone gets along.

It may help to think of the Internet as being a platform, much like Windows. Then each of these transfer methods is just another piece of software that runs on this platform. Word processors handle text in a way that suits long, visually bland documents. Desktop publishing handles text very differently, being more concerned with the position of the words on the page than with their spelling, or logical order. Yet both types of software can run on Windows, on your PC. In fact, each transfer protocol is just an agreed-upon standard for arranging data so that it can be accessed with a specific type of software—a Web browser, Usenet newsreader, ftp client, and so on.

It's not as complicated as it might be. For one thing, virtually all online protocols are based on the same *client-server* model. You, the client, request data, and the server provides it.

> **Client.** The software you run to access a server. Internet Explorer, Netscape Navigator, Forte Agent, Outlook Express, and CuteFTP are all examples of client software. *Browser* and *reader* are terms also often used to denote client software.

> **Server.** A computer and the software running on it, which offer data or services to clients. For example, a data server offers data. A Web server offers World Wide Web pages. A Usenet server offers newsgroups. These are all just types of data, which you access using the appropriate client software.

What's more, there's a big incentive to stick with established protocols that everyone already knows, or at least, to build on top of them in a seamless way.

The remaining sections in this chapter deal with the various streaming and downloadable music protocols, arranged roughly in order of difficulty. Since most of us will first encounter online music on the World Wide Web, we'll start there, looking first at downloads. Since the streaming technologies are mostly designed to launch from Web pages, we'll deal with those next. Finally, we'll come back to some other important download protocols that don't depend on the Web, especially Usenet and ftp.

World Wide Web: Downloads

Most people today are familiar with the Web browser, or the concept of surfing the Web. The two main pieces of software that let you do this are Netscape Navigator (now part of the Netscape Communicator suite) or Microsoft Internet Explorer (included with Windows). For our purposes, there's barely a nickel's worth of difference between them. A Web browser is basically a hole through which data passes, provided that the data has been formatted for the HTML protocol.

HTML. Short for HyperText Markup Language. A simple standard for inserting codes into text to control how it will display on a computer screen. HTML allows graphic images to be mixed with the text, specifies presentation of tables, and allows choice of colours and fonts. It has also been extended to include active elements—essentially pieces of software that do simple tasks when the page is displayed. All Web pages are coded in HTML.

Most of what happens in a Web browser is controlled by the server. Therefore, how you get music is determined not so much by anything you do, but by how the page was set up by its creators. Sometimes you can click on a highlighted *link* and music will stream and play; other times, clicking on a link will initiate the download of a music file in MP3 or other format.

> **Link.** Short for *hyperlink*. Within a Web page, a word, button or other area that, when left-clicked, switches your Web browser to a new page. All Web pages have specific Internet addresses, and hyperlinks can take you to any of these, displaying additional pages within the current site, or jumping to related information within another site. Links can also have other functions, such as launching software remotely on the Web site, starting a file download or causing multimedia content (including music, video or animations) to play.

Downloading Files

Most of the downloadable music you'll find on the Web is in the form of sample files—individual songs, or even parts of songs, made available for free download in order to promote a complete album. The idea is that you'll either spend enough time on the Web page to make the advertisers happy, or you'll like the sample enough to buy the performer's commercial audio CD.

When music is available on a Web page, it may be in one of several different formats. If the link shows a RealAudio logo, the music is meant to stream live over the Net. Liquid Audio links behave similarly. When you click on these, assuming you've installed the appropriate software, the music will simply play. You probably won't have any opportunity to save the music as a file on your system.

If you're looking for complete files you can download, you'll need to look sharp. Often the fine print on the page will specify "play" or "download." Another way to tell what you're getting into is to hold your mouse pointer over the link—whether it's a highlighted word or a button—and read the text in the status bar at the bottom of the screen. You don't need to decipher all of it. Just look at the right-hand end, widening the browser window if you need to, in order to display the entire text. If it ends in ".mp3" then the link points to a file.

Anything else is harder to guess. Sometimes, the status line will actually spell out the function of the link, if the Web page's creators took the trouble to include their own text message.

Typically, clicking a link will start the download, or take you to another page where you'll have to supply your e-mail address, at which point the download will start. Be careful about giving out your real e-mail address; even sites that make a clear statement about privacy may leak your address to spammers, who will bombard your mailbox with unwanted advertising.

Most site operators are aware of the lack of trust that this practice has created, and are working to improve the situation, but for now you may want to be cautious. Usually there's nothing stopping you from giving a false address. If you do this, however, have some consideration for other Internet users, and try to make one up that couldn't possibly exist!

Downloadable samples may also be in Liquid Audio format. In this case, the Liquid Player will give you the option of saving the file. If the save option is grayed out, the publisher has elected to withhold this privilege from the rights that are electronically imprinted in the file.

The directory at the end of this book will steer you to lots of sites that have downloadable sound files. You can quickly amass a remarkably interesting collection of music just by browsing these kinds of sites. Keep an eye on retail sites for special download offers, and visit your favourite musicians' home pages on a regular basis.

Improving Your Downloads

The advantage of downloads, of course, is that you actually get the data in your hot little hands (or on your hot little hard drive), to do with as you will. The drawback is the curse of the broken connection. All too often, you'll start downloading a big music file, get a quarter of it, and then something wacky happens to the connection and the data stops coming in. Since a quarter of a file is just about as useful as none at all, you'll probably need to start over from scratch.

This is particularly annoying with traditional modem transfers. Not only do your downloads take much longer than with the newer high-speed connections, and hence waste much more time when they fail, they're also more likely to fail! Talk about adding insult to injury.

Fortunately, there is a way you can improve the situation. *Before* you start downloading anything, install a program such as GetRight, US$20 from Headlight Software (www.getright.com), or Go!Zilla, US$24.95 from Aureate Media (www.gozilla.com). These download managers keep track of what's coming in, storing the data in a temporary file. If the connection is interrupted, they can request the server to start where it left off, and ensure that the new data is correctly dovetailed with what you already had.

This doesn't always work, mainly because some servers don't allow it. Also, you'll occasionally have trouble with servers that try to bypass the download manager for security reasons. Be sure you know how to temporarily disable your download manager, or some of these pages won't allow downloads at all. (In Go!Zilla, hold down the Alt key when clicking on the download link on the Web page.)

When they are allowed to work, both Go!Zilla and GetRight can also do things like shutting down your connection and/or your computer when the download is finished—perfect for those really big overnight jobs. Of the two programs, Go!Zilla has a few extra features. For example, with pages that allow it, you can drag links from the page onto the Go!Zilla window to download them. Go!Zilla can also "leech" all the files from a page, even allowing you to re-create the entire page on your own computer. By default, Go!Zilla is free, but runs an advertising banner within its window. Registration kills this eyesore.

GetRight, on the other hand, is slightly simpler to use, and includes the ability to download a file simultaneously from multiple servers, if more than one is available. If you have a fast Internet connection, this can help you get the most from it. (Go!Zilla does the same thing with multiple files, but doesn't try to split single files.)

If you're on a modem connection, you absolutely must use one of these programs to avoid driving yourself crazy with frustration. If you're lucky enough to be on a high-speed link, use one anyway, to get all the download performance you're paying for.

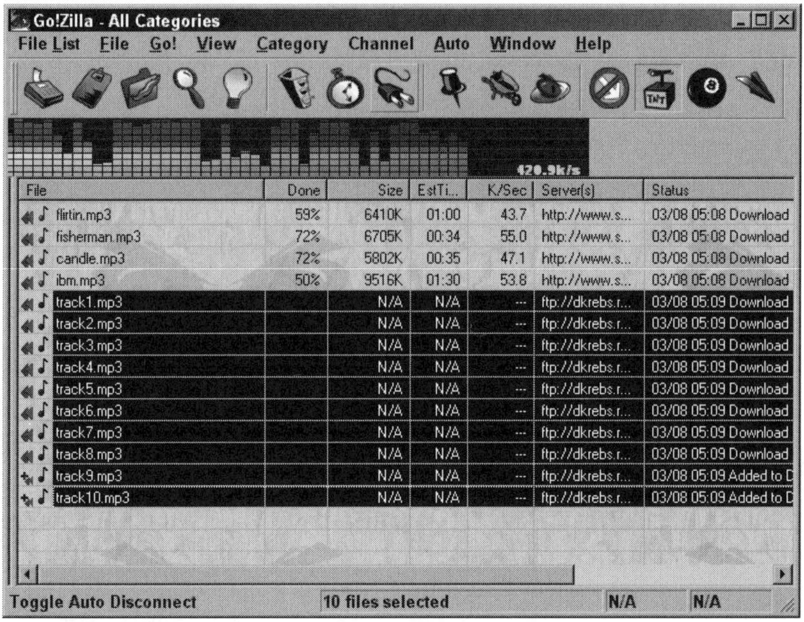

Figure 2.1 Getting files using Go!Zilla

World Wide Web: Purchases

Although you may have assumed that this book would just be about acquiring music electronically, you've obviously overlooked what is still the most common and, arguably, the most efficient way of getting music online—breaking down and buying the darn CD. There are already some definite advantages to doing this online, as opposed to over the counter in a retail store. There are also some pitfalls, which you should definitely know about before unleashing your credit card.

Security

A lot of consumers probably feel that security is the biggest problem in buying things over the Internet, and are therefore leery of the whole concept. This trepidation is almost totally unfounded.

The first fear, that your credit card information will somehow be electronically hijacked while in transit, is without any basis in reality.

Snatching credit information on its way to a Web site is so technically difficult that anyone capable of doing it could make a much better living selling their expertise legitimately. Providing your credit card number to a legitimate online retailer is no more of a risk than providing it over the counter in a traditional store.

Of course, that's not completely safe, either. Which brings us to the second fear, that you'll be ripped off by the vendor on the product you're buying. This one is more reasonable. Again, however, it's no more of a concern than when shopping downtown, and the preventative measures are the same. In fact, the main remedy was known to the ancient Romans, who summarized it in the phrase *caveat emptor*—which translates loosely as "let the buyer read the fine print carefully and count his change twice." Better yet, shop only with *e-tailers* who've built up a reputation for delivering what they promise, and who aren't likely to vanish overnight, along with your (electronic) cash.

> **E-tail, e-tailer.** The electronic equivalent of a retail store. Sites that sell stuff.

Privacy

Privacy is always a concern when you're giving out information about yourself. To place an order on a Web site, you must provide at least your shipping address, probably a telephone number, and certainly an e-mail address. All of these are valuable to promoters, and site operators can make a nice supplement to their core income by selling such information. Before you know it, you're up to your keyboard in spam.

> **Spam.** Advertising messages, posted, cross-posted, and e-mailed in large numbers, with callous disregard for their actual relevance to the groups or addresses that are being bombarded.

There's very little you can do except keep your eyes open. All e-tail sites should have a page describing their privacy policy. But you can't really believe this, especially as most have some sort of disclaimer, often a statement to the effect that "we can change this policy any time we like, but if we do we'll notify you." By which time it will be too late. If a site does start to spam you, shop somewhere else! Vote with your dollars—help elevate the standards for all of us. Retailers who think it's clever to abuse their customers' trust shouldn't have any customers.

A reasonable precaution is to set up a free e-mail address on a service like Microsoft's Hotmail (www.hotmail.com) or Yahoo! (www.yahoo.ca). When asked for your e-mail address, use this one. If it gets crammed with spam, you can quickly close it down and open a new one. (Some sites no longer accept this type of e-mail address. We can only wonder why. . . !)

Prices

One of the advantages of shopping online is that it's easy to comparison shop. You should definitely take advantage of this opportunity. Prices can vary considerably among various e-tail sites, and special discount offers are plentiful.

Unfortunately, prices overall tend to be no better, and in many cases much worse, than you'd find in a big urban retail store. Vendors claim that despite the savings on warehousing, retail premises, and staff, selling CDs online is just as expensive as doing it the traditional way. One suspects that, if there's any truth to this claim, it's only because the volume has yet to challenge the bricks-and-mortar outlets, when economies of scale will really kick in.

With site operators trying to draw new business to their sites, promotions are common, and well worth looking out for. For example, Sara Ross, Internet marketing manager for HMV North America, cites the availability of autographed copies of a 54–40 album. Or a live sample of Natalie MacMaster, posted immediately after her performance during Canadian Music Week. Fans who bought Sarah McLachlan's Mirrorball video or DVD also got a CD music sampler that included an unreleased version of the song "Sweet Surrender."

Naturally, prices on the Web will look a lot more attractive if you happen to live in a smaller town, without easy access to the competitive urban megastores.

Many sites have a negative-option approach to privacy. Somewhere, usually down at the bottom of a long questionnaire, there's a check-box that says something like "*Don't* sell my name to every huckster and sleazy e-mail spammer on Planet Earth." The box is unchecked by default; it's up to you to find it, decipher the inverted logic of the language, and correctly either check or uncheck it.

Delivery

Delivery is a more fundamental problem. Shipping anything by mail should scare anybody. I once ordered $120 worth of CDs from the U.S., and they arrived with $120 of duty payable—someone at Canada Customs had misread the value of the package as $1200. I had to refuse delivery, and wait two weeks (on top of the month I'd already waited) while the package was returned to Customs and revalued. This problem is greatly alleviated if you order from Canadian sites. You can also make the expense less burdensome by accumulating one large order instead of placing several smaller ones.

You'll definitely recognize the better, and more experienced, e-tailers by the quality of their shipping options. They may offer courier delivery, or at least guaranteed delivery by some method of their own choice. They should have something to say about Canadian delivery, including specific extra costs and a word about how Customs is handled. At the time of writing, both HMV.com and SamsCD.com were offering free delivery on orders of over a few discs. CDplus lets you pick up your order at one of their retail outlets across Canada.

While HMV.com promises delivery within "two to seven business days," marketing manager Sara Ross mentions that customers have been surprised just how quickly orders arrive, typically at the short end of this span. She does mention a potential problem, though: the package may not fit in your mail slot. This may be part of the reason that many HMV customers seem to use their business address for delivery.

Unfortunately, some e-tailer sites make it difficult to find out what their shipping options actually are. You may have to actually enter an order before the options appear. This is annoying, but not a huge concern; obviously, you can back out as long as you haven't entered any credit card information. You'll only have to do this investigation once per site.

Buying a CD from CDplus.com

Here's a good example of a Canadian e-tailer site. Shipping information is available by clicking on Customer Service, in fine print at the bottom of the screen, then on Shipping Info in the menu at the left side of the screen. (It's interesting that the New Visitor Guide page has no link to Shipping Information.)

When I checked, early this year, CD Plus was shipping by Parcel Post, and specifically absolving itself of responsibility for losses in transit. The cost was $3.50 for 1–2 discs, and $4.50 for 3–4 discs. There was also an Express/Priority Post service, which cost $15 for the first four discs, and $22.50 for 5–11 discs.

However, being Canadian with a nationwide base, CD Plus also offered a neat pick-up option. You could have your order sent to one of many company locations across the country, and be notified by a phone call when it was ready. I did need to enter a dummy order to get to a list of pick-up locations. However, once I found it, the list turned out to be surprisingly lengthy, including Brandon, Manitoba, Whitehorse, Yukon, and even my old hometown of Weyburn,

Saskatchewan (although they did spell it wrong). Quebec, *malheureusement*, was conspicuously absent from the list. Obviously, however, these things do change, so don't give up without checking the site for the latest info.

Alternatives

Even if you avoid these pitfalls, which isn't difficult, after all, buying CDs online remains an unsatisfying experience, lacking the immediate gratification of taking a disc home and popping it in your CD player. One potential remedy is a scheme introduced by MP3.com in January 2000. If you sign up on the My.MP3.com page, you can hear any CD you've bought from the site, immediately.

MP3.com followed this service with an even more inventive extension, dubbed Beam-It. This allows you to listen online to *any* CD that you physically own. Beam-It software on your computer checks the CD once to confirm that you do have it, after which the MP3.com site gives you access to a copy that resides on their own system.

An obvious advantage is that you can listen to your CD anywhere you've got an Internet connection. Unfortunately, counterbalancing this are several significant drawbacks. First, it only works with CDs that MP3.com has added to its collection. If your tastes run to the mainstream, no problem. Those with more esoteric musical proclivities may find themselves out in the cold.

Second, MP3.com was promptly sued by the Recording Industry Association of America (RIAA), who didn't like the fact that a) MP3.com copied the CDs onto its own servers; b) the service allows consumers to listen to the music without using the physical disc, even if they do own it; and c) consumers need only borrow a CD long enough to Beam-It in order to have unauthorized access to it thereafter. So by the time you read this, Beam-It may be defunct.

Finally, regardless of how the legal dispute turns out, there are some more fundamental uncertainties with the entire MP3.com approach. For one thing, it assumes that playing music over the

Internet (from their server) is going to work reliably, which is not likely, even if you have the best Internet connection available. Second, Beam-It assumes that you'd rather listen to a CD on your computer than just carry it around with you.

Nonetheless, the move by MP3.com is an important one, showing another way that CD purchases can become part of the online experience. As connections get quicker, we'll undoubtedly see more ideas of this sort.

Downloading CDs

Having CDs mailed to your home is nice, but the truly futuristic option is to download the entire CD on the spot. You can then store it on a recordable disc yourself, and have a complete album in under half an hour (if you've got a fast Internet connection).

Downloading a CD from EMusic.com

One site specializing in CD downloads is EMusic.com. Shopping is temptingly simple.

1. Set up an account, by providing credit card information and a password.
2. Browse the site and select the music you'd like. You can search by genre, or alphabetically, and you'll definitely see a few selections not available via conventional retail outlets.
3. Don't forget to grab the album covers, available for download in Adobe Acrobat (PDF) format. This really enhances the experience.
4. After that, go to the checkout. You'll be asked to confirm your order, and then taken to a page containing links to download the music. You can select each track individually, or click one link to get them all.

> 5. Find the tracks on your hard drive, and you can listen to them immediately using your MP3 player. Or unpack them to WAV format and record them to a recordable CD, then print the cover on your inkjet printer and you've got yourself a real professional album. This will be explained in more detail in Chapter 5.

The process of buying albums directly over the Internet still needs smoothing out, unfortunately. When I ran through my own version of the above EMusic example, I immediately bumped into a number of issues.

1. It took about 14 minutes each to download the two 70MB tracks from EMusic. That averages out to about 85 kbps—not very good for my cable connection, which has been known to exceed 300 kbps. The bottleneck was almost certainly on the EMusic server, as the purchase was made at 8:00 a.m. on a Saturday morning, when the Internet would be about as uncongested as it gets.

2. The EMusic server doesn't get along with automated download recovery utilities such as Go!Zilla, and I used up two of my five allowed downloads before I realized what was going wrong.

3 Tracks arrived in my *Temporary Internet Files* folder, instead of my usual download directory. Fortunately, I knew where and how to look for them. An inexperienced user would probably have assumed he'd been ripped off, because that temporary folder is deliberately hidden and not easy to browse conventionally.

4. The music was sent in MP3 format, encoded at 128 kbps, so there's some sacrifice in sound quality compared to a store-bought CD.

5. The album I purchased was a live Phish concert, and it came as two files, each containing 11 songs. I ended up

splitting the files myself, so that track markers would show up when the CD was played. (I later found that EMusic had an option to purchase the album as separate tracks, but for some reason the link didn't show up on their main Phish page.)

6. The two files were both several minutes longer than the 74 minutes that fits on a conventional CD-R (CD-recordable) disc. I managed to fit the files on two CDs only by moving one track from Set II to disc one, then recording onto two 80-minute CD-R discs which, by a stroke of luck, I had on hand. (Most retailers have never heard of 80-minute CD-Rs.) Whoever set this up should have included a track lay-out, rather than allow every user to figure it out from first principles. The Web page implies it's a two-disc show, and burning on three adds the extra cost of one more CD-R.

7 The colour CD jewel-case insert had minor but annoying formatting problems. (The track times didn't line up in a column). Fortunately, I'd recently reviewed the full version of Adobe Acrobat, which allows text editing. Most users would have only the free Acrobat viewer, and have no recourse.

8. No insert was included for the *back* of the jewel case. This piece is rather important, as it includes the lettering that shows on the spine of the disc—your only way of identifying it when it's on the shelf. Also, no art was provided for circular CD sticky labels.

9. No liner notes.

It took me several hours and many hundreds of dollars' worth of software to rectify these errors and omissions and end up with a professional-looking two-CD set. Was it worth it? Heck, yes. The price was modest, and I acquired a truly fine live recording *unavailable anywhere else*. There's the key: this recording would never have existed if not for the Internet.

Even with all the drawbacks, there's certainly a sort of pioneering thrill to buying music with a click of the mouse. Once some of the bugs are worked out—and we all have high-speed Internet connections—this could really catch on. For now, it definitely helps if you have both patience and technical expertise to spare.

Streaming Music

Although there's quite a lot of music available for download on the Internet, there's probably quite a bit more available via several streaming technologies. The reason is twofold: first, streaming "broadcasts" full-time, which pushes a lot of content, compared to what even the busiest downloader can grab; second, streaming offers excellent protection to copyright holders, making it very difficult for users to retain the music beyond a single listen.

Along with this strong security is the availability of an obvious commercial model—a way of making money off the whole rigamarole. Streaming audio can work just like commercial radio, with advertising providing the revenue to fund "free" broadcasting. In fact, Internet radio can improve considerably on traditional radio in this regard, allowing not just audio ads inserted in the programming, but also graphical banners attached to the player, animated graphics, interactive forms and "click-me" response links, and much more. Because of all this, there's already a hotly competitive battle going on to establish *the* standard commercial transport for streaming music on the Internet.

MP3 is well ensconced among amateurs, for both download and streaming, and is being widely supported even by commercial sites. However, the format has some limitations in commercial applications, notably its lack of copyright protection. This has led several companies to promote their own improved music technologies, each claiming its own unique advantages.

Three of these formats are already commonly used, and you'll bump into them almost immediately when you start visiting commercial sites. These are Liquid Audio, from Liquid Audio Inc.; RealAudio (and RealVideo), from RealNetworks Inc.; and Windows Media, from Microsoft Corp. We'll deal with each of these in detail.

(It's worth mentioning that all three formats actually include covert support for the ubiquitous MP3, typically with their own enhancements.)

There's also a continual ferment of smaller ventures, each hoping to outdo the big guys on their own turf—quite conceivable, given the fluid nature of this whole new world. Nothing has crystallized as yet, and almost any technology could turn out to be the Next Big Thing.

Of the three big commercial schemes, RealNetworks and Liquid Audio are the most solidly entrenched on the Net and in the music marketplace. However, they have very different orientation. Microsoft is a relative latecomer to this high-stakes game, but is gaining ground at a scary pace. It has technology that even its competitors admit to be excellent, plus enormous computer industry clout, plus a marketing machine second to none.

Liquid Audio

The green Liquid Audio icon is what you'll see most often for downloadable music samples. The Liquid Track format is highly respected for its sound quality, but Liquid Audio sees its own chief strength elsewhere. "We are a music distributor," says Andrea Fleming, vice-president of corporate marketing for Liquid Audio. Unlike traditional distributors, the company owns no trucks, moves no boxes, and operates no warehouses. Instead, it's been working on making electronic music distribution a reality.

Liquid Audio was probably the first company to create a complete end-to-end solution for moving music over the Internet, from creator or record label, onto data servers, through numerous Web sites, and finally right onto consumers' desktops—and beyond, onto portable music players. "The music companies want to be able to outsource all of these technical issues to a provider," says Fleming.

The Liquid System consists of three components. Of these, only one is visible to consumers—Purchase and Play. This includes the Liquid Player software, which lets you preview, play back, and purchase music, then export it to CD-R or a portable player.

Figure 2.2 The Liquid Player

Backing up this compound is the Syndicate and Sell layer. This includes Liquid Server software, which lets site operators deliver streaming audio clips or sell downloadable tracks. However, according to Fleming, few sites really want to operate these servers themselves. As of early 2000, Liquid was actually supplying the downloadable music for about 300 different Web sites directly from its own servers. The list includes such major e-commerce sites as Amazon. com, CDnow, Tower Records, and Yahoo!

Finally, at the far end there's the Create and Publish layer. This includes the Liquifier Pro software toolkit, which allows creators or publishers to encode their musical offerings, and optionally add graphics, text lyrics and, most important, security. However, Fleming reports that many content providers aren't bothering with Liquifier, instead letting Liquid Audio handle all of this work.

Here's how it works. Let's say you click on a link at the CDnow site, asking to download a song you want to hear. This actually connects you directly to the Liquid Audio server, which sends out the music to your computer. Currently, the company has a server "farm" in San Jose, California. An East Coast server should come online soon, improving access speeds for the other half of the continent, and server locations are also planned for Europe and Japan.

Liquid Audio has been working with music giant EMI to encode and put online that company's entire catalogue, including hundreds of thousands of individual songs. On the other hand, any band or musician who can afford a fee of US$99 can get the Liquifier Pro software and space on the Liquid Audio server for five songs. Those songs will instantly become available to all 300 sites that use the Liquid Audio distribution service. Not all give consumers access to the entire Liquid Audio catalogue, of course, but according to Andrea Fleming, most do.

There are currently about 50,000 individual songs available on the Liquid Audio system, supplied by about 1,000 record labels. This includes varying degrees of participation by the big music publishers, ranging from the massive EMI project mentioned above, to specific smaller-scale endeavours. It also includes a lot of smaller publishers. "A very large number of independent labels have handed over their back catalogue to us," Fleming notes. For example, the well-known band Little Feat has taken some of its old albums and put them on the Liquid system as individual songs.

Liquid Audio can also handle special events. For example, Alanis Morissette used Liquid Audio to offer free samples for four weeks leading up to her MTV Unplugged show. The offer was set to time out, about the time her new album became available.

"We really are focused on creating an economic model around downloads," says Fleming. "The reason people use Liquid Audio is they can make money." Here's how it works. When a music publisher puts a song on Liquid Audio, they set a price. Liquid Audio then tacks on a distribution fee. Finally, Web site operators decide on a retail price, allowing a profit margin of their own. So everybody gets paid. The typical split is about 50 percent for the publisher, 20 percent for Liquid Audio, and 30 percent for the site operator.

For publishers, Liquid supports full security and copy control. Publishers can build in specific rights, so, for example, you might only be allowed to play a track, but not burn it to a recordable CD. Music can also be imprinted with a digital *watermark*, which could include the identity of the purchaser, as defined by the credit card they used.

> **Watermark.** Extra information embedded in a digital music file, which is not audible to the listener, but which can be decoded using appropriate software. Music branded in this way would be traceable to the copyright holder, and possibly also to the purchaser of the specific music file.

The limiting factor on this scheme is bandwidth—the ability to move the huge amounts of data involved. Fleming asserts that the Liquid Audio system can handle entire albums—as it did for David Bowie, for example—but they'll take as much as six hours to download on a 56 kbps modem. Until the average consumer is on a fast Internet connection, this kind of distribution will remain focused on the sale of single tracks.

Liquid Audio, like most of the major players in this business, is trying to be neutral when it comes to digital formats. The company's Liquid Track LQT format is based on MPEG AAC encoding by default, but it can include material encoded using various other techniques, including MP3 and Dolby Digital AC-3. The company has built a plug-in to allow Real Networks' RealJukebox and Real Player to play Liquid Tracks.

In January 2000, Liquid Audio and AOL announced that Liquid would be providing a plug-in to allow the popular WinAmp player to play Liquid Tracks. In the same month, Liquid and Microsoft announced that the Liquid Audio delivery system would support the Windows Media Technologies (see page 64). The move will include encoding of the entire Liquid catalog of 50,000 songs and 1 million preview clips in Windows Media format, installation of Windows Media servers, and addition of support for Windows Media to the Liquid Player.

> One drawback of the technologically open-ended schemes such as Liquid Audio is that music purchasers are rarely informed what technology has been used, and at what bitrate. This means that you'll have little or no idea of the quality of the recording you're buying. As the market evolves, we'll have to demand our rights, and reward content providers who prominently display this sort of information.

With this widened reach, Liquid should be in a strong position to ride the coming wave of commercial music distribution online. However, they're facing at least two strong competitors, and final dominance is still very much up for grabs.

RealMedia

A large and rapidly increasing quantity of music is being "broadcast" over the Internet using streaming audio technologies. The first of these to gain wide acceptance was the Real Audio system, from Real-Networks Inc. That early start accounts for the company's main strength today: an estimated 90 million users, according to product manager Rob Grady.

Grady further reports that there are more than 1 million "media accesses" per day launched from within the company's Real Player software. Grady adds that this does not include people clicking on

Real links within Web sites. "These are people who aren't just surfing the Net and coming across a clip," he observes. "They're thinking of it as a fundamental part of the Internet, an actual *destination*."

The Real Player software was the first to use error correction and intelligent negotiation with the server to deliver good-quality sound even over a modem. That's given it a huge user base, but has left it with a legacy of older technology that's starting to look a bit tame. Developed for streaming over slow modems, Real's own codec tops out at 96 kbps. For encoding at 128 kbps or higher, the Real system switches to MP3, using the Xing codec, which RealNetworks recently bought.

"We are very much codec agnostic," says Grady. Support for MP3 was added in 1999, but he estimates that over 85 percent of the content distributed via the Real technology is still in RealAudio or RealVideo format. However, in a quick check it seemed that a lot of the content was streaming at a mere 16–32 kbps, which sounds about like muddy old AM radio, usually in mono. Classical music streaming off CBC Radio Two sounded particularly crackly and hollow.

Even when I found stations broadcasting at 96 kbps, stereo separation tended to be insufficient. Sound was clear, but lacking in sparkle. On the other hand, most connections came in very reliably. I had no trouble tuning in stations in Europe, during off-hours at least.

With the RealPlayer Plus version 7, you get a categorized list of stations in a small window at the left. You can update this at any time from the Real server, and choose "favourites" that appear in a separate listing. The list isn't as long as it might be. Although Grady cites 100 entries for the free version of RealPlayer and 150 in RealPlayer Plus, many are actually different services by single providers. Still, there's a lot to listen to, covering classical, country, jazz, pop, rock and several varieties of talk.

Figure 2.3 RealPlayer 7 Plus

You also get a list of "channels," represented by colourful logos. According to Grady, this list includes over 100 partners, who have signed contracts with Real. Some channel providers pay a fee, but more likely they are major names that Real is happy to have on their service. Think of these as "deluxe" stations." They're more likely to have video content, be updated more frequently, and generally be more elaborate.

You can customize your own channel list. This involves popping up a Web listing from Real, and picking the stations you want. The most popular are included by default, but there are many specialized channels available, such as Australian Whoopi!, or SCI FI.COM.

Real did take a bit of a hit late in 1999, when it was revealed that its RealJukebox player was surreptitiously sending user data back to the company. Real maintained that this information was being used for aggregate statistics only, to improve the quality of its service. Nonetheless, a patch was quickly issued, and the company promised that future versions would be free of this tendency. Version 7 of the RealPlayer was current when the controversy blew up, but Grady states that the company is "working hard" to improve version 8. "We are focused on one thing when it comes to privacy," says Grady. "And that is explicit consent of the consumer."

This may be true, but the consumer currently has no choice but to "explicitly consent" to quite a lot in order to use the Real software. For example, even the fully licensed and paid-for version of Real-Player wants to automatically check its home base for upgrades; you can turn this off, but only for 30 days at a time. Many other settings default to communicating with Real, unless you switch them off.

In fairness, it may be that Real has honestly been trying to create a seamless environment in which "local" and "remote" capabilities are indistinguishable. However, the more astute Internet consumers may not be willing to go down this path quite so wholeheartedly, if it means giving up even a tiny particle of their privacy.

Real has a lot of market momentum, and its technology is well proven. However, it's about to face its biggest challenge: the looming presence of the world's largest software company.

Microsoft Windows Media

Although Microsoft has been less visible in the streaming audio field than Real or Liquid, it hasn't been idle. Its Windows Media strategy was launched in the spring of 1999, and less than a year later was already a massive force in what it refers to as Digital Media.

Built on previous technical forays such as the Tiger video-on-demand server developed about five years ago, the new Windows Media Technology includes both audio and video capabilities. More important, it offers a complete end-to-end business solution for anyone wanting to provide content online.

At the consumer end, there's the Windows Media Player, included with Windows 98, Windows NT, and Windows 2000. Not surprisingly, Microsoft's technology is also integrated into its own

Web browser, Internet Explorer. (See Figure 2.2). Right-click on the toolbar area of the IE window, and check the Radio option to display the Radio toolbar. From this you can conveniently find stations and control playback.

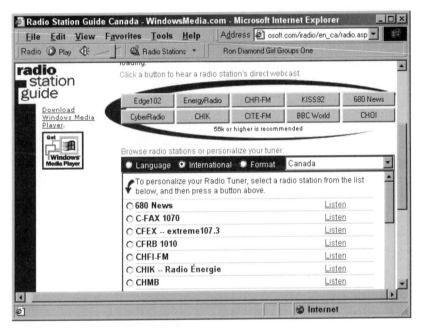

Figure 2.4 The Radio toolbar in Internet Explorer 5

At the back end, there's Windows Media Server, included as part of the standard Windows NT Server or Windows 2000 Server packages.

The back end is key. A content provider can simply buy a copy of Windows 2000 Server, and have everything needed to set up a Web server and a streaming media server. "I think we have a unique position in the industry to provide a *complete* end-to-end solution," emphasizes Michael Aldridge, product manager with Microsoft's Digital Media Division.

That end-to-end coverage is nowhere more important than with Digital Rights Management (DRM)—the ability to provide music securely from publisher to consumer. A DRM system is only as strong as its weakest link, and only Microsoft is in a position to ensure total security at the desktop. DRM services are being built into

Windows, so that a song that's marked "cannot record to CD-R" will either not copy at all or not play if it is copied.

At the client end, Aldridge is quick to counter Real's claims of end-user market share. Microsoft claims more than 50 million downloads of its Windows Media Player, which is obviously not to be sneezed at.

The audio component of Windows Media Technology is Microsoft's own WMA (Windows Media Audio) format, based on work done by Microsoft Research. WMA is claimed to be twice as efficient as MP3, and Microsoft has independent tests that seem to corroborate their claims. This means you can have the same sound quality with half the data, or dramatically better sound quality with the same amount of data. The upshot is better-sounding music, no matter what your connection speed, plus other benefits such as being able to fit twice as much music onto your portable player. Of course, this claim has to be put in perspective. Other formats also claim twice the performance of MP3, which probably makes WMA roughly comparable to Liquid Audio's AAC-based encoder, or to Yamaha's TwinVQ.

Nonetheless, some of the best-sounding streaming broadcasts I've come across have used Microsoft's technology. Perhaps the best place to experience it for yourself is at Launch (www.launch.com), operated by LAUNCH Media Inc. The site uses a customized pop-up browser window that includes fancy controls and bears no resemblance to Microsoft's drab Media Player. And sound quality really is excellent.

Tipping the scales is Microsoft's marketing push. After only a year, Aldridge reported that the WMA format was being adopted by portable-player makers including Sony, RioPort, Thomson and others.

Another very significant factor is Microsoft's benign approach to royalties on its WMA technology. In short, there aren't any. Software developers can download all the tools they need to create custom applications based on the Windows Media format simply by signing a licence agreement. Content providers can distribute material in WMA format without paying a cent. This is in very dramatic contrast to the stance by Thomson/Fraunhofer, detailed in Chapter 1, under which commercial users of the MP3 format must pay a percentage on every song.

If you want to play around with WMA, you can download the latest version of the Windows Media Player or a complete encoding and content-creation toolkit from Microsoft's Web site (msdn. Microsoft.com.windowsmedia, not to be confused with www. windowsmedia.com, which is a content-oriented site, Microsoft's answer to MP3.com).

Using Microsoft's software, I had no trouble creating WMA files from my own WAVs. They certainly seemed to bear out Microsoft's claims, with excellent sound quality and small size. However, MP3 lovers aren't about to switch overnight. For now you're more likely to bump into the format in streaming applications than for downloads.

SHOUTcast

Although it's not really a commercial format as such, Nullsoft's SHOUTcast (www.shoutcast.com) is very similar to systems such as RealAudio, Liquid Audio, and Windows Media. The difference is that it's designed from the ground up to cater to amateur basement-level broadcasters.

SHOUTcast is based on free MP3 server software published by Nullsoft, creators of the popular WinAmp software player (see Chapter 3), and now owned by AOL. It's a bit like the Real or Windows Media streaming systems, but with no corporate overhead at all. If you want to be a broadcaster, just download the software and follow the instructions on the Web site to configure it. Of course, there's nothing stopping commercial broadcasters from getting in on the act, although they'd presumably have to pay a royalty to Thomson/Fraunhofer for use of the MP3 format.

Since it's amateur-driven, SHOUTcast is cleaner and simpler than the commercial systems. To listen, all you need is WinAmp, or another compatible MP3 player. To find a station to connect to, just go to the SHOUTcast home page and pick one from the list. (See Figure 2.5.) You can search on any word, or by genre, which makes it relatively easy to find the kind of music you like. When I tuned in late in January 2000, the site was quoting 3,414 servers.

Figure 2.5 Using WinAmp to listen to SHOUTcast

Sound quality is remarkably good, provided you get a stable server—one that has a connection equal to its owner's aspirations. A nice feature of the SHOUTcast site is that stations are listed with the current number of listeners and the maximum number allowable, so you can pick one that's not overloaded. You can also see the bitrate, which helps you pick a station with either good sound quality, if you have a fast connection, or efficient throughput, if you're still on a modem.

Although 24 and 32 kbps are probably still the most common speeds, many stations are broadcasting at 56 kbps and a few are even going for 128 kbps. At 56 kbps, on a cable connection, you get excellent stereo separation and sound that's only slightly less crisp than you'd wish for. However, note that servers also use various sample rates. You'll find that many use 22 kHz, rather than the 44 kHz CD standard. (See Chapter 1.) At 128 kbps or above, sound is superb; this is where I found some of the best classical and jazz music on the Net, for example.

You will find that listening is variable throughout the day. During peak hours (the evening), audio does tend to break up, even if you have a fast connection.

You can get a very comprehensive station listing on the SHOUTcast Web site. To return to a favourite station, be sure to create a bookmark. In WinAmp, right-click, select Bookmarks from the pop-up menu and "Add current as bookmark," or just press Alt + I.

RadioSpy

Not a streaming technology itself, a useful accessory for streaming listening is RadioSpy, from GameSpy Industries Inc. This piece of software searches for all SHOUTcast, Windows Media, and RealAudio servers, sorts them by genre, number of listeners, or other parameters. RadioSpy thus attempts to be a one-stop front end for all Internet audio broadcasting. The software is available as a free download, but runs an advertising banner until such time as you pay up US$20.

Whether or not its worth it will depend on the kind of listening you like to do. If you want to see all audio sources in a particular genre, regardless of the technology they're using, RadioSpy will do it. It also provides extra connection information, such as a *ping* rating, which tells you how clean the Internet path is between you and each server. If sites support live chat, or offer extra information, it can all be accessed directly from the RadioSpy window. You can also set up a favourites list, which is definitely helpful. Once you've found a few stations you really like, this makes it simple to go back to them.

The drawbacks are relatively minor. RadioSpy is a bit complex and cumbersome onscreen. There's a lot of text staring at you, and no good way to turn any of it off. There are no conventional Windows menus, so the controls can be a bit confusing. However, once you get used to it, it all works quite well.

If you do find yourself listening to more and more material online, RadioSpy is definitely worth a few minutes to download and try out.

Usenet

Okay—so much for the Web. It's a wonderful place, and definitely the focus of activity as far as commercial distribution and promotion of music are concerned. But as pointed out at the beginning of this chapter, there's a lot more to the Internet than just the Web.

The richest, liveliest—and most confusing—place to get music is Usenet, or "the newsgroups." Usenet is to the Internet what cheap saloons are to a port town. It's a freewheeling, often barbaric place where the rich and famous can rub shoulders with people of doubtful character, and everyone can freely exchange opinions protected by a modicum of anonymity.

In order to brave these hazards without getting stung, you'll need a bit of preparation—acquiring the right equipment and a general awareness of the local customs.

The problems with Usenet boil down to:

1. **Bad software.** Unfortunately, there isn't any really *good* Usenet software. So most users' perceptions are tainted by their horrible experience with the user interface. Just remember, Usenet, like the World Wide Web, is simply a data resource that exists independently of how you access it.

2. **Bad Service Providers.** The sad fact is that most Internet Service Providers (ISPs) offer lousy Usenet service. Instead of looking upon Usenet as a way of offering added value to their customer base, most see it as an unnecessary expense, and take every excuse to reduce service.

3. **Bad users.** Some of the people you'll bump into on Usenet are jerks. Not most—you'll be amazed how polite

and reasonable most users are. But a few jerks go a long way towards spoiling the experience, posting things inappropriately, heckling those with less experience, arguing interminably over things that don't matter. You've got to learn to ignore these dimwits.

4. **Naive users.** That's you, when you first start out. *Newbies*, new users, all tend to make the same mistakes, and experienced users get really bored seeing them do it. However, you can easily raise the average, if you finish reading this chapter.

> **Newbie.** A beginner. On Usenet (or the rest of the Internet), someone just starting to find their way around. Usually identified by certain obvious errors. There's nothing wrong with being a Newbie—everybody was one, once. Just remember to tread softly at first.

What's on Usenet

Why delve into Usenet? Why not just stick with the colourful, user-friendly world of the Web? One reason is that, as noted earlier, while ftp and the Web work fine for commercial distribution of music, where users pay their own way, they're ill adapted to noncommercial distribution, where operators get stuck with the bill.

Usenet gets around this problem. Because of the way Usenet works (see page 74), data-transfer expenses are shared by all users, uploaders and downloaders alike. ISPs aren't crazy about this, but the better ones have learned to live with it, and perhaps even come to realize that good Usenet service is a terrific way of distinguishing themselves from their competition.

The upshot is that a *lot* of music gets transferred via Usenet. You can find more of what you're looking for, quicker, by spending a few evenings on Usenet than you can by weeks of searching the Web.

A second problem you'll have with the Web, and with ftp, is in the area of information sharing: no one will ever point you to their best sites. (That includes me! But don't worry—I'll do something even better.) The reason is pure self-preservation. Popular sites don't last long, so users "in the know" tend to be secretive.

As discussed earlier, a really good Web or ftp site will rapidly become popular. Popularity means lots of downloads, and that means moving lots of megabytes. Ultimately, that means a whopping big bill for the site operator. Bing!—the site is gone, and the folks who told you about it are sorry they ever heard of you.

So how does *anybody* find these great sites? The hard way. By being patient and building trust. The community that creates sites (or arises around them), will put up just enough of a barrier to entry to keep "membership" at a stable level. It's actually quite fair; only those who demonstrate a sufficient devotion to the culture eventually reap the benefits.

Usenet is one of the primary ways that this kind of information is shared, directly or indirectly. You'll either meet the people who operate sites, or you'll find out where they congregate. Not all of them will tell you everything day one, but many will, if you ask politely.

A number of Usenet newsgroups are devoted to posting music files. (See Table 2.1, and the more complete listing in the Appendix.) These are denoted as follows: first by the word "alt," indicating that these are unsupervised amateur groups; then the word "binaries," indicating they're not just for text; then usually the word "sounds;" then a word such as "mp3" or "AAC," indicating the preferred format of postings. The main MP3 group, for example, is alt.binaries.sounds.mp3.

Binaries. Files containing any kind of binary data, as distinguished from plain-text Usenet postings. Binaries on the Internet are generally of three types: graphic images, music files, and executable programs. The latter are often contained within compressed archive files, ending in .ZIP or .RAR.

Major binaries groups have an associated discussion group, typically with the same name but with ".d" appended. This is to keep text postings separate from the binaries. If there is a .d group, definitely limit your text postings to that group. A good music discussion group to start with is alt.binaries.sounds.mp3.d.

Table 2.1 The main music groups on Usenet*

Group	Content
alt.binaries.sounds.mp3	main MP3 trading group
alt.binaries.sounds.mp3.d	main MP3 discussion group
alt.binaries.sounds.mp3.requests	requests for posting
alt.binaries.sounds.midi	main MID trading group
alt.binaries.sounds.d	general music discussion
alt.music	general music discussion

* Note: beware of groups with very similar names. You may find a group with "sound" in the name and another with "sounds;" typically all but one will be abandoned and unused.

Caution: a lot of the music posted by individual users to Usenet is in violation of copyrights. As explained in Chapter 6, both poster and downloader are potentially liable for such violations. If in doubt, assume that music postings are not legal. Support your favourite artists by buying their albums, and stay out of court by not infringing on copyrights. You have been warned!

Although much of the music you'll see on Usenet is posted in violation of copyrights, there is more than enough legal music to justify the entire effort. For example, the Grateful Dead newsgroups alt.binaries.gdead and alt.binaries.gdead.highspeed move gigabytes of music weekly, yet contain zero pirated material, and are rigorously policed by the users themselves. The same is true of the Phish news-group, alt.binaries.phish. These bands allow free trading of their live music, and have no piracy problem at all. Most fans purchase all the bands' commercial albums despite the availability of live recordings. Other music creators are adopting a similarly open attitude, and other newsgroups will undoubtedly appear that will be similarly copyright safe.

For now, other groups that should be safe are the alt.binaries.midi series and alt.binaries.mods. These contain mainly amateur works, most posted by or with permission of the authors. In cases where works are "interpretations" based on copyrighted material, they are at least marginally "fair use." Certainly, they don't infringe on sales of the original material, and hence cause no financial damage to the copyright holder—the ultimate test.

> **Fair Use.** A legal term, referring to certain uses that can be legally made of copyrighted material without the permission of the copyright holder. The most often cited example is the right of an author to quote brief passages from copyrighted works, for the sake of discussion. Whether specific cases do or don't constitute fair use is often a subject of heated disagreement, or litigation. (See Chapter 6 for a more complete discussion of copyrights.)

Also, some or all of the material in the Old Time Radio group alt.binaries.sounds.radio.oldtime is likely to be copyright free. For now, be careful what you download! If you want to be absolutely safe, use Usenet for information only. In some of the smaller, more specialized groups, there's no harm in asking about copyrights. No one can shoot you for asking.

How Usenet works

There are numerous *FAQs* and similar resources on the Net that will explain in painful detail what Usenet is and how it operates. We'll take the ten-cent tour, keeping to a moderate level of technobabble, and focusing on what you'll need to know to specifically download music. Further information can be found in any good book on the Internet.

FAQ. Short for Frequently Asked Questions. This term is used a lot on the Internet, but probably originates on Usenet. New users to each discussion group invariably ask the same two or three questions, which appear in the message list day after day as users steadily arrive. Habitués of the group post a list of basic questions and answers in self-defence.

If humanly possible, always read the FAQ before asking *anything*. Your first ten questions have almost certainly been answered thousands of times over. There's just one exception. The one question that's never out of order in any newsgroup is "Where can I find the FAQ?"

Usenet started out as a discussion forum for early Internet users. However, unlike Web sites, or the newer discussion areas that are hosted on some Web sites, Usenet doesn't physically exist in any one place. It's more like group e-mail (or Lotus Notes, which is basically a commercialized and refined version of the same thing). As with e-mail, when a message is posted by a user, it goes onto that person's local server. That server, like a busy gossip, is constantly exchanging information with other servers all over the Internet. Messages pass among this community of servers like nasty rumours on the kaffeeklatsch circuit. Once sent, messages will be seen. But they *can* be *cancelled*. This involves sending a second message that tells servers not to propagate the first. A good Usenet browser (if there were such a thing) should include a Cancel command.

Part of the power of Usenet as a discussion forum is that successive messages on a single topic can be viewed as *threads*. This makes it easy to follow the "conversation" and locate specific contributions.

Most Usenet readers let you expand threads, to see the entire sequence of posted messages, or collapse them, so you see only a single line giving the subject of the thread.

> **Thread.** A sequence of Usenet messages on a single topic. A thread starts with a single posting. When readers reply to the posting, their messages are posted with the same subject line. Most newsreader software lets you view the postings in a thread like a point-form text outline, with responses indented under the original posting. Threads can also be collapsed, hiding all but the original subject line. (This is very similar to the Outline view in most word processors.)

Usenet Survival Guide

Before you dive into the deep and murky waters of Usenet, there are a few simple precautions you need to take. Every regular Usenet user knows these as second nature, but nobody is going to want to stop and explain them for you—and the other 10,000 newbies who arrived today.

For starters, remember always that Usenet is a very public forum, something like the old market square, but much, much bigger. Everything you post on Usenet will be visible to *millions* of people around the world. Try to keep that in mind, and cultivate a little healthy stage fright.

Here are some more specific rules.

1. Never, ever, *ever*, enter your real e-mail address into your newsreader configuration. You may want to enter a garbled address, but even then use a free address, such as Microsoft's Hotmail, rather than your own home e-mail. There's nothing more public than Usenet, and posting your own e-mail address is like posting your phone number on a billboard by the highway. (For more about privacy issues, see page 48.)

If you really must provide a return e-mail address, mess it up in a way that humans can figure out, but software can't. A popular ploy is to embed a word such as NOSPAM in the middle somewhere. Since no two users will do this exactly the same way, spammer software prowling for e-mail addresses isn't likely to get it right.

For example, you might become joeNOSPAMblow@hotmail.com. A human will know exactly how to use this address, but a piece of software won't.

Mostly, however, you should expect people to respond to your postings in the same way, by posting follow-up messages. Asking people to contact you by e-mail tends to sound like you're too lazy to come back and check for replies.

When posting a text reply to a Usenet posting, read the original message carefully. Quote only the pieces that are relevant, and keep your overall message length to a dozen lines or so. Write carefully, reread what you wrote, polish and repolish until your language is brilliant and your wit devastating . . . then press Cancel and forget the whole thing. Nine times out of ten, you'll be glad you did. Most messages just aren't worth it, serving an immediate emotional need rather than advancing the group discussion.

2   Lurk before you Flame, Don't Feed the Trolls. Leech if you must, but never nibble at the Spam. Usenet has become home to some very strange forms of behaviour. You'll need to watch out for several of these.

Lurker. Someone who reads a newsgroup but does not post. The term isn't derogatory; it comes from the fact that these people are effectively invisible to the other members of the group. Judicious lurking lets you get the feel of a group so you don't make an ass of yourself.

Flame. To dash off a negative, knee-jerk response to someone else's newsgroup post—thereby "flaming" them. This rarely advances the discussion, and thus wastes everybody's time—one of the classic ways of making an ass of yourself on Usenet.

Troll. The term comes not from mythology but from fishing, as in "trolling for bass." It denotes malicious individuals who post deliberately inflammatory messages, often to groups they don't like, just to stir up everybody's blood pressure and generate endless message threads as one reader after another flames back.

Leech. To grab all the binary postings in a group while contributing nothing. Although the term is derogatory, there's actually nothing wrong with the practice, as it costs other users nothing.

The most important thing to remember about spam is to never, ever, ever respond to it in any way. This is true of both e-mail spam and Usenet spam, though for different reasons.

The instant you click on a Web link included in a Usenet spam message, you've made money for the spammer, and hence helped pay for the privilege of being inundated by further spam.

If you respond to Usenet spam, no matter how negatively, you've vastly increased the congestion it's creating. Most spam is cross-posted to numerous newsgroups, and if you reply to it your message will probably be cross-posted as well. All of a sudden, you've doubled the amount of useless data flying through cyberspace.

Moreover, if you reply to e-mail spam, you're simply confirming that your e-mail address is active, and hence guaranteeing that you'll go onto all the spam A-lists — even if your message was a request to be removed from those lists! By law, the spammer may have to remove you from the original list, but you'll certainly find yourself on 20 others.

3. Bottom line: bear in mind where everybody else is coming
   from, and avoid wasting people's time. Remember, anything dumb you do to waste one person's time is going to
   be multiplied by thousands.

For example, posting a big binary file incorrectly can fill a newsgroup with hundreds of useless message headers. These make the
useful messages harder to find, and basically get in everybody's way.
Not a good way to win friends and influence people.

> If you're trying something for the first time, and you're not sure
> how it works, don't do it in your favourite group and take a
> chance on alienating everybody there. Instead, go to one of the
> test groups, such as alt.binaries.test, and try it there first.

How Music Is Posted

Just about the most common posting on Usenet music groups is
headed "How do I load these MP3 files?" Usenet is a confusing thing,
partly because the available software is so unfriendly, and partly because Usenet itself was never intended to carry anything like the kind
of huge data files that are now being sent in crushing daily volumes.

Usenet was originally a text-based bulletinboard, where Internet
users around the world could exchange views on various topics. It continues in this role; there are now between 30,000 and 50,000 topic
groups (depending on whether you count some of the really silly ones),
where you can debate anything from petit point to political science.

Some of the groups are as politically incorrect as it is possible to
be, but at least they're well sorted, so you can easily steer clear of subjects that you find offensive. (Ironically, this is the best argument I've
heard for retaining the really objectionable groups—it keeps this
material from spilling into other groups, so it can be easily avoided.)

The one thing that you can't really avoid is *spam*. Spam infests all
groups to some degree, although the music groups are relatively free

of it. The overall level of spam seems to be declining, perhaps be-cause Usenet experts are getting better at stamping it out, or perhaps because the advertisers who supported it are realizing that spending money to alienate prospective customers is a lousy value.

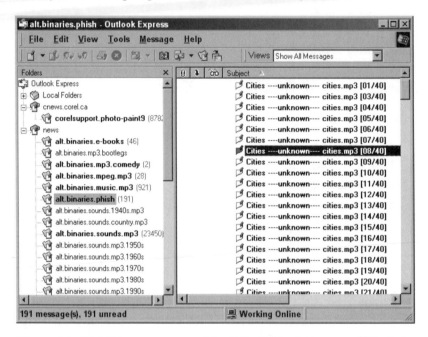

Figure 2.6 Multipart message subjects in Outlook Express. (All of the messages in the right frame are part of one music file.)

As time went on, Usenet users found more and more occasions when it seemed desirable to transfer the odd data file—just little things, generally relevant to the topics under discussion. The trouble was, Usenet could pass only text. So a technique emerged, called *uuencoding* (pronounced "you-you-encoding"), of translating binary data into text characters.

Uuencoding doesn't involve any compression. It works just like one of those secret Captain Midnight decoder rings, substituting particular text characters for particular strings of bits. Once data is uuencoded, it can be passed through Usenet just like a text message, as long as that message doesn't get too long. Most Usenet servers will filter out messages beyond a certain length.

Just about all Usenet browser software is capable of automatically detecting and decoding uuencoded data files. They're typically shown as attachments, just as you'd see in e-mail messages. You can save to your hard drive with a right-click or a menu command. When you save them, they're automatically converted back into their original binary form.

This works great for all sorts of data files: tiny DOS programs, spreadsheets, even graphic images. However, it doesn't work too well for music files that typically bulk 5MB or more. So yet another work-around was found: *multipart* postings (see Figure 2.4). Very large binary files, such as MP3 music files, are uuencoded as usual, but the resulting text message is split into smaller messages—ideally of no more than about 7,500 lines each. The average music file will consist of 10 to 20 such messages.

Multipart posting. Binary postings on Usenet that are broken across multiple messages.

To decode multipart files, your Usenet software needs to first assemble all the messages into one long text message, then uudecode the whole thing. (In fact, you could do it manually by saving the text from each message, combining it all in a simple text editor, then running any of the many public-domain uudecode programs on it. But this is a major pain, and definitely not recommended.)

Fortunately, pretty much any Usenet browser can do this for you automatically. The better ones are set up so that consecutive messages that obviously constitute a single multipart posting are shown as just one subject line in the message list, marked with some sort of icon or other indication that this is actually a multipart binary message.

Keep multipart parts short! If messages get over about 7,500 lines long, they won't propagate well across all Usenet servers, many of which have size restrictions.

Subject	Lines	Date	From
☐ ATTN Squanto Many thanko for REPOST: Phish - 9-28-99 - ph99-09-28d3t01.mp3 !!!!	1	03-07=07	No Man
☐ Can someone tell me where i can get these?	8	03-05=17	YllwSub
Cities ----unknown---- cities.mp3 [01/40]	[39/40]	03-07=21	Some Guy
☐ Hello anyone out there?	3	03-05=15	Some Guy
Phish 7-1-99 - ph1999-07-01-d1t06 Doin' My Time.mp3 (01/42)	[42/42]	03-06=04	Squanto
Phish 7-1-99 - ph1999-07-01-d1t07 Roggae.mp3 (49/58)	[10/58]	03-06=04	Squanto
Phish 7-1-99 - ph1999-07-01-d1t08 Water in the Sky.mp3 (01/34)	[34/34]	03-06=04	Squanto
Phish 7-1-99 - ph1999-07-01-d2t01 Get Back on the Train.mp3 (01/37)	[37/37]	03-06=14	Squanto
Phish 7-1-99 - ph1999-07-01-d2t02 Poor Heart.mp3 (01/34)	[34/34]	03-06=14	Squanto
Phish 7-1-99 - ph1999-07-01-d2t03 Down With Disease.mp3 (001/106)	[6/106]	03-06=15	Squanto
☐ Phish 7-1-99 - ph1999-07-01-d2t03 Down With Disease.mp3 (001/106)	7501	03-06=15	Squanto
☐ Phish 7-1-99 - ph1999-07-01-d2t03 Down With Disease.mp3 (002/106)	7500	03-06=15	Squanto
☐ Phish 7-1-99 - ph1999-07-01-d2t03 Down With Disease.mp3 (003/106)	7500	03-06=15	Squanto
☐ Phish 7-1-99 - ph1999-07-01-d2t03 Down With Disease.mp3 (004/106)	7500	03-06=15	Squanto
☐ Phish 7-1-99 - ph1999-07-01-d2t03 Down With Disease.mp3 (005/106)	7500	03-06=15	Squanto
☐ Phish 7-1-99 - ph1999-07-01-d2t03 Down With Disease.mp3 (006/106)	7500	03-06=15	Squanto
REQ:dajozz please i need 12-16-99 d2t4(tweezer) TIA	[3]		
☐	7	03-06=18	Nym
☐	17	03-07=05	DaJozz
REQ:dajozz please i need 12-16-99 d2t4(tweezer) TIA - ph99-12-16d204.mp3 (001/1[147/147]	03-07=05	DaJozz

39115/39115	354/364

Figure 2.7 Multipart message subjects in News Xpress. (Each subject line in the list represents one complete music file.)

Usenet Software

As mentioned earlier in this chapter, there is no good Usenet software. It's hard to believe: one of the oldest and most heavily trafficked facilities on the Internet, and yet all the software available for accessing it truly stinks.

Well . . . actually, each of the few products worth mentioning is good at *something*. It's just that none of them is good at everything you're going to want to do. The following sections discuss the various choices in some detail, so that you can make an informed choice according to your own interests and level of experience.

My recommendation is that you look at the available products in roughly the order they're described. Outlook Express is a great starter, but awkward for downloading music. News Xpress and Xnews are both good all-round choices. Agent is the most powerful, and the one that most experienced users end up with. Gravity and NewsRover are solid but idiosyncratic, and will appeal only to that minority of users who find their approach suits their own way of thinking.

If you decide to change newsreaders, you'll need to synchronize them. Run a session with your old newsreader and finish up all outstanding business, as far as humanly possible—downloads, message threads, and so on. (Assuming you can reduce the number of loose ends to manageable proportions, make a note of them.) Then run your new newsreader, carefully resubscribe to all your favourite groups, and use the Catch-Up function (or load each group and mark everything "read") to clear the slate. Now when you get new messages, you'll be starting more or less where you left off!

Outlook Express, Netscape Communicator

If you've never used Usenet, the best way to start is Outlook Express 5. It's by far the cleanest, most elegant, and easiest to use of the popular Usenet "client" products. It's also completely free. You'll get it along with Internet Explorer 5, which you can download from Microsoft's Web site, or you'll find it included on many software CDs.

Setting up Outlook is quite painless. You enter the address of your news server, and Outlook Express presents a list of the available newsgroups, from which you can select the ones you'd like to subscribe to.

Outlook Express is particularly good at handling multiple servers, something that few other newsreaders can do at all. Just set each one up the same way, then select the one you want from the Windows Explorer–like tree view at the left of the Outlook Express window.

Unfortunately, when it comes to music, Outlook has a crippling, near-fatal limitation. Most large files, music included, are posted as multiple messages. Any intelligent newsreader should identify when, say, 50 messages belong together, and contain a single music file. Outlook Express doesn't. Instead, you see 50 separate yet virtually identical message entries in the message list. This means that binaries groups display as an unreadable mess. Identifying individual posted files is a nightmare. A newsgroup containing hundreds of music files becomes a list of thousands of individual messages. What's more, downloading binary files is a multistep process. You have to carefully select exactly the correct messages, then get at the Combine and Decode command, then save the file.

So, while Outlook Express is great to learn on, and a fine way of exchanging information with other users, it's virtually useless for getting music from Usenet. This could change. If Microsoft addresses this one problem in its next release, Outlook would become as powerful as it is pleasant to use.

Beginners who shun Microsoft's Internet software may start their Usenet browsing with Netscape Communicator. Unfortunately, Netscape's Usenet reader is even less powerful than Microsoft's—only adequate for browsing text messages, and pretty much a write-off for downloading binary attachments, let alone for managing huge multipart postings. Like Outlook Express, Communicator is okay for exploring Usenet and getting used to discussion groups, but when you're ready to start downloading, start by downloading some more capable Usenet software.

News Xpress, Xnews

It's typical of Usenet that the most elegant, friendly, usable newsreader of all is an obscure freeware product called News Xpress, a relatively tiny piece of software created by a single programmer in Hong Kong, Ken Ng. It's a great tragedy that Ken stopped upgrading his product in early 1997 with the release of version 2.01, and a bitter irony that it has nonetheless remained one of the best newsreaders you can get.

In fact, News Xpress is possibly the best all-round newsreader, combining power and ease of use. It loses out to Agent only in a few advanced features related to handling big multipart binary postings. It's also not 100 percent bug free; the problems are subtle, but after a long session with News Xpress, it's not a bad idea to reboot your computer.

For some reason, News Xpress is virtually the only newsreader that looks and works just like any other Windows program. The list of newsgroups appears in a sub-window within the News Xpress window, and can be filtered by entering search text in a small field at the bottom. For example, if you type "mp3" you'll see only groups that have "mp3" in their name. You can then subscribe to groups you like, and switch to the list of subscribed groups by clicking on a tab at the bottom of the groups window.

Double-click on a newsgroup and you'll see a new sub-window showing a list of the messages. Multipart messages show up with a little cube icon. If there are parts missing, one corner of the cube will be missing.

To view a text message, double-click on it. To retrieve binary attachments, just select the subject lines in the list, right-click, and select Decode from the pop-up menu.

The most serious drawback of News Xpress for music fans is that it has no provision for storing and later manually recombining pieces of multipart postings. The next most serious drawback is that it supports only a single news server. You can get around that to some degree by running two or more separate copies of News Xpress, each with its own configuration files, but this is hardly ideal, and still won't let you combine message parts from different servers.

News Xpress has become enough of a legend to spawn an illegitimate successor—Xnews, another rogue freeware product, this one created by lone programmer Luu Tran. "I'm a fan of News Xpress, so I liberally stole ideas from that program," says Luu's excellent online help file. However, Luu goes on: "That said, Xnews is *not* News Xpress. I didn't try to clone it. I have my own weird ideas of doing things."

Fortunately, most of Luu's "weird ideas" are pretty clever. Xnews is more powerful than News Xpress, but that power comes at the cost of difficult configuration and some new kinds of odd behaviour. I haven't hit anything identifiable as a bug in Xnews, but Windows seems to behave itself much better when I don't use the program. My advice is to try it carefully, and see how it works for you.

Xnews has several features that really set it apart. It lets you organize your favourite newsgroups into folders, which is a tremendous help once you're regularly browsing a couple of dozen groups. It also lets you connect to multiple news servers, all at the same time if you like, and, with a bit of manual setting up, will even combine parts of multipart message from different servers.

Further, Xnews lets you set up multiple online identities for yourself. This may seem a bit paranoid, but it's actually a very useful feature; as explained earlier in this chapter, on Usenet anonymity is highly advisable. Using multiple identities won't conceal you from law enforcement authorities, or even a really determined hacker, but it makes it easier to keep the wackier Usenet denizens at arm's length.

For music downloading, Xnews works much like News Xpress—simple and practical. Accumulating missing multipart segments is possible, but more difficult than in Agent.

My biggest complaint with Xnews is how difficult it is to set up simple things like filters, which screen out unwanted messages. For example, it's very desirable to hide all short, nonbinary messages in a binary group. Xnews doesn't handle this particularly well. You can work around the problems, but this takes some skill in editing the program's various configuration files.

Xnews is an excellent choice for both browsing and downloading, provided you're willing to do some studying and tinkering.

Agent and Free Agent

As you browse the newgroups, you'll frequently see distraught postings of the form "How do I do . . . . in my newsreader?" The posters who are using Agent quickly get answers: often obscure answers, but useful answers nonetheless. Those who are using any other newsreader are typically told, "Get Agent!"

This is good advice, as far as it goes. Agent, a US$30 shareware product from Forté Inc. is certainly the most powerful Usenet reader available. Unfortunately, it's also incredibly difficult to learn and uniquely awkward to use. You may want to get a feel for what Usenet is all about before tackling Agent, but ultimately it's where experienced users end up.

The big virtue of Agent is that it gives you total control over most every factor you could imagine. You can sort and filter message headers in a variety of ways, copy messages to folders that you create, and automatically follow specific discussion threads. You can download messages for reading later off-line, instantly decode multipart binary postings, and set up complex filters to screen out the spam.

When you find a multipart binary message for which some of the parts are missing, Agent lets you download and save the available parts, then add the missing bits later.

Unfortunately, once you've acquired the last piece of the file, Agent leaves the crucial step of ensuring that the pieces are complete and properly sorted up to you. To get the pieces in the right order, you have to manually move them up or down in a tiny list window, by repeatedly pressing Up and Down buttons.

Aside from such petty annoyances, Agent has two more significant shortcomings. It doesn't support multiple Usenet servers, as do most other recent newsreaders, so gleaning message parts from a variety of sources becomes a risky ordeal. (See the Tip for a detailed explanation of one procedure that seems to work.) And it lacks any system for organizing newsgroups. You can subscribe to the ones you wish to follow, but you can't combine them into groups according to categories, or even sort them your own way. Agent displays groups only in alphabetical order, stubbornly placing alt.binaries.sounds.mp3.beatles at the opposite end of the list from rec.music.artists.paul-mccartney.

The worst shame is that Agent seems to have stopped evolving several years ago, so the problems are unlikely to be fixed any time soon. If you want the most powerful tool for grabbing music off Usenet, you'll use Agent. But you may not like it.

If you're manually assembling the parts of a big binary posting, be sure to make a backup before you Join the parts. You can create a new folder called Backup, and use the Message. . . Copy to Folder command to copy all the parts. If there's an error when you Join, for example if you've got a part out of order, you don't get a second chance—the original parts will no longer be available, unless you save them yourself.

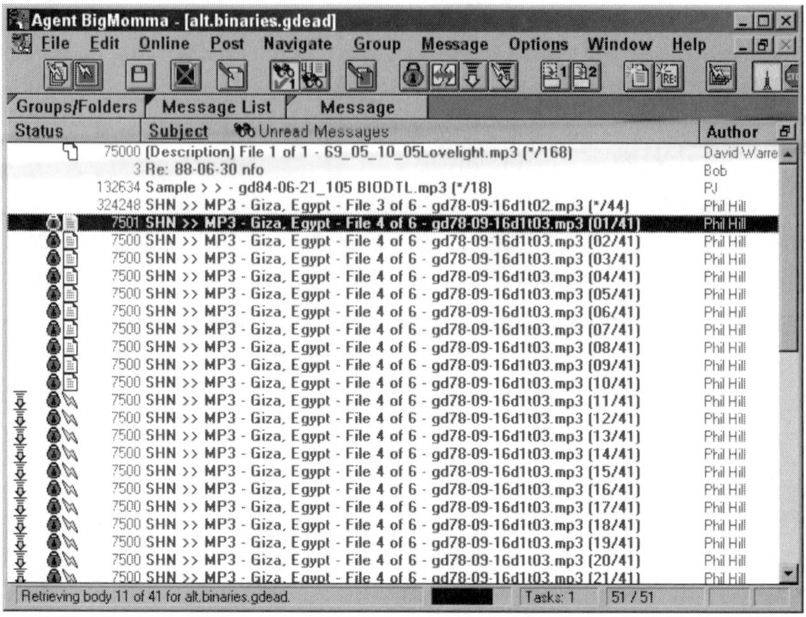

Figure 2.8 Getting separate message parts in Forté Agent

You can use Agent to collect message parts from multiple news servers (provided you have access to more than one). Here's the process:

1. Select the message listing for the incomplete posting. Set Message . . . Keep to ensure that your downloaded parts won't be purged if you have to quit at any time during the following procedure. Check the message window to see which parts are missing, and *write down the numbers*. (This is the only time that Agent will actually tell you; later, you'd have to check all the numbers manually.)

2. Split the multipart message into its component messages. Select and retrieve all the parts you can, then use Message . . . Move to Folder to store them away.

3. Log off. Ensure that the Group . . . View Messages . . . All Messages option is checked. Then select all the messages and delete them using the Message . . . Delete command.

4. Go to Options . . . User and System Profile, and enter the address for your alternate Usenet server. Log on using the Online . . . Online command. Make sure the correct newsgroup is still selected, and then select the Online . . . Get all Headers in Selected Groups command.

5. The message subject you're interested in should reappear. (If it's complete on this server, you've just wasted a lot of time—you could just retrieve it now.) Select the message, and check the message window to see which parts are missing. Hopefully, these will be different from the ones that were missing on the first server.

6. Assuming that the parts missing are different, set Message . . . Keep, split the message apart, then select and down-load the parts that were missing on the first server. Move them to the same folder with the other parts you collected previously.

7. Important! Log off. Display all messages in the group and delete them, as you did before! Change the server address back to the original server. When you next log on, again use Online . . . Get All Headers in Selected Groups to re-fresh the message list. (This will help prevent the header database from becoming garbled by combining message numbers from the two different servers.)

8. Make a backup of the parts you downloaded, and, assuming you now have them all, Join them and save the file. Congratulations—you did it! Simple, huh?

(Note: this procedure seems to work very well, but there is a possibility that your message database could become corrupted, especially if you miss one of the more impor-tant steps. *Use at your own risk!*)

CHAPTER TWO

By the way, Forté also offers Free Agent, which, as the name suggests, is entirely free. It omits several features of the full product, the most significant being the ability to create folders, a major drawback when dealing with large numbers of postings, especially multipart binaries. It also lacks the powerful sorting and filtering tools of Agent, which can help you wade through masses of messages. The bottom line is that, while Free Agent is fine for a tryout, serious user—the only kind who should be using either Agent at all—will definitely want to pony up for the full version.

If you visit the Forté Web site, you can download a complete manual for Agent, in Adobe Acrobat PDF format. This is not only an excellent way to assess the program, it's a great resource for learning about Usenet.

NewsRover, Gravity

If none of the preceding products tickles your fancy, another one that's worth a look is NewsRover, a US$29.95 shareware product from S&H Computer Systems in Nashville, TN (www.newsrover.com).

Shareware. Software that you can download and try out for free, but which requires payment of a (usually quite modest) *registration* fee if you continue to use it beyond a specified period. This approach allows small publishers or individual programmers to sell their software online, and allows customers to try before they buy. Most shareware pops up registration reminders, or *nag screens*, until you pay the fee.

The strength of NewsRover lies in its ability to filter messages based on numerous criteria, including size or presence of a binary attachment, as well as to set up "interest groups" for automatic scanning. A massive bonus is that the software can check automatically multiple news servers for missing parts of multipart postings.

The downside, as with most newsreaders, is an awkward set of controls. Annoyances include "menus" with only one option on them, nonconfigurable toolbar and window layout, and status information that's often unreadable.

Even with these faults, however, NewsRover is worth keeping an eye on. Depending on your own way of working, you may find that its strengths outweigh its quirks. The overall impression is that this is a project that's outgrown some of its early design; if the publisher were to redo some of the basics, it could be a very compelling choice.

MicroPlanet Gravity is another newsreader that has a few devoted fans. It fits somewhere in the middle of the pack—slightly easier to use than Agent, but also less powerful and more cumbersome at dealing with binary postings. It bears mention mainly because it's one of the few newsreaders that's capable of downloading and storing individual parts of a multipart posting for later decoding.

Unfortunately, Gravity stumbles on the basics. Like Outlook Express, it defaults to displaying all the parts of multipart postings. Although it is possible to hide the parts under a single subject heading, to do so you have to treat the entire posting as a message thread. Using the same visual approach to handle both text discussions and multipart binary postings is confusing. Worse, Gravity doesn't provide a reliable indication of whether all the parts of a multipart posting are available, leaving you to open the "thread" and count, if you want to be sure.

On the plus side, Gravity does allow you to set up more than one news server, and quickly switch between them. However, it has no provision for combining multipart binaries from multiple servers.

Overall, Gravity is a fairly attractive product, but hardly ideal for music buffs. It sells for a very cheeky US$10 more than Forté Agent—registration is US$39.95 from MicroPlanet Inc. (www. microplanet.com).

There are a few other newsreaders out there, but, alas, the above are the cream of the crop. Again, the best advice is to try Microsoft Outlook Express to get a feel for text discussions, then move up to News Xpress or Xnews, ultimately ending up with Forté Agent . . . like everybody else.

Getting Big Binaries

Downloading huge binaries can be tricky, even if your Usenet software is really good at it. The main problem is that messages propagate unpredictably across Usenet, and most Usenet servers are actually terrible. So it's all too common to find that a 20-part file has arrived on your server with only 19 parts intact.

Usenet servers are essentially under constant barrage, according to John Grimmett, network supervisor for, arguably, the best Usenet server in Canada, Look Communications Inc., which operates the Internet Direct service. The total volume amounts to about 14GB per day, but arriving in the form of tens of thousands of individual messages per minute.

According to Grimmett, the big trick is being able to spool—or temporarily store—this incoming volume. Outgoing data, to users, is a mere trickle by comparison. Storage for spooling in turn depends on the hardware budget. "The big differentiating factor is how much in the way of computing resources they've put into it," says Grimmett.

The other big factor in determining the quality of Usenet service is a service provider's ability to forge tight relationships with other Usenet servers, so as to get all the postings—preferably by multiple routes. For example, Grimmett notes that Internet Direct has five major news feeds plus several "regional" feeds.

According to statistics published in the newsgroup de.admin.lists for December 1999, alt.binaries.sounds.mp3 is by far the largest single group, accounting for around 7.5 percent of the total volume of Usenet. The runners-up include several movies groups, where users are posting entire feature films. However, about half of the top thirty or so are music groups.

Amazingly, alt.binaries.gdead—devoted to music by the Grateful Dead—comes in at number 24, with close to 1 percent of the total volume. That's a *lot* of music from just one band! Another interesting anomaly is that alt.binaries.sounds. mp3.jazz came in way ahead of both alt.binaries.sounds. mp3.dance and alt.binaries.sounds.mp3.heavy-metal.

When you start looking for music postings, you'll know very quickly how well your Internet Service Provider has done their job. If most of the music postings you see on your Usenet server are broken, you'll know you've got the wrong ISP. Drop them like a hot potato and get another one that respects its users enough to provide a decent Usenet feed.

If you simply can't change, or can't find a provider that does a good job, you can subscribe to a third-party Usenet-only service. There's a handful of companies that provide this, the better-known being Giganews, Netcene, and RemarQ. The cost is typically about US$10 to $12 per month, although you may get a better rate by signing up for a full year.

I won't go into great detail on this subject here, but you can find an excellent comparison of news servers at members.tripod.com/ ~newscompare/chart.html, and a page of tips on picking one at www.exit109.com/~jeremy/news/providers/. More resources are listed in the directory at the back of this book.

Dealing with missing parts is what really sets the top-notch Usenet readers apart from the also-rans. A good reader will help you accumulate parts across several sessions. If you're downloading by modem, for instance, it will save the parts you've got and let you start where you left off if the connection is broken for any reason. A really good reader should be able to combine parts from multiple servers. An excellent reader would let other users mail you parts, or get them to you some other way—but no newsreader available today does this.

Often a broken upload will be missing only the very last piece. (These are often quite tiny, and so don't propagate well.) If so, it may still be quite usable. You need to check carefully to spot this. For example, you may see a song for which 19 of 20 parts are available. This will be marked as an incomplete post in your newsreader. Look more closely. If the missing part is number 20, chances are, the song is actually intact. The better newsreaders, such as Xnews or Agent, will let you combine the parts that are there, and the missing bit may just be silence at the end of the song. Note that this *won't* work with an executable file or a conventional archive file, such as a ZIP, RAR, or SHN.

Dealing with Missing Parts in Agent

1. If only the last part is missing, try this first. Select the broken message. Use the Message . . . Split command to display all the available parts, then select all the parts and select Message . . . Join, then press the Save button. You'll get an error message, but just click OK, saying you do want to save the message with the error in it. If the song plays, great. If not, go on to step 2.
2. After trying step 1, you'll probably need to delete the message from your listing, then reload all messages for that group to redisplay a clean version of it. This in itself can display parts that didn't show up before, so check again that there are missing bits. If there are still some missing, use Message . . . Split again.
3. Select all the parts, then select Message . . . Keep, or press K. (This prevents the parts from being deleted.) With the messages still selected, go to Online . . . Get Selected Message Bodies. The selected parts should download.

4. Right-click on the Groups listing, in a separate pane of the Agent window, and select New Folder from the pop-up menu. Now drag the downloaded parts into the folder, or select them and use the Message . . . Copy to Folder command.

5. Post a polite text message either in the music group itself, or in the associated discussion group if there is one. Put the title of the song in the message subject, as well as something like "PLS REPOST parts 3, 9, 18." Then wait for the parts to show up. (Users of the more close-knit groups, such as alt.binaries.gdead, or alt.binaries.phish, are very good at reposting when asked nicely.)

6. Repeat the above procedure for marking and downloading the missing parts. Move them to the same folder as the others. When you've got all the parts, go on to the next step.

7. Create another folder, and name it Backup. Copy all the parts to that folder. (You only get one chance in Agent; after that, the parts are gone.)

8. Select all the parts, right-click and select Join Sections . . . , or choose Message . . . Join Sections . . . Ensure that the sections are in correct order by moving them up and down in the dialog list. (Be *very* careful about this! Parts that were reposted may have slightly different subject lines that won't sort alphabetically.) Then click Save.

Exhausting? Definitely. And doubly so because most of the difficult parts could be automated so easily by the software.

Other Internet Protocols

There are numerous other techniques for moving data over the Internet, and all of them are used for moving music. We'll run over a just two of the better-known options.

ftp

The uninspiringly named "file transfer protocol" dates back to the early days of the Internet. As the name suggests, it was originally intended as a quick way of moving files around, and it's still useful for that purpose. A fair amount of music gets moved by ftp, so it's worth knowing something about this almost forgotten Internet facility.

Early ftp software was run by typing simple text commands. In fact, Windows still includes a version of ftp. If you run an MD-DOS Prompt window and type ftp -h, it will respond by displaying a help-screen listing of the available commands and options. (It is possible that your specific Windows installation doesn't include it.)

Fortunately, you don't have to use this barbaric variety of ftp anymore. There are many programs that provide a graphical interface, similar to Windows Explorer, while still using the standard ftp commands to communicate with ftp servers. Two of the best are Bulletproof ftp and CuteFTP. Both are available as shareware, so you can try them out before investing.

CuteFTP is particularly interesting as the most recent version, 3.0, includes MP3 search capability. You type in a song, file, or group name, and the software tries to find it using a number of major search engines.

> When you see a posting on Usenet saying something like "FREE FTP SITE!! THOUSANDS OF FILES!!" it's either spam or a troll. For reasons that should be obvious (such as basic economics) there *are* no "free ftp sites with thousands of files." Some of these messages will go on to explain what they're actually trying to sell you; others are simply trying to annoy you by pointing you to invalid addresses—or trying to annoy someone else by pointing you to *their* address.

The main thing to know about ftp is that it mostly works by invitation, much like mailing lists or tape- and CD-trading groups. The reason is cost. The operator of an ftp site will end up picking up all the charges relating to usage of the site. If hundreds of people show up and start leeching gigabytes of music, the online bill is going to be astronomical.

Despite this difficulty, ftp is such a convenient way of moving large music files that many devoted fans do operate sites. However, most are not wide-open. You need to: get to know the people involved, via Usenet or e-mail; reassure them that you use the site correctly and not monopolize the connection; and give some indication as to whether you can and will reciprocate, by uploading occasionally rather than just downloading everything in sight.

Surprisingly, it's not that difficult to win this kind of trust, but it does take a bit of time and a willingness to become part of the fan community.

If you expect to get involved with cult bands, and particularly the jambands that allow trading of huge volumes of their live music, expect to find a use for some ftp software. Otherwise, you'll find that your Web browser can actually connect to ftp sites. (These have "ftp://" at the start of their address, rather than the "http://" used for Web pages.) Also, download manager software such as Go!Zilla can handle a lot of ftp chores, especially if the downloads are initiated from a Web link, as they often are.

A major problem encountered by ftp site operators are people who use the default *retry* setting in their ftp software. If it fails to connect to the selected server address, most ftp software is very happy to keep trying over and over and over, every few seconds, until it gets in. That's fine for you, but unfortunately these retries clog the server's connections and slow down access for everybody. If you're connecting to amateur-operated sites, set the retry time to about five minutes, or better yet, ask site operators about their preferred procedure.

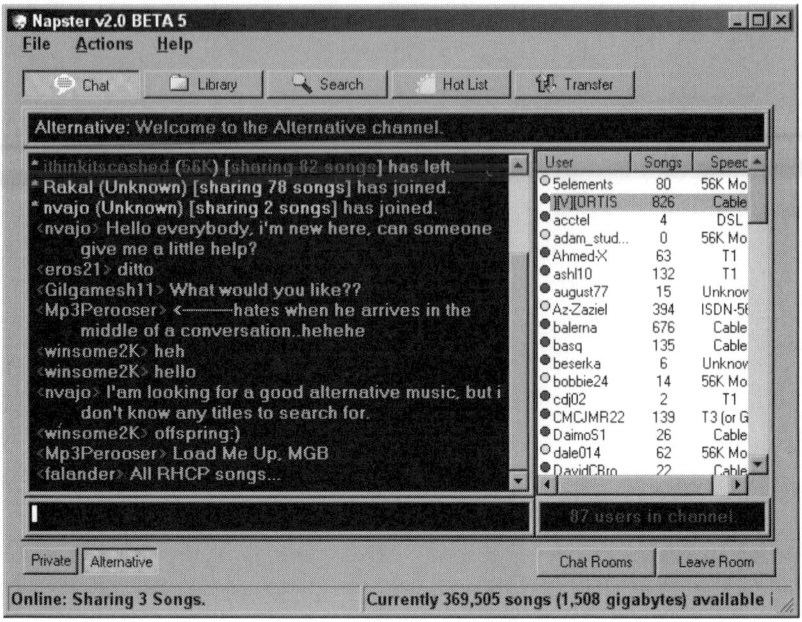

Figure 2.9 The Main window in Napster

Napster

Napster is a seemingly innocuous piece of software that became notorious late in 1999 when its publisher, Napster Inc., was sued by the Recording Industry Association of America (RIAA), for promoting copyright infringement.

Napster is sort of a special-purpose spinoff of ftp. It lets you share a designated area of their hard disk with others on the system, for the purpose of sharing and trading MP3 files. The software also integrates a chat facility that lets you type messages back and forth, and an audio player, to let you hear your downloads right away.

Once installed, Napster lets you search for and download MP3 files from other users' computers. There are two drawbacks to this. The first big one is the RIAA, which contends that Napster encourages copyright infringement. Napster Inc. counters that all they do is provide the software; they have no control over what files users trade with each other. In this they seem to have the U.S. Digital Millennium

Copyright Act on their side. It shields companies that provide a service on the Internet from being held liable for the applications that their users may find for the service.

It's hard to predict how the courts will rule, but equally hard to see just how Napster can be uninvented now that the concept is proven. Even if the company were forced out of business, the software could continue to circulate among individual users, or be replaced by an amateur-written equivalent.

The second drawback with Napster is technical. Basically, in drawing files from other users, your download speed will be limited to those users' upload speed, which is likely to be pretty slow. Even with ADSL or cable modems, the upload speed is typically limited to about 128 kbps, which is a lot less than you'll get from Usenet or most of the better Web servers. The only exception is likely to be students, who may be able to set up Napster sites on fast servers at their schools.

Whatever the outcome of this controversy, Napster vividly demonstrates the sort of things that can be done over the Internet, and how the number of transmission options is likely to keep broadening. If you want to try it out, Napster is a free download from www.napster.com.

Home Recording

Another major source of digital music—very definitely not to be forgotten—comes from within your home, from music you already own or have access to. This could include the following:

- **Live recordings** of yourself, your talented friends, your garage band, or just the family Christmas-carolling sessions. These would likely be on tape, but could easily be transferred to CD using desktop audio technology.
- **Digital transcriptions** of your precious (and all-too-irreplaceable) vinyl record collection.
- **Do-it-yourself compilations** culled from your audio CD collection.

Although the music industry maintains a standoffish attitude about the latter two items, it is currently considered acceptable to make compilations from albums you already own. While everyone concerned has stopped short of saying it's legal or permissible, home recording is allowed to exist in a sort of limbo. Bottom line, you are not going to be sued for it.

Vinyl and Tape

One of the great things about digital desktop sound is that it finally gives us an opportunity to preserve and even improve our cherished vinyl records. We've all got 'em: stacks of LPs that we bought as teenagers or inherited from our parents (after spending our impressionable years listening to them).

Like many music fans, I used to buy LPs and play them just once: in order to transcribe their contents to cassette tape. If and when the tape wore out I'd play the original album a second time. Now you can do the same thing, only with digital quality, preserving those old recordings, too many of which have become virtually irreplaceable.

To record from an analog device, such as LP or tape, you need to connect it to your computer's sound card. If you're connecting a tape deck, you can just plug its output into the sound card's Line In jack, although you'll probably need an adapter cable. Most stereo components offer their output via two separate RCA-style connectors for left and right stereo signals. Most sound cards get input via a single tiny jack, like the ones used by headphones on portable music players. However, any Radio Shack store can provide an adapter.

If you're connecting a turntable, things are different. Turntables put out a very weak signal, and need a pre-amplifier to strengthen it before your computer can use it. The best solution is to get a cheap amplifier (save your older living-room amp when you replace it!) and sit it between the turntable and your computer. Connect both tape deck and turntable outputs to the amplifier inputs, as usual, but take the amplifier output that would normally go to the tape deck and connect it to the Line In jack on your sound card.

Using an amplifier has an additional advantage: it lets you connect standard stereo speakers rather than the self-amplified computer-style speakers. This gives you lots more choices in setting up your computer sound system (see Figure 2.7). Just connect the speaker output from the sound card to the input of the amplifier, again using an adapter cable.

To record, run your sound editor software—something like Cool Edit 2000 or Sound Forge XP is ideal, and probably came with your sound card. (Sound editors are discussed in Chapter 4.) Select File . . . New to create a new sound file, then press the record button, usually marked with the same red dot used on tape recorders. Be sure to have lots of hard disk space set aside. You'll need about 10MB per minute of music.

How to Get a Good Recording

Before you set your software in motion to capture the incoming sound on your hard drive, there's one major adjustment to make, the *record level*. This can make an enormous difference in the quality of your recording, and isn't particularly difficult to do.

Basically, you need to set the level as high as the recording medium can handle, but no higher. Setting levels too low will not only give you quiet music, it will give you muffled and indistinct music, even if you later turn your playback volume all the way up. That's because the recording hasn't taken full advantage of the resolution available. It's a bit like taking a photo in dim light. Even if you get the photo lab to brighten up the print, you'll find that there's no detail in the shadows, because the film just didn't capture it in the first place. The whole picture will tend to look either murky and dark, or pale and vague. The same is true of music. If you don't use the full range of amplitude (volume) available, you're reducing the resolution of the recorded image.

In the case of tape, the available volume range was determined by the physics of the metallically coated tape. With digital recording, it's much simpler. As described in Chapter 1, music is sampled 44,100 times per second, and the amplitude of the sound wave at each sample point is assigned a numeric value between 0 and 65,536. If you record at too low a volume, you're reducing that number, and capturing much less detail.

On the other hand, setting the levels too high is even worse, bringing down on your head the curse of digital audio *clipping*. This is like measuring with a ruler that's too short for the job. As you can see in Figure 2.8, clipping destroys the original wave shape. The effect is a horribly harsh, broken-up sound in the loudest parts of the music.

Clipping. When the amplitude (volume) of the recorded sound wave is greater than the capacity of the recording medium to contain it, the tops of the waves are literally clipped off.

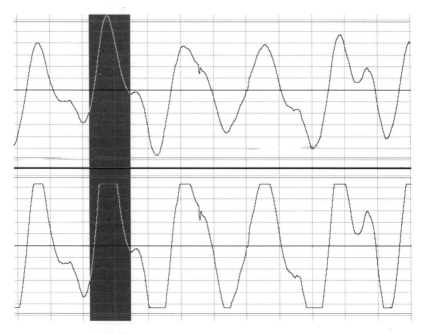

Figure 2.10 What clipping does to a sound wave

Clipping was an issue with home tape decks too. When the VU needles (or LEDs) swung too high into the red, it meant that you were recording at a louder volume than the tape could handle—a bit like pressing too hard with a felt marker while printing on absorbent construction paper. The music "blots" and detail is lost.

However, this is nothing compared to *digital* clipping. With tape, the peaks of the waves get at least slightly rounded off, since there's some vagueness in just how strong a magnetic pulse the tape medium can absorb at any given point. (In fact, with higher-quality tape, you can go further up into the red.) But with a digital recording, sample values go up to 65,536 and that's it. Anything higher is sliced clean off, producing a ghastly distortion in the music.

The idea is to record as loud as possible, so as to use the full range of data values, yet not to exceed the allowable maximum, so as not to clip. It's a bit like playing blackjack. You need to draw cards totalling as close to 21 as possible, without going over. Draw 22 (65,537 in this case) and your recording goes bust!

Most software that you might use for analog recording doesn't attempt to control these levels directly. Instead, you set them using either the Mixer software that came with your sound card, or the Volume Control that's built into Windows. Generally, these control exactly the same system setting within Windows, so if you make a change in one, it will be reflected in the other.

Setting Windows Record Levels

1. You can view the Windows volume controls by opening the Play Control dialog. If you've got a little yellow speaker icon in the Tray area of your Windows Taskbar, double-click it. If it's not visible, open your Control Panel window and double-click the Multimedia Properties icon. Select the first tab, Audio, and ensure that the box is checked next to "Show volume control on the taskbar."

2 In the Record Control dialog, select the Options . . . Properties command. In this dialog box, under "Adjust volume for," click the round radio button next to Recording. In the list, ensure there's a check mark next to Line-In.

3. In the main Play Control dialog, ensure there's no check mark in the Mute box under the Line-In slider, or the Mute all box under Play Control.

4. Now you can change the record level by moving the vertical Line-In slider up and down. It's quite sensitive, and unfortunately there's no numeric scale, so you have to make a note of the position against the little horizontal marks if you expect to need the exact setting again. (Complete albums should always be recorded at the same setting.)

5. Set up your recording software. Play a number of snippets of your source material, trying to pick the loudest passages. Be sure to check both sides if you're recording an LP. Gently tweak the Line-In level up and down so that the audio levels in your software go almost to the top of the scale without touching it. (This is particularly easy to see with the long horizontal indicators in Cool Edit 2000 or Cool Edit Pro; just ensure that Options . . . Show Levels on Play and Record and/or Monitor Record Levels are checked before you start.)

The Creative Labs Mixer that comes with recent Sound Blaster Live! Cards (LiveWare 3.0) mostly duplicates the Windows Record Control dialog, but it does have one very handy extra. If you hold the mouse over the REC slider, it will pop up a Windows tooltip box, saying something like "Record Slider Volume: 68%." This gives you a repeatable setting, and it's worth writing down. If you record one side of an LP, then find that the settings have been changed before you can do the other side, it's going to be very difficult to re-create them without some sort of indicator like this. (You can eyeball the setting using the Windows slider, but this approach is annoying and inaccurate.)

Once you've got the music in a big WAV file, you can do all sorts of things to it. We'll discuss these in Chapter 4. Ultimately, you can record it to audio CD, as explained in Chapter 5.

CD Rippers

If you start with music on CD, the process is considerably simpler. Since the music is already digitized, you just need to transfer the data to your hard disk.

A *ripper* is a piece of software that transcribes the contents of an audio CD onto the hard disk of your computer. Audio CDs use a different recording format than computers, so it's tricky to extract it back out as a computer data file. Fortunately, virtually all modern CD-ROM drives are capable of reading music as data.

> **Ripper.** A piece of software that does Digital Audio Extraction of sound data from an audio CD.
>
> **Digital Audio Extraction (DAE).** The process of pulling music off an audio CD in the form of a digital audio file that can be freely read, played, and manipulated by your computer.

The quality of your recordings from CD will depend a lot on the hardware you're using. Old or cheap CD-ROM drives will copy music more slowly, and may create errors that will spoil the recording. Newer CD-ROM drives handle the process more efficiently and reliably.

The speed of your computer may also play a role in your recording quality. There's less you can do about that, but just about any Pentium II or Celeron PC should be able to handle the job, and even a classic Pentium may get by, depending on the amount of memory, speed of the hard drive, and quality of the CD-ROM drive. (Your biggest problem may be that many original Pentium-era CD-ROM drives simply weren't capable of ripping audio.)

There's a fairly wide choice of CD ripping software available. In fact, recent players such as RealJukebox and MusicMatch Jukebox include ripping capability. So does Adaptec's CD-R recording software, Easy CD Creator. These products are friendly and quite easy to use, but sacrifice some of the precision and control of dedicated tools.

One significant feature to look for in a CD ripper is the ability to automatically check audio CDs against the Compact Disc DataBase

(CDDB) Disc Recognition Service (DRS), operated by CDDB Inc., in Berkeley, CA (www.cddb.com).

The problems is that audio CDs don't include any text information, such as the name of the album or the names of the individual tracks. (There are moves to change this for future CD releases.) CDDB is a database containing track listings, titles and artist names for over 500,000 audio CDs. Using unique code information on an audio CD, the software can look up and display the full track names, and automatically include artist, album and track name in the file-name of tracks that are ripped to your hard drive. (The actual CDDB Web site includes lots of other music-related information, and is well worth a visit in itself.)

Ripping a CD with MusicMatch Jukebox.

1. Load the audio CD in your CD-ROM (or CD-R) drive, and start MusicMatch Jukebox. From the Options..View menu, ensure that Show Recorder is checked.
2. If you're connected to the Internet, the software will query the CDDB database and display a listing of the track titles in the Recorder window. Otherwise, you won't see the names, but you will see track numbers and times. Click next to the tracks you want to record, placing a check mark in the white box. You can also press the All or None buttons to quickly select or deselect the entire album.
3. Press the Start button.

Much better tools for this purpose include AudioCatalyst, from Xing Technology Corp., Easy CD-DA Extractor, from Poiksoft in Finland, and Exact Audio Copy (EAC), from Andre Wiethoff. The latter is particularly attractive, as it has an unrivalled reputation for accurate transcription, and is entirely free for the downloading (at www.exactaudiocopy.de).

The process for ripping with EAC is similar to that described above for MusicMatch Jukebox. Insert the disc, query CDDB to get track titles, then select the tracks you want. However, EAC is both faster and more reliable. While Jukebox ripped at little better than realtime speed on my system, EAC managed about 5X, ripping about five minutes of music in one minute.

EAC also provides a detailed report of any possible errors in the transfer. This lets you fine-tune the process, adjusting for inconsistencies in the way each CD-ROM drive reads audio data.

AudioCatalyst is somewhat friendlier and more colourful than EAC, and places more emphasis on speed and direct encoding to MP3. Both are useful features, but should be taken with a grain of caution. Speed may mean a sacrifice in error levels; the difference may be inaudible, but it's always a concern. MP3 encoding while ripping equally involves an emphasis on speed. Owned by Xing, Audio-Catalyst naturally uses the Xing MP3 encoder, which is known for its speed, but not its audio quality. It's been improved a lot in recent months, but demanding users may still be cautious.

Ultimately, for convenience, you may want to choose either of the popular Jukebox products, from Real or MusicMatch. For both precision and value, Exact Audio Copy is hard to beat.

Conclusion

As you can see, there are a lot of very different ways of getting music onto your computer. You can download it, stream it, or buy it and have it shipped. You can assemble it from Usenet postings, record it from LP, or rip it from CD. And there are more options still to come.

It may seem confusing, but the great thing about all these choices is that there's bound to be a route through the technological maze that will suit your own personal needs and experience level. So dive in where you feel most comfortable and start exploring.

Then, as you begin accumulating lots of great digital music, you can move on to the next chapter, which will tell you everything you need to know about actually *playing* those acoustic treasures.

3

Playing It

In this chapter we'll look at everything you need, both hardware and software, to turn your PC into a desktop audio powerhouse. The field is huge and changing fast, so we can't possibly cover every product, nor keep up with all the new and revised products sure to be released in quick succession. However, we can offer a lot of useful information on each product category, pointing out obvious market leaders, and helping you to establish some basic criteria for judging future products that you come across.

To play music on your PC, you need to have the right accessories, and these are described in detail, as follows:

Hardware
- Computer basics
- Sound cards
- Speakers

Software
- MP3 players
- Jukeboxes

Accessories
- Portable and home-stereo MP3 players

S O, YOU'VE MASTERED all the background, got your download software going, and grabbed some great music off the Net. Now comes the fun part—listening to it.

Hardware

Computer manufacturers are just starting to recognize that the humble beige desktop PC has acquired yet another facet to its already dizzying versatility. You can buy a computer pre-equipped to be an electronic-game system, graphics workstation, financial number cruncher, word processor, study and reference aid, or Internet-surfing terminal . . . but not as a home stereo component.

Yet.

That's going to change. We're already seeing manufacturers offering improved speakers, higher-performance sound cards, and more convenient audio controls. But that's just the beginning. Today, very few PCs right out of the showroom have everything they need to play really great-sounding music.

Even as this gap is inevitably closed up, there will always remain a big advantage to tailoring your own configuration, rather than accepting the off-the-rack PC that some manufacturer has guessed will suit the lowest-common-denominator purchaser.

Computers

The good news is that you definitely do *not* need some sort of jet-propelled sci-fi computer to get started with all this audio stuff. Most of the software and hardware testing for this book was handled by a generic 450 MHz Pentium III, which wasn't leading edge the day it was purchased (for about $1,800), and which will be decidedly passé by the time you read this.

In fact, virtually all of the products and procedures discussed in this book can be handled by any PC newer than a classic Pentium running 200 MHz—most will work fine on even older systems. Any Celeron-based machine will do just fine, as will any Pentium II. And with the right extras, your old Pentium 90 can be rehabilitated as a dedicated music player.

What's more important than the raw speed of the processor is the exact hardware configuration—the mix of accessories that you install. Here are a few basic suggestions:

1. First, get a big hard drive—a *big* one. A really *BIG* one. Get the biggest hard drive you can afford. That probably means spending a whole extra $100 when you're buying a new system. The sweet spot (in major urban centres, at least) seems to be between $300 to $400. The latest and literally greatest drives are introduced at about $400, and rapidly drop toward $300. Anything priced much below $300 is probably smaller than you really want.

Naturally, if you live in Elk's Elbow, northern Saskatchewan, or anywhere on Baffin Island, prices may be slightly higher. But the relationships will be about the same.

Within the next year or so, it's possible that hard-drive sizes and prices will bottom out as far as audio is concerned. A very few years ago, graphic image files seemed huge, and tended to swamp our "gargantuan" one-gigabyte hard drives. Today, we hardly even bother to check the size of a graphic file. The same will doubtless happen with audio. In a year or two, the average hard drive will seem huge compared to the amount of audio we're likely to have around. (Then we'll start worrying about video.)

2. Next, get yourself plenty of RAM memory. A good minimum would be 64MB, but 128MB is much, much better, and will speed up virtually everything you do. In particular, if you plan to do much manipulation or editing of sound files, having at least 128MB on hand will be a big help. It seems likely that the real hotshots will be moving up to 256MB configurations this year, and 128MB will become the minimum standard. You may want to watch the fluctuations in the price of RAM chips, and pick the best moment for your purchase.

RAM. Short for Random Access Memory. It comes on little circuit cards called SIMMs (single-inline memory modules) or DIMMs (dual-inline memory modules). It serves as
the "working scratch-pad" area used by your computer's
main processor chip to do its work. (It is *not* the same as
hard-drive space, which is used to permanently store software and data, even when the computer is turned off.)

When you buy RAM, either as an upgrade or for a brand-new
system, *ask* to have the smallest number of largest-capacity
modules installed. This will leave the maximum number of
memory slots open for future expansion. Often there's little or
no extra expense in getting one high-capacity RAM module instead of two smaller ones. But if you don't ask, you may end up
having all the slots filled up with low-capacity modules the system vendor was eager to get rid of.

3. Be wary of systems with a limited number of expansion
   slots. Often, a cheaper computer shaves costs by including
   a motherboard with fewer slots. This is a false economy.
   Slots can fill up fast, and you can't add more. For audio
   applications, you'll need a sound card. You'll probably
   want a fast Internet connection, and that usually requires
   a network card. (If not, you may want to use an internal
   modem card.) If you want the fastest CD-R recorder, you
   may decide to get a SCSI interface card (see Chapter 5). All
   this can add up, and leave you slotless. The difference in
   cost really isn't worth the compromise on future capacity.

4. Accessories can really make life easier. Get a good multi-
   media-ready keyboard, with audio controls built in. If you
   buy a name-brand computer, you may get this type of control built-in, or at least located on the front of the PC box itself. However, most PCs include execrably flimsy keyboards.

If you buy a local brand, the retailer will typically be happy to upgrade you to a decent keyboard.

Frank's Pick: Microsoft Natural Keyboard Pro

This book was typed on a Microsoft Natural Keyboard Pro, and would have been much more difficult to type and to research without it. This keyboard has complete audio controls, so when the phone rings you can just hit "Pause" to stop the music. You can also change the volume with the "Plus" and "Minus" buttons, and go forward, back or Home in your Internet browser all with single buttons. This really makes life easier. I even programmed a button to open the Windows Control Panel, for quick access to audio settings.

At the back, the keyboard includes two USB ports. As more and more peripherals use this type of connection, having these ports easily available is going to mean a lot.

On top of all this, the Natural Keyboard Pro is the best keyboard for touch-typing that I've used in many years. The ergonomic split design is odd at first, but pays off in the long run. (There's also a traditional rectangular model without the split.) Other keyboards offer extra multimedia buttons, but none currently matches the feel of the Natural Keyboard Pro. (Logitech and IBM are close competitors, however, and worth watching, especially if typing feel is less important to you.)

5. If you're tight for cash, disregard the preceding items, and spend the most money on nonupgradables—processor and motherboard. Although these can theoretically be upgraded later, in practice the economics are almost always against it. Next, spend money on the physical, permanent items. A good monitor will outlast more than one computer, and your eyes will thank you for it. Similar reasoning applies to speakers. These devices will continue to enrich your computing life long after your current PC is obsolete.

There's more, but we're going to deal with the most significant and specialized components separately: sound cards and speakers immediately ahead, and CD-recordable drives in Chapter 5.

PC Sound Cards

It may seem trite, but it needs to be said: a PC needs a sound card to actually produce sound. There are good sound cards and rather a lot of mediocre ones. The difference in cost isn't much, so you might as well go first class.

Several factors differentiate sound cards.

1. **Sound quality.** Most brand-name cards have been producing excellent sound quality for some years now, so this is pretty much a solved problem. However, some cheap cards still do turn up that won't quite make the grade. Stick with recent, top-name products, and you can't go wrong. Names to look out for include Creative Technology Ltd. (Sound Blaster Live! series); S3 Inc. (Diamond Monster Sound MX300, MX400); Aureal Inc. (Vortex series); and Guillemot Corp. (Maxi Sound series).

2. **Sound features.** This lumps together a variety of sound-related extras. For example, any good card today should be able to drive at least four satellite speakers, each with a completely independent sound stream. (Some audio schemes feed the same audio signal to both rear speakers.) Most of the top-end cards also include processing ability that optionally adds ambience or special effects to the sound.

3. **Connectivity.** The better sound cards have lots of plugs—*inputs* and *outputs*. For example, you might look for SPDIF digital connections, which will allow a card to talk to state-of-the-art stereo components over a completely noise-free connection. The bare minimum you need is two Line Out plugs (each driving two speakers), one Line In and Microphone In.

4. **Bonus features.** Some cards include extra connections, or special-purpose options. For example, some "pro" cards handle more inputs and outputs simultaneously. Some models in the Creative Sound Blaster Live! series include extra connector cards or bays, to enable easier hookup to various devices outside the PC.

5. **Software bundle.** Good name-brand cards typically include a fistful of software, ranging from games to professional sound-editing products. Look for both quality and quantity. You can expect to get several games plus some decent recording/editing software. Look carefully to see which are full versions rather than limited demo versions.

Frank's Pick: Creative Technology Sound Blaster Live! Platinum

There are lots of good sound cards on the market, but at the time of writing, the best all-round product for amateur music playback and recording was the Creative Labs Sound Blaster Live! Platinum. This card is an easy recommendation for several reasons:

- *Sound quality is excellent, and four-speaker 3D sound is well supported. The basic software is comprehensive, and upgraded frequently. (Creative is practically unique in adding major new software features to its existing products, at no charge.)*
- *Support, both from the manufacturer and embodied in third-party products, is unsurpassed.*
- *The software bundle is extensive, and right on the mark. In addition to a combination CD/MP3 player, you get Sound Forge XP, an excellent audio editor, and Cakewalk Express Gold, a complete MIDI studio. (Oh yeah: you also get three best-selling 3D games.)*
- *This particular model of the Live! series introduced the Live! Drive, a panel that installs like a CD-ROM drive in the*

*front of your PC, and provides convenient front access to
much-used input and output connectors, the best of all being
a headphone jack. This can really save the wear and tear on
your family and neighbours, when you're doing some sound
editing and end up playing the same ten-second test clip fifty
or sixty times.*

*Other strong brands to watch in this area include Diamond
Multimedia, Guillemot, and Yamaha. However, as yet none
rival the all-round convenience of the Live! Platinum.*

For professionals, there's a whole other range of cards, which typically offer more inputs and outputs and other features that most of
us don't need and which will only complicate things. Unless you
know of a specific reason to push the limits, it's best to stick with the
best-known consumer brands. Audio can still be a troublesome thing
to configure properly on Windows-based PCs, and by wandering
away from the mainstream, you make it much more likely that you'll
encounter these sorts of problems.

PC Speakers

A sound card creates electrical signals corresponding to sounds.
Think of it as just another stereo component, like a tape deck or CD
player. In fact, it can act as a CD player if you stick an audio CD in
your CD-ROM drive and you have everything wired up properly.

Like a tape deck, your sound card still needs to be connected to an
amplifier. The signals the card produces are too feeble to produce sounds
as they are. After the signal is amplified, it can drive a set of speakers.

In home stereo systems, the amplifier and speakers are very dis-
tinct components. With computers, it's proven convenient to build
the amplifier into the speakers, rather than have a separate box clutter-
ing up your desktop, or shoehorned into the inside of your PC, where
it's bound to create electrical interference. This is one reason you can't
simply plug any old speakers into your PC—home stereo speakers
expect a stronger signal than your sound card alone can produce.

There's also a second reason. PC speakers are shielded, so that no signals leak out. A speaker is a big electromagnet, and when operating, it tends to kick out not just acoustic noise, but electromagnetic noise as well. This can play havoc with the much more delicate electrical signals in your computer equipment. In particular, the speakers' magnetic fields can do funny things to the magnetic fields that control the picture on your monitor, since they're often placed adjacent to it.

Bottom line, the simplest way of equipping your PC for sound is to buy a good set of PC speakers. Note that I said "a good set." The key mistake most consumers make when shopping for a computer is to settle for cheap, tinny-sounding speakers. Almost no PCs come with good speakers. In fact, if you spend much less than about $150 on speakers, you're really shortchanging yourself. Spending $200 or more could be the nicest thing you ever do for your ears.

That may seem like a lot of money, but you have to put it in perspective. Half-decent home stereo speakers start at about $100. With PC speakers, you're paying for the amplifier as well. What's more, a good set of PC speakers will almost certainly outlive several generations of PCs. They don't wear out, and they don't become obsolete at the same rate as digital electronics.

There's only a handful of companies making good speakers at the moment. If you don't see one of their names on the box—or if you see no name at all!—you should probably keep looking. The brands to look out for are: Altec-Lansing, Bose, Cambridge SoundWorks (owned by Creative Technology), Labtec, Logitech, MIDIland, and Yamaha. A very interesting newcomer is Vancouver-based Sonigistix, which makes the radical Monsoon series. Another relative newcomer is Klipsch LLG, in Indianapolis IN, well known in home stereo.

Of these brands, you'll find that Altec-Lansing and Labtec tend to go after the low end, starting under $100 and topping out below $200. If you go for the higher-end of this range, you can get quite a good value. However, if you plan to really listen to your PC, rather than simply cranking out CDs for play in your stereo system, it's truly worthwhile to spend a bit more.

Bose, Cambridge, Klipsch, MIDIland, Sonigistix, and Yamaha go for the middle and high ground, starting at about $150 and going on up to about $400. Each of these companies makes some very nice-sounding units.

Note that you probably won't see more than two of these brands at any given retail outlet. In fact, you'll be very lucky to see two, and often you won't see any at all. The sad fact is that speakers are not yet marketed as well as they might be. It seems there's a perception that consumers don't really value good PC sound. Hopefully, we'll prove this wrong. You only need to hear a really fine set of speakers once to be spoiled forever.

The biggest choice in configuration will be how many speakers to get. Low-end speaker systems tend to include just two speakers. You might think that's enough, but not so. The trouble is that desktop speakers have to be so small, it's difficult to get enough range of sound out of them. So the better speaker systems are *three-way*, including two desktop *satellites* and a big *sub-woofer* that sits under your desk.

Satellite. A desktop speaker, usually quite small. This refers to the complete housing, with actual cone-shaped speakers inside it. Typically includes a modestly sized mid-range speaker and possibly tweeter and woofer as well.

Tweeter. A small, often button-shaped speaker, designed to reproduce high notes. Not often seen in PC speakers.

Woofer. A large, usually cone-shaped speaker designed to reproduce low notes. There's no clear distinction between a mid-range speaker and a woofer; it really depends on the design of the individual system.

Sub-Woofer. A large speaker designed to reproduce only very low notes. It gives the low rumble to games, music, or movies.

The term "sub-woofer" is really a misnomer. With three-way PC speaker systems, the sub-woofer actually supplies a lot of the mid-range sounds. This gives a fuller sound than could be achieved with two tiny desktop speakers. However, most PC speaker systems have underpowered sub-woofers. This is the first thing to listen for. You should get enough bass to rattle your paper clips, *without* turning the sub-woofer volume level all the way up.

The next step up, or rather sideways, is to a five-piece system. This isn't vital for music, but it does expand the sound, and lets you have true 3D sound for games or DVD movies. If you're primarily interested in music, a five-piece system is nice, but you won't want to compromise on the sound quality just to get those two extra rear speakers.

The easiest way to test PC speakers is to run them too loud, especially with music that stresses the extremes of high and low. Poor-quality speakers tend to buzz or distort under these circumstances. In fact, physical construction is a pretty good indicator of sound quality. Speakers with cheap plastic cases are more likely to rattle than ones with solid metal or even wooden boxes.

Frank's Pick: Klipsch ProMedia v.2-400

Introduced in 1999, the Klipsch ProMedia v.2-400 is a five-piece speaker set that literally blasts all other speakers off the desktop with 400 total watts of power for truly no-compromise sound quality. This is the first PC speaker system to bear the coveted THX certification, issued by LucasFilm to mark home theater systems that meet their demanding specifications. At $400, the price is high-end but definitely not out of line.

The massive power output of the ProMedia system lets you play your music quietly and yet still have sharp audio detail. That detail is further enhanced by the two-way design of the four satellite speakers, each containing its own woofer and tweeter and hence sounding very robust even without help from the sub-woofer. That leaves the subwoofer, for once, to be truly "sub," dealing with bass so low you tend to feel it in your bones rather than hear it with your ears.

Controls are convenient, with volume and sub-woofer volume knobs both mounted under one of the satellite speakers. A

Figure 3.1 The Klipsch ProMedia v.2-400 system, with four satellite speakers and a subwoofer

third knob is a fader, *controlling the balance of sound between the front and rear satellite pairs.*

Klipsch has been selling ProMedia v.2-400 systems as fast as they can build them, so it would appear that consumers are ready for this kind of sound quality. Hopefully, other manufacturers will take note.

Meanwhile, as of early 2000 two older speaker systems remained worthy runners-up, both offering excellent sound at somewhat lower cost than the intentionally top-end Klipsch.

The Cambridge SoundWorks Four-Point Surround five-piece system, from Creative Technology, is very solid and clean-sounding, with lots of bass and a good mid-range. The system loses out just slightly as far as the brilliance of its high notes, but gains real-world points for its robust construction, which will withstand desktop use better than most.

Also very definitely worth a listen is the Monsoon line from Vancouver-based Sonigitstix (www.sonigistix.com). These radical flat-panel speakers sound as cool as they look, with amazing clarity and presence, limited only by somewhat underpowered sub-woofers, and the lack of a five-piece configuration for full surround sound.

Although PC "multimedia" speakers are certainly the easiest solution, you certainly can consider connecting your PC to a home stereo amplifier, and thence to proper stereo speakers. This can give you excellent sound at a reasonable price, since you really don't need to spend much on the amplifier. Just be sure to place the speakers a few feet apart, well away from your monitor.

One drawback to going this route is that unless you use a very fancy amplifier, you'll only be able to run the two front speakers through it. However, if find you do want 3D sound, you can always get an inexpensive set of self-amplified PC speakers for the rear. Either way, you probably won't need a sub-woofer, since home stereo speakers tend to be designed with sufficient oomph in the low end without extra assistance. Of course, a good-quality sub-woofer is nice to have anyway, but it becomes an optional expense.

One final option that's worth looking out for is Yamaha's @PET RP-U100 Receiver. This is essentially an amplifier that's specifically designed to work with your PC. It doesn't even need a sound card; just connect it directly to your PC's USB port. The computer sends audio data directly to the unit, which decodes it, amplifies it and sends the result to any speakers you like. (Yamaha will happily sell you a matching set.)

At about US$500, the @PET is definitely a high-end product. Even so, it's an exciting foretaste of the things we can look forward to as more manufacturers start taking PC sound seriously.

Software

To actually play music in MP3 or other digital formats, you need a little piece of software—a *player*. There are quite a number of these available. Many are completely free for the downloading. A few add powerful extra features and still sell for no more than about US$30.

Whichever player you install in Windows will become associated with the MP3 file type. From then on, double-clicking on an MP3 file in Windows Explorer will cause the player to load and play the file. Alternatively, players have their own File . . . Open commands, and in some cases massive file management features as well. In almost every case, you can also drag and drop music files onto the player.

MP3 Players

It may not be the fanciest player, but Microsoft's Windows Media is likely to be the one you'll encounter first, simply because it's already on your system. Versions have been included with Windows for years, and the latest release is usually included with any Internet Explorer upgrade. (If you're not sure if you have the newest version, you can use Internet Explorer's Tools . . . Windows Update command to get it.)

The nicest thing about Media Player is that it will play virtually any digital audio (or video) format, including MP3, WAV, WMA, MID, and even many of Real's RM files (depending on the respective versions of Media Player and the encoding used on the file itself). It also plays streaming music or video in the increasingly popular Windows Media format.

When playing an audio file, Media Player shows your position in the file using a slider, which you can grab with the mouse and use to select a specific point in the track. There's another little slider to control volume and a mute button to quickly silence the player.

However, as you play more music on your computer, you'll quickly bump into the limitations of Windows Media Player. You can't set the left-right speaker balance. More important, you can't queue up multiple sound files for playback or save playlists to repeatedly play back the same group of files.

Microsoft has a much fancier Media Player, version 7, scheduled for release sometime in 2000. Meanwhile, developers are already using the Media Player technology to create their own more elaborate or specialized products.

If you want a really nice player specifically for audio, there are lots of free ones to choose from. One of the oldest and best-known MP3 players is WinAmp, developed by Nullsoft Inc., now owned by AOL. WinAmp earns its reputation as *the* default music player. None of the others seems to combine quite the same proportions of versatility and convenience. There's very little that WinAmp can't do, yet it remains plain and simple to operate.

The main display is designed to look as much like a typical CD player as possible. WinAmp replicates the usual controls (see Figure 3.1). These same buttons can be found in most every software player. Play, Pause, Stop, Next Track, and Previous Track. There are also several others. Sliders let you set the volume and the balance between left and right speakers. A larger slider shows your position within the current track. You can skip to any point in the track by dragging this slider.

The PL button pops open the Playlist window. Here you can queue up a bunch of tracks to be played consecutively. Simply drag the tracks from Windows Explorer onto the Playlist, or push the Add button.

Finally, the EQ button opens the Equalizer. Here you can raise or lower the volume of low, middle, or high tones. You can even save your configuration, and have it load automatically when a particular track is played.

WinAmp includes the ability to use *playlist* files. Loading a single playlist file lets you play a selection of MP3 files in a specified order. Playlists can be created by saving from the Playlist window in WinAmp. However, they're really just text files containing the file names, even though they're saved with the.M3U extension.

Playlist. Generally speaking, any ordered list of tracks that you want a software audio to play. Most players let you store playlists as files that can be re-used. The best playlist files simply list the name and location of each track on a separate line, and hence can be modified with any word processor.

That's more than you really need to know just to play music. But there's a pile of other features, tucked out of the way. Right-click on the main window to see the menu.

The Play Location command lets you enter a URL address to access SHOUTcast streaming audio (see Chapter 2.) It's a shame that this isn't a bit friendlier, with a list of "favourites" or bookmarks. As it is, the player remembers the most recent addresses, but only in numeric IP form, offering no clue as to what sites the cryptic numbers represent.

An easier way to use SHOUTcast is to go view the SHOUTcast site in your Web browser and double-click on a link there. (You can also use WinAmp's own built-in Minibrowser.) The music will start streaming and play just like a local file.

One of the most useful options is Double Size. Without this, most players are unusably tiny on a high-resolution monitor. (Apparently their authors all use old 640x480 VGA monitors.) Another neat trick is WinAmp's ability to "click" onto the sides of your Windows desktop, making it easy to position down in a corner, without having it disappear entirely.

WinAmp also has amazing expandability. You can add *skins*, to completely change the appearance of the WinAmp window. You can also add plug-ins, which can perform a variety of functions, ranging from displaying hypnotically dancing graphics in time to the music, to translating music in different formats, such as AAC or VQF, to modifying the music with various acoustic effects.

> **Skin.** A graphic file containing the entire surface appearance of a program window. Installing a skin lets you change the look but not the underlying operation. Most music players now include skin capability.

You'll find a good (though far from complete!) catalogue of plug-ins and skins on the WinAmp Web site (www.winamp.com).

There are just a few very, very tiny annoyances with WinAmp. The most obvious is that when you drag MP3 files into the Playlist Editor, they display only their embedded ID3 text tags, and sort according to these. Unfortunately, few MP3 files are intelligently tagged so as to fall in the correct order. So you've either got to retag a lot of the files you get off the Net, manually tell WinAmp to sort by file name (and then ensure that the file names are more logical than the tags!), manually rearrange the files each time, or, best option, ensure that you have a correctly sorted playlist file for each group of MP3 files that are meant to play together.

Otherwise, WinAmp is a near-perfect player, and definitely the one to start with when you're not sure what you want.

Frank's Pick: DFX, from Power Technology

The Internet is littered with add-ons for WinAmp, but US$29.95 DFX is one of the most useful. It works with both WinAmp and RealPlayer, and can greatly enhance the quality of music played by either program, whether it's from MP3 files stored on your own system or streamed directly over the Internet.

DFX provides the equivalent of the DSP (digital signal processor) effects you'll find on any recent home stereo amplifier or receiver—those buttons that give you "concert hall ambience," and let you select from a variety of cavernous echo effects.

A digital signal processor, or DSP, is exactly what the name implies—a processor chip that can modify digital music data as it's being played. Most DSP effects are nice for a few minutes, but tedious in the long run. After all, the DSP doesn't do anything for the music that the people who recorded it couldn't have done—if they'd thought it really needed it.

Surprisingly, however, DFX actually not only sounds quite natural, it gives you a lot of control that you wouldn't find on any but the most ultra-expensive hardware amplifier.

With many of the recordings you'll pull off the Internet, aural quality isn't going to be first-rate, and a bit of DSP processing is very welcome. Used in moderation, DFX can really brighten up a dull recording, adding pep to the high notes and a lot of depth and clarity to the overall sound.

DFX also does a lot to compensate for any shortcomings in your audio hardware, and the usually less-than-perfect environment most PCs end up crammed into.

If you're playing music in Windows 95/98, you may sometimes find that you have to set your volume control higher than usual to get the same amount of sound. The basic problem is that there are many separate controls in Windows that all affect sound. This is mostly good — it gives you lots of control over how things work. However, you do have to be sure to set all the controls correctly.

Ensure that you have the Taskbar icon for volume control enabled (open Multimedia in the Control Panel and check the Show volume control box) and *double*-click on it. You should see the Play Control window. Check that the Wave/Direct-Sound slider is all the way up. Most volume controls affect only the Play Control slider at the far left; but Wave/DirectSound also controls MP3 and WAV playback volume.

Similarly, if you find that you have trouble getting *any* sound, or getting your microphone or line input to record properly, check the full Play Control settings to see if any sliders have been muted.

If you don't see all the sliders we've shown, you can enable them using the Options . . . Properties command, as shown in Figure 3.2. You may not have all the same ones available that we show — this depends on what sound hardware you have installed.

It's not a bad idea to enable the Mute checkbox on any sound sources you know you're not going to be using. For example, you can mute the Microphone and Line-In sliders if you're not doing any recording. This may help keep out extraneous buzzes and noises while you're listening to music.

So why are all these sliders here? Not just to mess up your life, surprisingly! If you play sound from several sources—for example, from audio CD, MIDI instruments, and software MP3—you may find that some of the volume levels are too high or too low. For example, the audio CDs may be barely audible, while your MP3 player tends to rattle the windows. In this case, open up Play Control and tweak the individual sliders—for example, dropping the Wave/DirectSound volume relative to the CD Audio volume.

Aside from WinAmp, there are numerous other players you may want to look at. We'll mention just a few; you can find lists of players at any of the major MP3 sites.

- **Sonique**, from MediaScience Inc. This is a nice player to try if you're interested in something a bit more futuristic-looking than WinAmp. It does a nice job of integrating graphic light-show effects into its own window, and offers an extensive collection of visualization plug-ins. The controls are a bit smaller and more confusing than in WinAmp, though.

- **K-Jöfol**, from aEGiS cORP. Despite the unpronounceable name, this is a neat little player with a unique organic appearance, lots of features, support for AAC and VQF music files, and the ability to use plug-ins designed for WinAmp. The only fault is that the player is permanently in testing. A new version K-Jöfol 2000 is being released before the original version ever reached a final release. Despite this peculiarity, the player works well and is certainly fun to use.

- **FreeAmp**, sponsored by eMusic.com, is a free player being developed by a large group of programmers dedicated to the Open Source philosophy, which maintains that the original program code for all software should be available to users. Regardless of this background, it has now reached a level of refinement that makes it quite competitive with the other players we've mentioned. Its basic controls are clean and clear, and it includes music-library features similar to the jukebox programs we'll look at next.

Jukeboxes

Jukeboxes are a newer category of player, defined so far mainly by just two products. However, they're different enough from the basic player to be worth considering separately.

The two products in question are RealJukebox Plus, from Real Networks, and MusicMatch Jukebox, from MusicMatch. These are virtually clones of each other, and seem to be locked in an anything-you-can-do battle of features.

Figure 3.2 MusicMatch Jukebox 5

Jukeboxes start with playback, but also include several other features:

- **MP3 encoding.** This is a very useful feature, obviously. Using either of the two jukebox programs, you can convert WAV files into MP3 or Microsoft WMA format. Predictably, RealJukebox also supports the RA RealAudio format, although there's no real reason to use it, unless you're preparing music for streaming from a Web site. Both juke-boxes use high-quality encoders, although they seem to be optimized more for speed than audio fidelity.

- **CD ripping.** Both MusicMatch Jukebox and RealJuke-box offer the ability to capture tracks from CD. This is, again, handy if you want an all-in-one product. However, free products such as Exact Audio Copy (see Chapter 4) are easier to use and do a better job.

- **Audio recording.** So far offered only in MusicMatch Jukebox, this is the ability to record from analog sources, such as tape or LP—anything that can be plugged into the Line In or Mic jacks of your sound card. This is handy to have around, although a full sound editor is really a neces-sity if you're going to do much recording.

- **Library management.** These programs want to or-ganize your library of playable music files on your com-puter. Unfortunately, neither of the developers seem to be aware that this is a really dumb idea, since most of us won't keep our music files *on* our computers, but on removable CD-recordable discs or other media. Compiling a library takes ages to search your hard drive, then comes up with a list that essentially creates a new view of your files. What's wrong with Windows Explorer?

Aside from these features, both MusicMatch Jukebox and Re-alJukebox are very competent players, handling MP3 and CD play-back nicely. They can be expanded to show nice large controls, or contracted into a barely visible bar. Both support skins, although the available selection for either product doesn't seem as dazzling as it might be. (Most skins are just variations in color, with less-usable control buttons.)

Of the two players, MusicMatch is slightly simpler to use and bet-ter organized. RealJukebox Plus continues to display ugly advertising in its main window, even after you've registered by paying your money. Worse, these ads are clickable, so one wrong move with the mouse sends you to an advertiser's site. However, these are cosmetic issues, and the underlying player is powerful and comprehensive.

Although MusicMatch Jukebox is generally very well designed, it does have a flaw that can lead to confusion. If you reduce the volume in MusicMatch Jukebox, then quit and play music using another program, you may find that the sound is much too quiet, no matter how high you set either the program's own volume control or the Windows volume control.

This happens because MusicMatch Jukebox adjusts the Windows settings for Wave/DirectSound and CD Audio, rather than the master volume level. To restore the setting, you have to either re-open MusicMatch Jukebox and set the volume all the way up, or open the Windows Play Control dialog (by double-clicking the speaker icon in the Tray area of the Windows taskbar) and set the appropriate sliders all the way up.

By the way, this procedure is worth trying once, even if you don't bump into the specific issue with MusicMatch Jukebox. Many audio problems in Windows are a direct result of incorrect settings in the Play Control dialog.

On balance, the extra features of these jukebox products—CD ripping, MP3 encoding, and music downloading—do justify the modest purchase price. In particular, if you're planning to limit your investment in audio software to the absolute minimum, they offer an excellent way to acquire virtually all the necessary tools for one low price.

It doesn't seem likely that a huge number of other competitors will join this market. However, even if the two current jukeboxes remain unchallenged, this will remain an important product category, simply because it's so central to the entire online music phenomenon. For example, RealJukebox directly supports hardware players such as the Creative Nomad and RCA Lyra. In fact, RCA uses the jukebox as its default software for loading files into the player (see page 135).

MID and MOD Players

Just a quick word about MID and MOD players. Many people will delve into online music without sampling the creative outpourings of the MID/MOD community, but it's really very easy, and well worth a listen.

If you just want to play the odd MID file, WinAmp or Microsoft Media Player will do just fine. WinAmp will also play many flavours of MOD files. However, MODPlug Player (www.modplug.com) is really the nicest way of playing MOD files.

MODPlug resembles WinAmp, although the main window is cluttered by extra controls. The main thing is that it will play practically any MID or MOD you throw at it. It's got the usual options, including playlists, graphic plug-ins and EQ controls.

It's definitely worth taking a quiet evening to check out MODPlug and this whole unique world of music.

MIDI Set-up

Something to check if you're interested in MIDI is the size of the General MIDI library that comes with your sound card. Generally, the more megabytes the better. This file stores all the instrument sounds (*voices*) that will be used to reproduce MIDI music. It's like the difference between a high-quality set of fonts and one of those $29.99 packages of 10,000 public-domain fonts. The latter are going to have some rough edges.

If a MID file specifies a piano sound, your synthesizer (the sound card and software that you installed with it) looks in the standardized General MIDI library for a piano voice, and uses this to produce the required notes. If you've got a good piano voice, it will sound rich and resonant, almost like a real concert-hall instrument. A cheap voice, on the other hand, will sound like an electronic imitation of a piano. The difference is the amount of acoustic detail stored in the library file, and more detail means more data.

Look for a GM voice file of at least 2MB, and 4MB or 8MB if possible. Creative Technology ships all three sizes, but you may have to search for the larger ones on the software CD-ROM, and you'll also need to reconfigure the card, via the Audio HQ controls, to use the larger file. Other cards behave much the same way.

Accessories

Hardware MP3 Players

A recent development, portable MP3 players are proliferating like toadstools. They look similar to a portable tape player (such as Sony's Walkman), but they're quite a bit smaller, have no moving parts and produce noise-free digital sound.

Given the availability of music in computer-readable form, these devices are a natural consequence. All you need is a processor chip that can decode the music and a bit of memory to hold the data. You download the music from your PC to the player, then take the player with you wherever you like. The device can be tiny, the biggest single component being the batteries that run it. And having no moving parts, it can get dramatically longer battery life than a tape or CD player, with no fear of jamming or skipping if its shaken around a bit.

The main problem is the memory. Memory chips are still much more expensive than tapes or CDs—more expensive even than the drive mechanisms you need to play tapes or CDs. Even at a low encoding rate (see Chapter 1), you need at least 30MB of MP3 files to contain the equivalent of an LP, and 50MB or more to contain some of today's tightly packed CD albums. That much memory is expensive, especially when it has to be *non-volatile*—able to retain the information even when the power is off.

The early players were made possible by memory products developed for use in portable computers and digital cameras—both rather

Figure 3.3 The Creative Nomad portable MP3 player

more expensive devices than the average portable tape or CD player. The two main types of storage used so far are Flash and Compact Flash. There's also the Memory Stick, developed by Sony and used in its own Walkman MS. Prices are still steep: as much as $100 for 32MB.

Of course, the price of memory is going to continue plummeting steeply. If *Moore's Law* holds, we should see 32MB drop to $25 within three years. In this case, the actual drop is likely to be quicker. The market for these memory products is growing so rapidly that economies of scale will help reduce the current cost.

Moore's Law. A famous rule of thumb coined in 1964 by Gordon Moore, co-founder of Intel Corp., which predicts that manufacturers will be able to double the data processing capacity of silicon chips every 18 months or so. This implies that computers (and all other chip-based products) will double in power, or drop in price by one-half, about every year and a half. At last report, this skyrocketing escalation in computing power was expected to continue for at least another 15 years or so.

So most of the problems are things that can and will be fixed, although the timetable is uncertain. Equally uncertain is just how the music industry will embrace this new class of product. The first steps were not auspicious, with the Recording Industry Association of America suing Diamond Multimedia for producing the Rio player, claiming it was a recording device and that it contributed to music piracy.

The suit was eventually resolved. Courts sided with Diamond in ruling that the Rio wasn't a "digital audio recording device" under the law, and hence not subject to the controls that the RIAA had invoked. (In fact, the Rio can't record, only play back.) Diamond by this point was promising strong support for the Secure Digital Music Initiative (SDMI), the industry's master plan for piracy prevention (see Chapter 6).

The Major Players

Assuming you're interested in a portable player, there are a number of things to look for. Unfortunately, some of the most desirable features are largely unavailable in the first-generation players—but a second generation was coming to market early this year, with promise of more to come. Here's what to look out for:

- **USB connection.** One of the most annoying things about the early players was their reliance on the PC's parallel printer port for transferring data. This is both slow and an invitation to compatibility problems, since the port was never meant to be used this way.

It seems likely that second-generation players will all support the USB (Universal Serial Bus) connection, which is designed for exactly this kind of use. USB allows devices to be plugged in while the computer is running, and lets the computer automatically recognize them.

- **Larger memory capacity.** Small memory capacity is another big issue. The fact is that 64MB would still only be barely enough even if you could afford to have several 64MB Flash memory cards with you. Next-generation players will have more memory, perhaps enough to hold several albums at once—all the discs of a live concert or a Wagnerian opera, for example.

- **Multiple audio standards.** Support for various new encoding systems will soon be a necessity, as more music is delivered via Liquid Audio or Microsoft Windows Media. The RCA Lyra is one current player that already has the ability to download software to play almost any conceivable audio format.

- **SDMI support.** Like it or not, the music industry has determined that all new players will include support for its new anti-piracy scheme. This is great in principle, as it allows for wider commercial distribution of music in digital form. But the exact implementation may be troublesome.

A prime example is the Lyra, an otherwise excellent device that's seriously hindered by the need to encrypt all music before it can be played. The Lyra is thus not an MP3 player at all, since it can only play this unique encrypted format. This is true regardless of the origin of the music. If you rip a few tracks off a CD you just bought, they're still going to need processing before the Lyra will deign to deal with them.

This chore is handled by RealJukebox. It's quite slow, even on a reasonably fast computer. The software also creates extra PMP files on the Lyra's Flash card. These are the "keys" that allow files to be played. Files can be copied off the Flash card, but the copies won't play.

Creative seems to have a better solution with the original Nomad—it simply doesn't allow music to be copied *off* the player's memory card. Since the device can only play back, it can't actively contribute to piracy. If you have pirated music, it will play it, true enough, but it won't help you to acquire it, so it creates no security breach.

- **Descriptive display.** The Lyra has a large LCD text display, but unfortunately truncates all file names to 16 characters, making it very difficult to tell what's playing. If (like me!) you put the band's name at the start of the file name, all the tracks end up looking alike. The Nomad scrolls the MP3 file's ID tag, which is a much better solution. Future devices will doubtless give you more information and more accurate control over the playback.

- **Ruggedized construction.** Early devices were quite fragile. Expect to see future models with tougher cases. Housed in resilient plastic, there's no reason one of these players couldn't survive being dropped, kicked, and otherwise abused.

Naturally, manufacturer will come up with even more ideas over time. If this type of device prospers at all, there's virtually no limit to the kind of capabilities that could be built in.

Frank's Pick: None of the Above

Sad to say, the current crop of digital music players is very much a first generation harvest. There are just too many obstacles on the way to enjoying the music.

However, if you're really sure you want this type of device, and you know up front the compromises you'll be accepting, then the Creative Nomad is a good bet. It's tiny yet solid-feeling, and comes with a reasonable 64MB storage capacity, and accepts standard Flash memory cards.

One totally unnecessary annoyance with the Nomad is the lack of a pass-through connector on the PC cable. Thus, you have to unplug your printer to plug in the Nomad. You can probably find a suitable cable, or use a printer switch-box, designed to let you connect more than one printer.

Of course, by the time you read this, a whole new bunch of players will be appearing, including the Creative Nomad II.

The sound of almost any portable player can be dramatically improved by replacing the original-equipment headphones with a really good set. You can buy these at most any stereo shop for anywhere between about $30 to $80, and it's well worth the investment. Portable digital players can produce sound that deserves better treatment than it will get from cheap $10 headphones.

Future Developments

Always assuming that the industry doesn't drop the ball, this current wave of "portable digital music player" is just a harbinger of the coming flood of digital devices.

One exciting development is the ability for handheld computing devices to play music. Already, units such as the Hewlett-Packard Jornada 430se have limited MP3 capability. The Jornada includes a third-party MP3 software player, and has a built-in headphone jack. Sound quality is great, the only limitation being battery life, and that depends more on the power-hungry colour display than anything else.

It seems inevitable that as the capabilities of Microsoft's Windows CE operating system continue to expand, it will acquire more support for Microsoft's Windows Media technologies.

Another potential breakthrough is presaged by a device called the Brujo, from netDrives, in Ithaca, New York (an offshoot of Glyph Technology, which builds high-capacity disk systems for professional music and movie production). The Brujo is a home stereo component that plays both audio CDs and data CDs containing MP3 files. This would let you store five or ten times as much music on a standard CD, without worrying about what format the material was in. At US$299.99, it's a relative bargain.

Sales manager Jim Spitznagel admits to one issue with the Brujo. The device doesn't recognize folders (directories) on the data disc, so all the MP3 files simply appear as track numbers. While this makes sense on audio discs having 16 or 20 tracks, a data CD can hold hundreds of MP3 files.

As of February 2000, the Brujo was being sold only direct from netDrives. Interestingly, Spitznagel stated that the company was feeling no pressure to incorporate security features.

The Brujo is such an attractive concept, its success can only be limited, again, by the music industry. If overly cumbersome copy-control measures are incorporated into future models, the original convenience could be lost. Otherwise, I can't see buying another CD player that doesn't have this capability.

Conclusion

Hopefully, after looking at the growing range of hardware and software products described in this chapter, you can see how quickly the PC is mutating into an audio device. Recall what happened when the PC became a typewriter (the word processor), a sketch pad (graphics software), a page-layout device (desktop publishing), and a communications tool (the Internet). These transformations have been almost literally earth-shaking, and seemingly irreversible. This is indeed the beginning of a new era in entertainment.

In this chapter we've looked at the equipment you'll need to join in the audio revolution. In the next chapter, we can get into some of the most exciting aspects of that revolution—all the ways you can *process* audio on your computer.

4

Processing It

In this chapter we'll move on to the more advanced topic of processing digital sound files on your computer. Sections will cover:

- Editing software, including the Cool Edit line from Syntrillium and the Sound Forge line from Sonic Foundry.
- Editing tasks, including cutting, pasting, mixing, normalizing, and equalizing.
- Noise reduction, to remove unwanted cracks, pops and hiss from old or imperfect recordings.

AFTER YOU'VE DOWNLOADED OR RECORDED some digital music, and the novelty of playing it has started to wear off, the time comes when you might want to do a bit of processing on it.

This chapter will give you a quick introduction to the software tools you'll need to do amazing things with the music files on your personal computer (PC). Some of this information gets slightly technical. But don't be intimidated. It's really just as easy as desktop publishing, or word processing—or cruising the Internet. Some of the concepts are new, but once you have the essentials down, it should all fall into place. The results are definitely worth it.

Personally, I never expected to become an expert recording engineer. The inner logic of music is largely a mystery to me, and I've always thought that recording was something that could only be handled by hirsute troglodytes (apologies to any actual recording engineers reading this) sitting behind glass windows in front of hundreds of thousands of dollars' worth of incomprehensible knobs and gauges.

Of course, 20 years ago I didn't expect to become an expert printer and typographer, either. But desktop publishing blew away all my previous expectations. Back in the early 1980s, typesetting and page layout were handled by skilled artisans using physically challenging machinery. By the end of that decade, little old ladies were laying out and illustrating their own knitting newsletters (seniors took to the technology faster than most of us), and you had to go to the Third World to find anyone who didn't know what a *font* was.

Very soon, the same will be true of terms like *sampling, mixing,* and *normalizing*. We'll all be recording engineers, limited only by our own talent and motivation.

The age of desktop audio is upon us.

A Bit of History

If you're like most people, the deepest interaction you've ever had with the music you listen to is to push the REC button on your tape deck—probably to make up a personal "Best of Abba" cassette tape you could listen to while your car is stuck in traffic. Well, good news: the tape deck is *finally* obsolete.

Good riddance. No more munched-up tapes, muddy sound, long rewind times. . . .

About ten years ago, I went into one of the best stereo shops in downtown Toronto, with $1,000 cash in my pocket and the desire to buy a tape deck burning brightly in my heart. To my vast disappointment, the salesman seemed incapable of telling me which of several then-current technologies was going to be The Wave of the Future—DAT (Digital Audio Tape), DCC (Digital Compact Cassette), DBX, or Dolby S.

At the time, it seemed certain that a quantum leap was imminent, and that one of these technologies would win out. Compact cassette is such a feeble technology, both mechanically and acoustically, that it was hard to doubt that when true digital recording became available—as with both DAT and DCC—analog tape would be swept aside overnight.

I left the store with $1,000 still in my pocket, feeling disappointed and bewildered, but determined to wait a few months until a clear winner emerged. The months stretched into years, and compact cassette remained the mainstay for home recording.

Imagine my surprise, when I find that a replacement for the venerable Compact Cassette has at last emerged—and I already own it. (Good thing—I can't seem to find that $1,000. . . .)

Of course, I'm talking about that big beige box on my office desk. Equipped with some fairly affordable software, the personal computer can now do everything that a tape deck formerly did—only with absolutely state-of-the-art digital quality, and with ease and flexibility that no cassette-deck owner ever dreamed of. The change is going to be at least as dramatic as the transition from paper to electronic publishing, and for many of the same reasons.

The biggest difference between a typewriter and a word processor is that on the latter, the backspace key actually does something useful. With a typewriter, the moving keys write, and having written, move on—neither all your piety nor correction fluid can wash out a word of it cleanly enough so your boss can't see it. With a word processor, you have total control over the writing process. You can write, delete, and move things around endlessly and almost without effort.

The relationship between a tape deck and a desktop audio system is much the same. With a tape deck, about all you can do is press REC and hope for the best. A few fanatical audiophiles actually stare at the VU meters and try to set the record levels properly. But if you make a mistake, the only recourse is to go back and painstakingly rerecord chunks of the tape, maybe even the whole thing. You can't rearrange songs, nor even access them in any sequence but the one in which they were originally recorded.

Desktop audio is more than just a quantum leap beyond the tape deck. Of course, it's also still in its infancy. The available tools are still a bit "techie" and cumbersome, and they do need some learning. But they're no more difficult to use than a good word processor, or a desktop publishing program.

The main thing is to take your time. Don't expect to be hugely productive in five minutes. Play with the various tools—you can download demo versions of virtually all of them. Experiment with some short pieces of audio, maybe 30 seconds at a time. And above all, as mentioned above, don't let yourself be intimidated. All these products are easier than they look, and based on the same few underlying principles.

Read through the rest of this chapter before selecting the software you want to try first. Follow through some of the hands-on exercises, and things will come together very quickly. You may never use a tenth of the power of the tools we'll be looking at, but you can have a whale of a time with that tenth.

And if you do get stuck, just think back to the tape deck . . . and how much easier it would be to use if it had an *Undo* button.

Types of Processing

As we saw in Chapter 2, desktop audio gives you total control over every phase of the recording process. But that's just the beginning. When I speak of "processing" I'm actually talking about several possible steps, some inescapable, some entirely optional. Of course, you need to actually have some music to start with. Check out Chapter 2 for information on how to record it or download it.

Once you do have some music on your computer, there are numerous processing steps you can take. Here are the main ones, more or less in the order you'd go through them in practice.

1. Audio Cleaning (optional). If the music comes from older sources such as scuffed and scratched LP records or cassette tapes afflicted by the characteristic tape hiss, you may wish to do some sonic cleanup. A number of products variously known as *de-clickers, de-noisers,* or simply audio *cleaners* can help remove unwanted background sounds and generally improve the quality of the recording.

2. **Digital Effects** (very optional). You can also apply *digital effects,* to enhance the sound quality or modify it to suit your own tastes. This is comparable to using the *DSP* settings found on today's high-quality stereo amplifiers. For example, you can make the music sound like it was played in a cathedral, if this is what turns you on. More usefully, you might attempt to widen the stereo image, so that there's more acoustic "space" between the left and right channels, or add emphasis to low bass tones in order to beef up a recording that's lacking in that area.

Digital Signal Processor (DSP). A silicon chip, similar to the processor that runs your computer, but designed specifically to modify audio in realtime (i.e. as it is being played). By applying various mathematical transformations on the waveform, a DSP can make music sound as though it's being played in anything from a palace to a padded cell. It can add echoes, emphasize high or low tones, or even play with *phase* to create a 3D effect.

3. **Wave Editing** (optional, but often desirable). This is the most complex possibility: actually editing the music. If you start with commercial recordings, you probably won't need to do this at all. But if you find yourself dealing with less-than-perfect recordings, you can accomplish amazing things, turning rough, amateurish recordings into professional-sounding tracks ready to burn onto an audio CD.

4. **Compression** (optional, but often desirable). Finally, if you're planning to use the music in a portable player or via a software player on your PC rather than, say, recording it onto an audio CD, you'll need to use a *compressor* of some sort. This can scrunch a huge WAV audio file down

by a factor of five to ten times by converting it to one of the popular compressed formats such as MP3, WMA, AAC, or RM.

Note that while the above constitutes the likeliest sequence of steps, you can do most of them in any order. However, compression always comes *last*, particularly if you're using one of the lossy compression formats, such as MP3. You definitely want to avoid opening a compressed file and then resaving it in compressed form. This means recompressing it, and since there's a certain amount of loss in quality every time you compress, it also means introducing an entirely unnecessary generation of loss. Compress only finished files, on which you plan to do no further processing.

Of course, there won't be any actual loss in quality if you save in a lossless compressed format such as SHN. However, you'd still have to go through the annoyance of uncompressing and later recompressing the file, so you might as well just get used to doing the compression at the very last. Think of compressed files in general as being *read-only*.

On the other hand, uncompressed WAV files stored on an audio-format CD can always be retrieved by ripping them back onto your computer, as described in Chapter 2. With a good CD-ROM drive and ripper software, there should be no loss in quality. But even this is a time-consuming extra step. Best to get everything done before you store the music away in either compressed or CD-audio format.

With any sound editing, there are some general rules that will make your life a lot easier:

1. First rule of amateur mechanics: *Keep all the parts!* Save your original file separately from working files, which you'll probably want to delete as you go, in order to save hard-drive space. It's not a bad idea to set your original file to Read-only (right-click on it and select Properties, then tick off the Read Only box). You can then load it and modify it,

but save using another name. Keep the original file intact until you're 100 percent sure you won't need it again. (Then save it for another two days!)

2. Keep an entire performance (concert, album, or whatever) in a single file. That way, all processing will be applied identically to all parts of the music, and you won't end up with audible variations between different parts of the recording.

3. If possible (as in Cool Edit 2000—see page 151), consider recording and editing in 32-bit mode, thereby making editing operations more accurate. This will be particularly worthwhile if you're going to make a number of successive enhancements, since errors will tend to accumulate. Save the working file as 32-bit, then convert to standard 16-bit format when you're done and ready to store it as CD audio or MP3.

Note that there are several drawbacks to working in 32-bit. First, you'll need even more hard-drive space, since 32-bit files are double the already beefy size of standard 16-bit WAV files. Second, you'll only be able to open the files in a program that supports the 32-bit format (such as Cool Edit 2000).

Finally, the eventual conversion from 32-bit to 16-bit must be handled very shrewdly by the software, or it could introduce an additional loss in quality. In general, however, any losses should be much less than the combined loss incurred by doing several successive processing steps on a 16-bit file.

Sound-Editing Basics

An audio editor, such as Cool Edit 2000, is to sound files as a word processor is to text files, or a graphics editor, such as Adobe Photo-Shop, is to image files. It lets you snip pieces out of the music and paste them in somewhere else. It lets you fade in at the beginning of a number, or fade out at the end. It even lets you get right up close to the sound wave and redraw it, moving individual sample data points by ridiculously fine amounts.

All this can be incredibly useful. Don't like that long intro on your favourite song? Snip! It's gone. Always thought that drum solo in the middle of "In a Gadda Da Vida" was too long? Slice, splice, and it's cut down to size. Got an amateur recording with lots of crowd sounds, or a too-abrupt ending? A cut here, a fade-out there, and you've got a totally professional-sounding piece of music.

Sound editors can seem daunting at first. Partly, this is because most were designed with professional musicians in mind. The day of the consumer-level audio editor has not yet dawned—but there is a gleam on the horizon, as software developers begin to realize the potential benefits of selling to *everybody* who listens to music, instead of only to the few who are capable of creating it.

Of course, if all you ever do is pull songs off commercial CDs, or download sample tunes off the Net and then make up best-of discs, you may never need to touch a sound editor. But if you want to make digital transcriptions of your aging LPs, or cassette tapes, you'll end up using some sort of sound editor, since these are the also the best tools for analog recording. (For digital recording, of course, you'd use a CD ripper, as described in Chapter 2.)

But don't be too quick to set limits for yourself. Bob Ellison, president of Syntrillium Software Corp., tells a story of one hobbyist who particularly impressed him by using Syntrillium's sound editor Cool Edit to literally "pick apart" a Beatles song, remixing it from mono to stereo.

This kind of manipulation becomes surprisingly natural, once you get familiar with the basics. If you can keep your head when first confronting the seemingly incomprehensible mass of control buttons and wavy squiggles presented by the average audio editor, it will all come into focus more easily than you might expect.

Especially after you've finished reading this section.

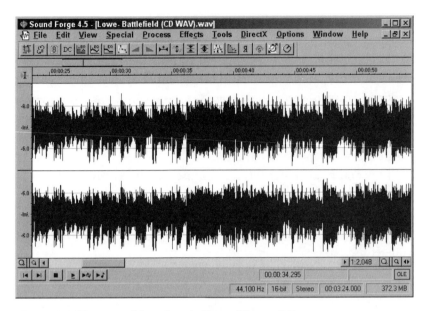

Figure 4.1 The waveform view in Sound Forge 4.5

Representing Sound

Aside from the fact that audio editors are largely designed for pros, there's a more fundamental problem with audio editing that makes it inherently more difficult than editing a graphic image or a text document.

With an image file, or a word processing document, what you see is what you get. But you can't actually *see* a sound file. What you hear may be what you get, but it would be very difficult to edit by ear alone.

Even worse, music doesn't happen in an instant. You can take in the largest and most complex painting in a single glance; the only way you can "view" a symphony is to sit down and give it your undivided attention for an hour or so. Impractical, if you're trying to make just a few small changes in the bassoon solo.

Sound editors get around this to some degree by allowing you to "preview" the sound at any point, in big chunks or tiny snippets of sound. But what's really needed is some sort of visual shorthand that will allow complex sounds to be manipulated intuitively and instantaneously.

Anyone who's taken high school physics knows that sound is a wave, and that this wave can be represented graphically, typically looking like a cross-section through the more familiar sort of wave on the ocean. In this case, the vertical axis represents *amplitude*, that is, the volume or intensity of the atmospheric displacement, while the horizontal axis represents time.

This graph, as represented in Figure 4.1, is exactly what sound editors rely on. It's a bit abstract, of course—just try to imagine the experience of hearing a symphony based on that random squiggle you see on your display! But this is actually a very useful view, once you get used to it.

Visual Representation of sound

If you load a sound file into any good sound editor, you can quickly get a feeling for the relationship between what you see on the screen and what you hear when the file is played.

1. Load a sound file into Sound Forge, Sound Forge XP, Cool Edit 2000, Cool Edit Pro, or any other full-featured audio editor. (Even the Windows Sound Recorder will help give you some idea. If it's not on your system, you can install it from your original Windows 95 or 98 set-up CD-ROM, using Add-Remove Programs from the Control Panel.)
2. Push Play (almost always shown by a right-pointing triangle, as on most CD players, tape decks, or VCRs.) Now look at the main waveform display. You'll typically see a vertical line—the *cursor*—moving from left to right, with the jagged music waveform moving past it from right to left. (In Sound Recorder, you'll see a green line that grows broader or thinner. That's the same thing, only with

much less detail.) Chances are you're seeing two wave-forms, of course, one above the other—those are the left and right speaker *channels* of a stereo recording. If you load a mono recording, there will be only one waveform.

3. Note how the louder passages are represented by broader sections in the waveform. Any sharp cracks or pops will be clearly visible as narrow *spikes* sticking out from the main body of the wave. Soft passages appear as very slender sections of the waveform.

4. Try zooming in (right-click in Sound Forge, the magnifying glass icon in Cool Edit) until you get right down to the point where you see the characteristic wave shape. Of course, by this point you'll be looking at only a tiny instant of the music. Notice that the blotchy, jagged shape normally seen in a wave editor really is a wave—it's just squashed sideways so tightly that you can't see the line of the waveform itself. This is necessary in order to show a useful amount of sound at one time. By the time you can actually make out the wave line, you'll be looking at a mere split second of sound.

5. Zoom in far enough and you'll see a bunch of little black dots along the wave line. These represent the actual digital *samples*—data points stored in the digital sound file—44,100 of them in each second of standard CD audio! Now you can see that this complex waveform really is just a graph, drawn through a large number of data points, each representing a measurement of sound amplitude at a particular instant in time.

You may also begin to appreciate the limitations of digital recording. Those discrete dots are the only points that are actually guaranteed to lie on the original waveform. The line drawn between them is only an educated guess, using mathematical interpolation to approximate the original.

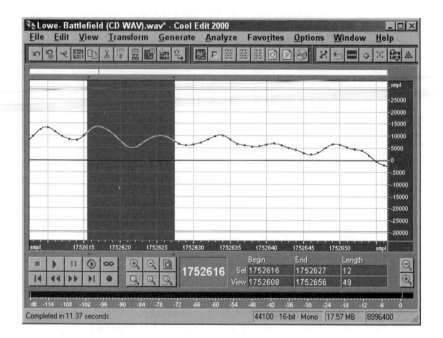

Figure 4.2 Cool Edit 2000 shows dots representing sample data in an audio file

Sound Editors

There are only a few audio editors that you really need to think about—and are likely to be able to afford—for basic home-audio applications. The better ones connect to a whole world of professional tools, and if you find you really want to go on, you can certainly get into more complex and powerful audio tools.

A word of caution: as with any product descriptions in this book, the following details are based on the latest editions of the software available at the time of writing. This market is changing at a frenetic pace, and you may find that newer versions dramatically expand the capabilities of any particular product. However, the features mentioned below will still give you a good guide for picking the product you need. The *types* of features you'll need aren't going to change much.

There are two main companies to watch in this field: Syntrillium Software Corporation, in Phoenix, Arizona (www.syntrillium. com), and Sonic Foundry Inc., in Madison, Wisconsin (www.sonicfoundry. com). Both produce editors that are widely used and much admired, and, equally important, are available in separate versions for pro and amateur users.

So let's look first at these main products, then check out in detail some of the wonders they can work on your sound files.

Cool Edit Pro and Cool Edit 2000

Let's start with Cool Edit 2000, from Syntrillium Software Corp. in Phoenix, Arizona. Released in the fall of 1999, this is a uniquely attractive choice, packing high-end power at the amazingly affordable price of US$69. This package includes virtually everything you'd get in a full professional-class sound editor. That's no accident, since it's based on the redoubtable Cool Edit Pro 1.2, one of the most popular professional sound editors.

Syntrillium has been extremely cunning in deciding what to leave out of Cool Edit 2000. The two main omissions are things that no professional would want to be without, but which no amateur is likely to care much about: *multitrack editing* and *DirectX plug-in* support. You may not even know what these terms mean! If so, you *are* the target user.

> **Multitrack editing.** The ability to display multiple synchronized sound streams at one time, to edit them individually or all at once, and to combine them into a single (i.e. two-track stereo) recording.

> **DirectX Plug-in.** A plug-in is any module that can be added on to a piece of software in order to add new capabilities. DirectX is Microsoft's multimedia support structure in Windows, which is exploited by many audio plug-ins, allowing them to be compatible with virtually any Windows software.

The basic Cool Edit 2000 has all the features you need to record from any analog source, such as LP or tape. It will let you adjust the audio level, cut and paste sections of the music, fade in or fade out, apply special effects, and much, much more. When we look at some of the basic editing functions later in this chapter, you'll start to get an idea how powerful this product really is.

What's more, Cool Edit 2000 is expandable enough that you won't easily outgrow it. While Cool Edit 2000 doesn't support industry-standard DirectX plug-ins, it does accept Syntrillium's own plug-ins, of which there are currently two very good ones.

The more important of the two for home users will be the Audio Cleanup Plug-In, which sells for US$49. This adds some very sophisticated tools to help with removal of unpleasant background noise, such as tape hiss or the cracks and pops of an old vinyl record. We'll look at these tools in detail later in this chapter.

The other optional add-on is the Studio Plug-In, priced at US$49, or US$20 if purchased together with Cool Edit 2000. This adds 4-track editing and mixing capability, which can be handy if you really get into editing and splicing audio tracks. Four-track mixing is probably plenty for most general applications, and the editing features are quite comprehensive.

My own recommendation would be to grab the basic Cool Edit 2000 and the Noise Reduction Plug-In. At the time of writing, this is absolutely the best value available in a full-featured audio editor. (Of course, these things can change quickly, so surf around a bit before pulling out the charge card!)

At first sight, aside from its hefty US$399 price tag, Cool Edit Pro 1.2 is almost indistinguishable from Cool Edit 2000. In fact, a non-professional user might never stumble across the significant differences.

The most obvious difference is that Cool Edit Pro includes full multitrack editing, with support for up to 64 tracks. This facility is invaluable if you're planning to record and mix your own album, but not likely to come up for casual users.

Non-destructive Editing. The main virtue of multi-track editing, especially for the average user, is that it allows

non-destructive editing. You can make cut-and-paste types of changes to various tracks without actually changing the data. Your edits are essentially programmed and applied as needed, without affecting the original tracks. When you've got everything perfect, you can mix the tracks into a single final version.

More significantly, for our purposes, Cool Edit Pro includes a wider range of special effects, and offers live preview of most effects and noise-reduction filters. In other words, while the noise-reduction features are almost identical to those in the Cool Edit 2000 Noise Reduction plug-in, you'll be able to immediately hear the effect of various settings, without having to run the filter and then play back the result.

Cool Edit Pro also accepts DirectX plug-ins, which opens it up to a wide range of extras. And it accepts recording input from multiple devices, so you can use two or more inputs at a time. Again, not something most non-musicians will care about.

On the negative side, Cool Edit Pro does *not* include the ability to save recordings in MP3 form. For that, you need an optional US$29 plug-in. On balance, Cool Edit Pro is a lovely tool for working musicians, but overkill for average folks.

One neat feature that's shared by Cool Edit 2000 and Cool Edit Pro is support for 32-bit resolution. What this means is that you can digitize music from LP or tape using 32-bit values for the sample points, rather than 16-bit values used by most software. This can improve quality if you do a lot of processing on the file. Of course, you can later save the recording in standard 16-bit format.

There is one other option, although it's no longer part of the Syntrillium line. The company's original sound editor Cool Edit 96 is still widely available as a free download on public software sites. You may need to do a bit of work with a good Internet search engine to find it, but it's worth the effort if you really want to minimize the cash outlay. (For example, I found it at http://www.rocketdownload .com/Details/Musi/C96setup.htm. Of course, I can't guarantee it'll still be there by the time you go to look; a lot of sites are replacing it with Cool Edit 2000.) If nothing else, it will give you a taste of the capabilities you'll be getting with the current product.

It's worth noting the drawbacks of these generally excellent products. Both Cool Edit 2000 and Cool Edit Pro use a very pleasant but slightly non-standard control layout. The toolbars aren't fully configurable, and don't act quite like the ones you may be used to in something like Microsoft Office. You can decide which tool groups to display, but you can't mix buttons from within the groups. It's all very logical, but just a bit different than any other piece of Windows software.

Many of the companies producing professional audio tools are now starting to go after beginning users. But with Cool Edit 2000, Syntrillium has been the most aggressive so far. Bob Ellison, affable company president, acknowledges that Cool Edit 2000 is a conscious effort by Syntrillium to go after the new low-end user. "A lot of people are way too focused on the audio pros," he says. "They're all trying to make the world's best *reverb*. We're saying that this kind of processing is not for audio pros exclusively."

Since much of Syntrillium's software is downloaded off multiple Web sites, and later registered by a relatively small proportion of downloaders, it is difficult to estimate the total number of users. However, Ellison theorizes that users of all versions of Cool Edit number easily in the hundreds of thousands, possibly in the millions, if casual users are included. When I spoke with him, 5:00 p.m. EST on a Thursday, there were about 300 people downloading software from the Syntrillium site alone.

Ellison mentioned that the company was deliberately not publicizing itself too widely as yet. "You have to be very careful," he notes. "You don't want to trip over your own feet as you run." However, it seems very likely that this market is about to explode, and Syntrillium is poised to take advantage.

Of course, it won't be alone. Let's look next at its closest competitor

Sound Forge and Sound Forge XP

Sonic Foundry Inc., in Madison, Wisconsin, puts on a slicker, more corporate front, but in many ways it's a mirror image of Syntrillium.

Its lead product, Sound Forge 4.5, selling for US$499, goes head to head with Cool Edit Pro, each having its strengths—and its devotees.

The junior version is Sound Forge XP. Selling for US$49.95, it's quite a bit easier to use than the slightly cluttered Cool Edit 2000, and sticks with a traditional Windows 95/98 layout, so many users will feel immediately more comfortable with it. The trade-off is that while there's plenty of power for most tasks, some of the neater features of Cool Edit 2000 are missing.

Sound Forge XP is perfectly capable of recording sound from any device you can plug into your sound card. It also has complete editing, including the usual cut and paste, and the ability to mix (overlap and combine) segments of music.

You can also normalize (an important operation that's covered later in this chapter), fade in, fade out, set markers at key points in the file, alter the left-right stereo balance, and add various special effects, such as reverb or flange.

One basic thing that Sound Forge XP can do that Cool Edit 2000 (or Cool Edit Pro, for that matter) *cannot* is to display two files at one time, using the standard Windows multi-document interface (MDI) (i.e. showing multiple files in separate sub-windows within the main Sound Forge XP window). This comes with the usual commands on the Windows menu, such as Tile Horizontally or Minimize All. This is comparable to what you'd find in any good Windows software, such as Corel Draw.

Of course, you can't perform editing operations simultaneously across both tracks, as you can using the Cool Edit 2000 Studio Plug-In. But frequently, all you'd like to do is just *see* several pieces of music at once—for example, if you're cutting a bit out of one to paste into the other. With Cool Edit 2000, you have to flip between the files, or go to the trouble of using the much more complex multi-track add-on.

What Sound Forge XP doesn't have are the more advanced features of Cool Edit 2000, such as the ability to create your own script files to automate repetitive procedures, or the ability to work in a "spectral" view, which shows the range of sound frequencies in the file.

Most sorely missed, however, are the capabilities provided by the two optional Cool Edit 2000 plug-ins—noise reduction and multi-track editing. Although the latter may only come up very rarely, noise reduction is a major plus for anyone transferring their old analog recordings to digital form. You have to go to the full US$499 version of Sound Forge and then add Sonic Foundry's US$499 DirectX plug-in to arrive at a comparable level of capability.

Nonetheless, Sound Forge XP is an excellent choice if you want a good all-round sound editor and care more about ease of use than some of the more advanced features available in Cool Edit 2000. You'll also save US$20 with Sound Forge XP. (You may save even more if you buy one of the more recent Creative Labs Sound Blaster Live! sound cards, since at least some models include Sound Forge XP—a not-insignificant bonus.)

It seems inevitable that these two products will play feature leapfrog, so check both Web sites before deciding. It would be surprising if the next version of Cool Edit 2000 wasn't easier for novices, or if the next version of Sound Forge XP didn't add things like a noise-reduction option. Of course, it's all up to the respective publishers. At least between these two editors, you've got a good choice.

Sound Forge 4.5, the full professional product, is more similar to Cool Edit Pro than Sound Forge XP is to Cool Edit 2000. Considering the price, we'll look at the features list mainly as a matter of academic curiosity.

In general, Sound Forge 4.5 has the same sort of basic editing capabilities and digital effects that you'll find in Cool Edit Pro. Where the product excels is in its support for various different music formats, including not just WAV and MP3, but also Real Networks' RealSystem G2. Sound Forge even works with video in the common Windows AVI format, allowing users to synchronize audio to the moving image.

Sound Forge includes a batch facility, that allows piles of files to be processed automatically, using any of the programs' effects or tools. And, of course, Sound Forge 4.5 includes full support for DirectX plug-ins. Sonic Foundry offers a good range of tools that musicians will appreciate, although at a substantial price. For example, the excellent Noise Reduction 2.0 package is a US$399 add-on, where Cool Edit Pro includes similar capability in the base product.

Another surprising omission in Sound Forge is any semblance of multitrack editing. Sonic Foundry sells an entirely separate multitrack audio editor called Vegas Pro for US$699. This is a very comprehensive package, and probably worth the extra expense for power-hungry professionals, who can take advantage of features such as support for multi-processor PCs for extra processing speed.

Generally, then, Sound Forge 4.5 is a somewhat slicker, yet in some ways simpler, product than Cool Edit Pro. Where it shines is in its ability to handle various types of media formats, including video. Given the close competition between these (and several other) contenders, then, expect features and prices to mutate rapidly in the coming months.

Basic Editing Tasks

If you've read the preceding sections, you should be able to pick a sound editor for yourself without too much trouble. No matter which you decide to start with, you're probably going to encounter the same editing problems, and solve them in much the same way.

The next section examines a few of the commonest editing procedures and demonstrates how you can put a sound editor to work. The examples include specific references to both Cool Edit 2000 and Sound Forge XP, but the procedures are largely the same in any good editor.

Normalizing, Equalizing, and Fading

One of the simplest things you can do to a sound wave is to modify its volume. This may seem like a no-brainer, but in the world of digital recording, the process can become just as sophisticated as you like. And in some cases, it can be vital to ensuring that you end up with a really nice-sounding recording.

We'll look at three basic kinds of volume change. *Normalizing* typically means raising or lowering the volume of an entire sound file by a constant amount. Equalizing selectively boosts or reduces specific frequencies within the file. And fading selectively causes sections of the file to grow or diminish in volume.

Normalizing. The process of changing the volume level of an entire sound file to a) ensure that various tracks play at what feels like a constant volume level, and b) ensure that digital sound samples use the full possible range of data values, from +32,768 to −32,768.

Normalizing is a bit like changing the contrast and brightness in a photograph, or on your TV or camcorder. If you turn the brightness too low on your TV, the image will be murky and lack detail; if you turn it too high, the screen will glare at you and detail will wash out. Similarly, normalizing ensures that you've got a full range of levels in the recording, so that it doesn't sound either quiet and dull, or overloud and harsh.

Here's another way to look at it. Remember that the digital waveform is defined by a large but limited number of data points. If your entire recording is created at half volume, then the loudest sounds will have sample data values of only about +16,000 to −16,000. By using only half the available values, you've lost half the available resolution—like creating a graphic with fewer pixels. Not only will everything sound too quiet, there's going to be less real detail in the music.

It's actually even worse than that. By reducing the overall volume, you've changed the subtle interrelationships between loud and soft, high-pitched and low-pitched sounds. No amplifier will reproduce them correctly, since they're optimized for sounds recorded at a full range of volume, and your ears won't respond correctly, since the full range was originally chosen specifically for its correspondence to what our ears and brains most enjoy. Hence normalization. All this means is stretching the waveform, making it taller or shorter, so that it fits nicely within the expected amplitude range, and uses

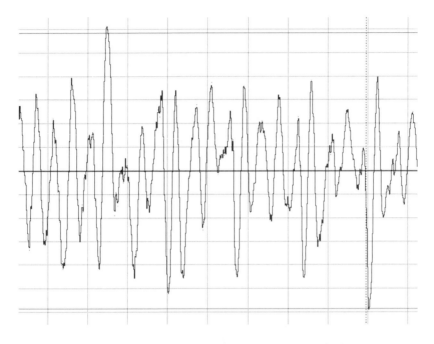

Figure 4.3 Using the full data range for maximum resolution

virtually all the available data values, from zero to around plus or minus 32,000.

Normalizing a quiet recording can't *create* any new data, it simply stretches what's already there. In fact, you're introducing new rounding-off errors as the old data values must be expanded to new, larger ones that will never fit exactly. This means that it's much better to record at a volume level that uses the full data range in the first place than it is to normalize later. You should probably resist normalizing except where it's clearly the lesser of the two evils.

On the other hand, if you've recorded at 32-bit resolution (as you can in Cool Edit), you've got a lot more data values to play with, and it may make sense to normalize every recording before converting to standard 16-bit format for transfer to CD or conversion to MP3. You'll probably gain more than you lose.

Of course, whether you're recording or normalizing an existing recording, the one thing you must avoid at all costs is *clipping*. Clipping changes the shape of the wave from rounded to square-ish, producing a horrible, harsh-sounding interference, especially in the high-pitched tones. (The effect of the squaring-off is like adding a lot of new high-pitched noise.)

Clipping. When the volume (amplitude) of a recorded sound wave exceeds the capacity of the recording medium, the peaks of the waves are literally clipped off. This makes the sound harsh and garbled.

Clipping occurs with tape decks, if your VU needles or LEDs go up into the red area. However, with tape, clipping is never totally sharp, since it depends on what the specific tape can handle, and that varies slightly from tape to tape, even from one section to another on the same tape. Digital clipping, on the other hand, is razor-sharp. This is very nasty, and it's the easiest way to totally ruin a digital recording.

So, to summarize: you want to normalize the waveform so that it's peak data values fall near the upper end of the data range, but don't exceed it. It's like playing blackjack—if you get close to 21, you win, but if you get 22 you go bust.

Normalizing should be done to an entire recording uniformly, assuming that the recording was created at a constant volume level, as it should have been. For example, with a professional album transcribed from LP or CD, all the tracks should be normalized at once, in a single large WAV file.

The only time you'd normalize tracks separately is if they've been recorded at noticeably different levels. However, it's very difficult to get this right, since no two tracks are meant to sound exactly equal in volume. If you just set the peaks to the same height in each waveform, you'll almost certainly get tracks that don't sound similar when you play them back. Start with ten tracks, and the problem grows exponentially. The only solution is a lot of trial and error. You can also use tools that try to expand or contract the waveform based on an average volume level, rather than on just the peaks.

Normalizing

Although we've gone through the theory in some detail, normalizing a reasonably decent recording should be very easy.

1. Load up a WAV file containing all of the album or performance. If necessary, splice the tracks back together temporarily.
2. In Cool Edit 2000, the command is Transform . . . Amplitude . . . Normalize. You can select a percentage, indicating how much of the available data range you want the wave to use. In Sound Forge XP, it's the Process . . . Normalize command, with a single slider control. It's okay to normalize to 100 percent most of the time, but some users prefer to use a little less than the full range.

Notice in Figure 4.3 that the file shown is already normalized, but doesn't seem to fill the entire range. This happens to be a very quiet piece of music. You can also see one spike in the middle that drops almost to the edge, indicating that the normalization is in fact correct.

Also, in Cool Edit 2000 you'll note a check box that sets DC Bias Adjust. In Sound Forge, this is a separate command, Process . . . DC Offset. This ensures that the waveform is actually centred along the zero line. Usually it will be, but occasionally you'll get one that isn't perfect.

Equalizing is simpler to explain. This is just like using the graphic equalizer you get with a lot of home stereo systems (usually with cheaper ones, for some reason), or the one that's built into the WinAmp player.

Equalizing. EQ for short. Altering the emphasis on high (treble), middle or low (bass) within a recording. Typically accomplished using a graphic equalizer, which consists

of a series of volume controls, each affecting a different range of frequencies.

If a recording has too little bass, lacking that proper oomph in the low notes, you can use equalization to boost it a bit. Similarly, it is possible to bring out a vocalist on a poor recording by making just some of the middle tones louder.

In Sound Forge XP, the equalizer is accessed using the Process . . . Graphic EQ command. This displays a dialog with the traditional slider controls, allowing you to increase or decrease the volume level of ten different frequency ranges within the file. If you push up the right-most sliders, you'll be increasing the high tones, while pushing up the left-hand sliders increases the bass.

Cool Edit 2000 doesn't exactly have an equalizer, as such. Instead, you use the Transform . . . Filter . . . Quick Filter dialog to accomplish much the same thing. There are the same sliders that boost or reduce eight frequency ranges, but because this is done using filters, the effect isn't exactly the same as in Sound Forge (see Figure 4.5). However, it's very close, and if you experiment a bit you'll be able to do the same sorts of things.

Use equalization, like all effects, with extreme restraint! It's much easier to ruin a recording than to improve it. However, if you're starting with a recording that has serious problems, equalizing can be an easy way to perk it up.

Note that you can also equalize files using WinAmp. If you use WinAmp to create a WAV file from an MP3 file, for example, you can tell it to use your current Equalizer settings in the resulting file.

Fading is no more difficult than either normalizing or equalizing. However, this is the first effect we'll talk about that is not applied to the entire file.

Fade. To gradually increase or decrease the volume of a recording. Typically usage is either *fade in*—to start from silence and gradually bring the sound up to full volume— or *fade out*—to start at full volume and gradually reduce the sound to silence. However, other fades are used when editing segments of music together. A cross-fade reduces the volume of the original segment while bringing up the volume of the pasted segment, to create a smooth transition.

We've all heard music that fades out at the end of a song. Obviously, this is much more pleasant than having it stop abruptly in the middle of a sustained note. You can easily apply fades to clean up the edges of a ragged recording, and generally make your work seem much more professional.

Applying a Fade

To fade in or fade out, in either Sound Forge XP or Cool Edit 2000, the procedure is roughly the same.

1. Select the piece of the wave that you want to fade. (Usually, five or ten seconds is plenty.)
2. In Sound Forge XP, select Process . . . Fade . . . In, or Process . . . Fade . . . Out. In Cool Edit 2000, the command is Transform . . . Amplitude . . . Amplify (there's also a toolbar button). In the dialog, select the Fade tab, then the appropriate item in the Presets list—for example, Fade In or Fade Out. You can adjust the various settings, but the defaults are good.

In either program, while the faded area is selected, you can listen to it by pressing the space bar.

Obviously, fades would tend to happen at the start or end of a track. They're a good way to soften a too-abrupt start or take out some unwanted crowd noise at the end.

Cutting, Pasting, and Mixing

With a text file or even a graphic image, cutting and pasting are just about the most basic editing actions you can perform. However, with music, it's not quite so straightforward. Simply snipping a piece out of a sound file and jabbing it in elsewhere is not likely to produce a pleasant-sounding result.

There's definitely an art to this, but it gets a lot easier once you know a few basic tricks. The main thing to realize is that you have to soften the transitions, or you'll end up with jarring discontinuities in your music.

The technique for doing this is *mixing.* Instead of just butting a pasted area against the music before and after it, you allow the edges to overlap a bit and mingle together. If you pick the position of these areas carefully, it's easy to make them virtually imperceptible. Crowd noise is great for this, since it's almost random, and the ear doesn't pick out the change from one bit to another.

Trimming Your WAVs

If you like live music, or any kind of semi-amateur recordings, one of the problems you'll quickly run into is that many audio tracks will include large amounts of crowd noise, or rough sound, or other unwanted material. Even with studio recordings, you may find that you disagree with the original edit and would like to make a few judicious "improvements."

With older recordings, you may have scratches or other unusable sections, and the only solution is to cut them out entirely.

It's not as hard as it seems, as long as you have the right tools for the job. In the following, the idea is to cut a piece off the end of a file, remove another piece and discard it, then take the first removed piece and graft it back on. This way you've rid yourself of an unwanted chunk, but retained the very end of the track, which we are assuming contains a transition to the next track. This way, your splice is inaudible, and tracks continue to flow into one another.

In Sound Forge XP, the trick is to use the Edit. . . Paste Special. . . Mix command.

Let's say that you want to cut some crowd noise off the end of a live song. Follow these steps:

1. Load the WAV file into your editor (first decoding it from MP3 or other compressed format, if necessary).
2. Ensure that Options . . . Drag and Drop Snapping is turned on (checked).
3. Identify the part to cut. (Don't cut too much! You might miss it later, once you've consigned it permanently to digital oblivion. On the other hand, anything over 15 seconds of non-content can seem to drag on, after you've heard it a few times.) Listen carefully for significant sounds that give a sense of time and place—tuning, comments by the musicians, announcements. . . In particular, check the very end of the track for significant material that serves as a lead-in to the next track. You don't want to lose this!
4. If the end of the file is of absolutely no interest, your job is easy. Place your cursor at the start of the boring bit, and select about ten seconds into it (to the right). Fade out the selection, using the technique previously described. Then grab the *left* edge of your selection and drag it (past the right edge!) to the end of the file, leaving the right edge where it was, so that it now becomes the

left edge. (In Cool Edit 2000, you need to hold the Shift key to move the edge of the selection.) Press Del to remove this piece, and Save. You're done.

5. Otherwise, if there is significant material at the end of the file, the trick is to grab the very tail end and graft it back onto an earlier portion, so only the boring middle part is lost.

   Carefully identify the minimum length at the end of the track that you'll want to keep. You'll need at least five to ten seconds of material. Select backward from the end of the file, to the left, stopping at the first convenient lull, or at the beginning of the transition passage that you need to keep. Usually, there's an obvious point you can use. If there isn't, don't worry, pick the best spot you can and we'll cover up the inconsistencies later.

6. Press Ctrl-C or select Edit . . . Cut, to copy this piece to the clipboard.

7. Locate the beginning of the boring segment you want to delete. Remember this location, then place the cursor about five to ten seconds past (to the right of) this point, and select from there to the end of the track. Press Del to discard this portion.

8. Now go back to the position you remembered from the previous step, which should now be five to ten seconds before (to the left of) the new end of the track. Select Edit . . . Paste Special. . . Mix (or press Ctrl+M). In Cool Edit, select Edit . . . Mix Paste.

   In Sound Forge XP, you can press the Preview button to hear the splice as it will sound. If needed, you can tweak the Source and Destination volume sliders up and down until you can't hear the end of the original track "under" the newly pasted-in tail-end. Normally, a setting of 0.0 dB works fine, but this depends a lot on the material you're trying to blend together.

In Cool Edit the volume sliders run horizontally, but the command works almost exactly the same way. If you chose the right piece to paste, you can usually leave the sliders at their 100 percent position.

If you followed all this, you'll end up with quite a professional edit.

Once you get a bit of practice, you can try longer mix edit overlaps. You can actually construct a whole new ending to a track using this basic technique, or even create new transitions between tracks. For example, you could merge the start of, say, track 5 onto the end of track 3, allowing you to drop track 4 entirely, while keeping the seamless feel of the live performance.

When performing any edits that can change the length of your file, enable the *snap* option in your sound editor. This is especially important if you're working with tracks that merge seamlessly, with no pause, as with live music or some "concept albums." CD tracks must start on an even *frame* boundary; if they don't, the missing partial frame will be audible as a pop or hiccup in the music. By cutting the file with snap enabled, you ensure that it will always end right on a frame boundary. (You may need to trim the end off files of dubious lineage, just to make sure.)

Frame. Data stored on audio CDs is subdivided into frames, or short segments. This normally doesn't affect anything we do, but when storing multiple tracks that should run smoothly together, it is important that their lengths are exactly divisible into frames, to avoid creating an audible pop between tracks.

Obviously, this type of editing technique is particularly valuable with amateur or bootleg recordings, especially recordings of live performances. These tend to have ragged beginnings and endings, and often include long stretches of uninteresting crowd noise or applause. You can take this kind of raw recording and with very little effort make it sound slick and professional, like a commercial live album.

However, even with commercial recordings, a little editing skill can come in handy. If you're recording from old LPs, you can silence out the noise between tracks, or clip off particularly bad cracks and pops that might result from a deep scratch in the vinyl.

Of course, when it comes to noise reduction, there's a whole range of specialized tools you can use. We'll try those next.

Cleaning Up Your Sound

In Chapter 2 we covered the process of recording music from a vinyl LP. But that's only half the battle, or, to look at it the other way, only half the fun. Once you've digitized the music, it's very tempting to use more digital technology to do some judicious cleaning up, eliminating or at least minimizing those annoying vinyl cracks and pops and background noise.

There's quite a bit of software available to aid you in this task. Products range from the simplistic to the insanely sophisticated. Somewhere in that range is the right one for you.

One of the simplest and easiest you may already own, and if you don't, you'll see in Chapter 5 that you really should. That's Easy CD Creator, from Adaptec Inc. Although this package is mainly aimed at storing software on CD recordable discs (see Chapter 5), it includes several extra modules, one of which is a basic sound cleaner.

Two of the more powerful options are actually add-ons to the leading audio editors: the Audio Cleanup Plug-in for Cool Edit 2000, the Noise Reduction Plug-in for Sound Forge 4.5. Cool Edit Pro has its own built-in noise-reduction tools.

There are also several stand-alone products, which for some reason tend to combine audio cleanup and CD recording. The most notable of these is DARTPro 98, from Dartech Inc.

All of these have roughly, but not exactly, similar features. If you do much work with low-quality recordings, you'll probably find it worthwhile to have two or more on hand. Fortunately, several are relatively inexpensive, allowing you to create a well-stocked arsenal of cleaning tools even on a limited budget.

Types of Filtering

When a sculptor was asked how he created such lifelike works, he answered that the secret was to chip away all the bits of marble that didn't look like his subject. With sound cleanup, the trick is to siphon off all the stuff that doesn't sound like music. If our ears can clearly distinguish the noise as a separate entity, why shouldn't computer software?

Unfortunately, sound is a complex phenomenon. Isolating a sound that to us seems to stick out like a sore thumb is not a trivial proposition. The noise and the music overlap and intermingle.

A large part of the solution lies in a field of mathematics known as harmonic analysis. This allows any complex waveform to be broken apart into simpler components. Thus, any real-world sound wave can be seen as the sum of a large number of pure sine waves of various frequencies. Some of those can be easily identified as being unwanted "noise" and discarded. The best case would be a noise consisting of a single pure tone of constant pitch. This could be eliminated simply by discarding the appropriate sine wave.

Of course, the reality is far more complex. These types of techniques yield various approaches, each appropriate to a particular type of noise. What's more, each technique offers many parameters that can be manually fine-tuned so as to zero in on the noise and nothing but the noise.

This is the real art of noise reduction, and you should realize that none of the products mentioned in this section can work miracles. With a badly degraded recording, you'll always come down to a choice between retaining some of the noise or losing some of the music. You can play with settings endlessly to improve the outcome, but none of the automated filters is going to do a particularly good job on its own.

On the other hand, backed by a bit of human judgment, any of these cleanup tools can do amazing things to resuscitate an old recording. The onus remains on you to apply the tool where it will do the most good.

Before we see how this works in practice, we need to check out some of the products that can do it.

Cleaning Software

CD Spin Doctor. While Easy CD Creator leads the pack for CD-R creation, the included CD Spin Doctor module comes across largely as a consumer gimmick, and yet it does work, and, in its favour, it's certainly dead simple to use.

What's more, CD Spin Doctor includes the highly useful option of previewing your filter settings live. This feature is hidden within the confusingly titled Option Properties dialog box, but works amazingly well, and does a lot to elevate the program above the gimmick category.

There are just two slider controls, one each for Noise Removal and Pop Removal, and nary a graph or numeric setting to be seen. As you move the two sliders up and down, you can easily hear the improvement in sound quality. First the noise fades out, then you get a subtle transition to declining sound quality as the filter starts eating away at the actual music.

This is pretty neat, but unfortunately, the program seems to have an awkward little bug. When the preview hits the end of the sound file, CD Spin Doctor quits abruptly, leaving you staring at the Windows desktop. This isn't totally fatal—just make sure you don't play the whole file when you're previewing!

The other concern with CD Spin Doctor is that the type of filtering being done isn't documented, and there are no detailed settings that you can adjust, so you may be losing more of your music than is immediately obvious, or even necessary. If you do much recording with this program, it would be a good idea to use extreme restraint, leaving behind much more noise than you may think is necessary. That way you'll at least know that you haven't eroded too many of the edges off your music.

CD Spin Doctor is certainly convenient, and would be useful in a pinch, but it's no substitute for full-featured cleanup software. This shouldn't worry Adaptec much, since Easy CD Creator would be a must-have product even without Spin Doctor.

Cool Edit 2000 Audio Cleanup Plug-In. Surprise: the best value in sound editors is also the best value in sound cleanup—a staggering one-two punch from Syntrillium. The Audio Cleanup Plug-In adds just US$49 to the US$69 base price of Cool Edit 2000, which means that you can have complete professional-quality editing and audio restoration for about C$175. This is bar none the best bargain in audio software.

What's doubly amazing is that none of the capabilities seem to be compromised. The noise-reduction features are virtually identical to those in Cool Edit Pro, and very similar to the much more expensive Noise Reduction plug-in available from Sonic Foundry for Sound Forge 4.5. (There's no comparable solution for Sound Forge XP.)

The one limitation of the Cool Edit 2000 Audio Cleanup Plug-In is its inability to preview the effect of your settings on the fly. For that you need to move up to Syntrillium's own Cool Edit Pro, or switch to a more specialized product entirely.

The big brother to Cool Edit 2000, Cool Edit Pro offers almost identical audio cleanup features, with the one significant difference that at least some of the tool dialogs give you the opportunity to preview the effect of your current settings. You can even alter your settings on the fly and hear an immediate change in the result. This is a great timesaver, allowing you to zero in on the magic settings that will remove as much extraneous noise as possible without damaging the music itself.

DARTPro 98. This somewhat daunting product, priced at the daunting price of US$399, at once represents both the high-end

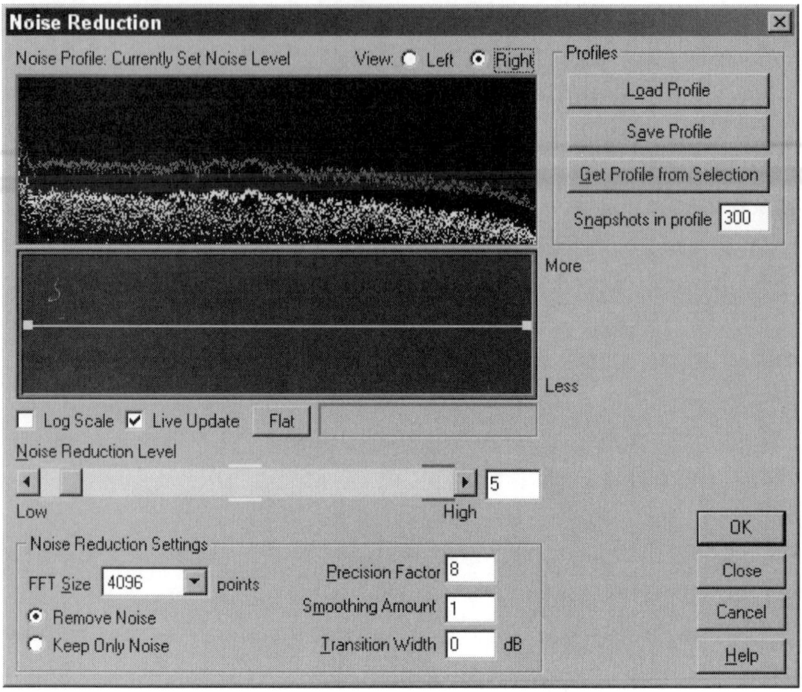

Figure 4.4 The Noise Reduction dialog in Cool Edit 2000

professional approach and the old guard in audio software. It seems to date back to well before the current consumer interest in digital audio, and is probably overdue for both a user interface revamp and a rethink on the price strategy. However, once you master its peculiarities, it turns out to be very efficient at its appointed task.

The DARTPro 98 user interface can seem particularly confusing if you've already gotten accustomed to one of the popular audio editors. Many of the controls look familiar yet behave in their own unique way. For example, the waveform view defaults to maximum magnification, rather than minimum, so when you first load a file all you see is a straight line across the screen. It's only when you zoom out to the minimum magnification that the characteristic jagged pattern appears. Also, for some reason, you're required to hold down the Ctrl key when using the mouse to select regions. Fortunately, you can turn off this dubious "feature" in the options menu.

Once you get past such annoyances, things do get much better. DARTPro 98 includes comprehensive cleanup tools, with excellent preview abilities for each, comparable to those in Cool Edit Pro.

DARTPro 98 also includes both recording and CD-R recording capabilities, combined in the separate DART CD-Recorder program. It's not exactly beautiful, but it does do the job. You can record (rip) from CD, or record from LP (or other analog source). DART CD-Recorder even supports DirectX plug-ins, allowing you to launch any that you have installed by pressing a button and selecting them from a menu.

Overall, DARTPro 98 is a very powerful but somewhat rough-edged and unfriendly package. At the time of this comparison, it's biggest drawback was its high price, up there with Cool Edit Pro, a complete editor that includes very similar cleanup features.

Dartech does offer two less expensive alternatives: DARTPro 32 and CD Recorder. DARTPro 32 is simply the previous version of the software, now bargain-priced at US$99.95. The major omissions are real-time preview, the DeHum filter and support for DirectX plug-ins. This puts it up against the slightly more expensive Cool Edit 2000/Noise Reduction combo. You'd have to check the complete feature lists to make a personal assessment of which you'd prefer, but my inclination would certainly be toward the comprehensive editing abilities of Cool Edit 2000.

CD-Recorder, as the name implies, focuses on recording from analog sources and recording to CD-R discs. DirectX plug-in versions of the DeClick and DeHiss filters are included. At US$49.95, it's a more interesting low-end option. If you want the cheapest noise-reduction product, this is probably it.

Others. There are several other products around that do similar types of cleanup. However, the three mentioned above cover the full range from high end to low end, so one of them will very likely fill your own needs.

Cleaning Up

Although each of these products has its own look and feel, the actual cleaning tools are remarkably similar. Before we look at the specifics, here are some general hints on how to get good-quality noise reduction without fraying your nerves.

1. Above all, use restraint! It's far better to leave some noise than to lose some music. You can always go back and try again to get more of the noise, but if you mess up the audio by overprocessing it, the damage is added to all its previous problems. Also, turning off as many options as possible will help reduce processing time.

2. Test noise-reduction settings on a few small, representative samples of the music, say, about 30 seconds each. You can really get to know a short sample, and start noticing subtle changes.

3. Listen to what you're removing! Some tools let you do this directly. For example, in Cool Edit 2000 the Noise Reduction dialog has a check box marked Keep Only Noise, and the Hiss Reduction dialog has one marked Keep Only Hiss. Enabling these literally lets you hear what you're (going to be) missing. Run the filter then listen to the result. What you hear should be pure static. If you can easily follow the melody by listening to what's being thrown away, you're obviously giving up a lot of valuable sound information.

   An alternative method of hearing your noise is to mix the processed version of your test sample with the original unprocessed version, at the same time inverting one or the other. You can do this by opening the original file and copying it to the clipboard using the Edit . . . Copy command. Then open the filtered version and select Edit . . . Mix Paste. A dialog appears; leave all the settings at their defaults, but tick off the two Invert boxes for L and R stereo channels.

When you click OK, whatever information is common to both versions of the file will cancel out, leaving behind only the changes made by the filter. This technique can be particularly handy if you want to test the effect of a complex series of filtering steps.

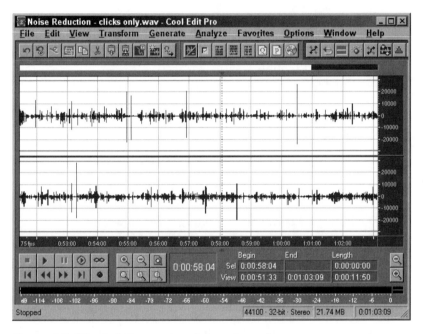

Figure 4.5 What's being removed: just the noise

Hiss reduction is about the simplest of the cleaning tools. It attacks one specific type of noise, although there are many parameters that decide how stringent the attack is going to be. With hiss, you can usually hear the "sweet spot" setting quite clearly. More vigorous hiss reduction will give dull, muffled music; looser settings will leave some hiss behind.

What's more, hiss reduction generally seems to work better than the more generalized types of noise reduction. For example, I found that DARTPro 98 hiss reduction made an astounding improvement in old tape recordings.

Hiss Reduction in Cool Edit 2000

Hiss Reduction offers relatively fewer settings, and is generally easier to get right, so it's a good filter to play with first. Here's how it works:

1. Select the Transform . . . Noise Reduction . . . Hiss Reduction command.
2. In the dialog box, select one of the Presets: High Hiss Reduction, Light Hiss Reduction or Standard Hiss Reduction. You can also manually set the Noise Floor Adjust slider, to determine how much noise will be filtered out.
3. Press OK. Or select the Keep Only Hiss radio button to eliminate the music and keep only the noise. You should definitely try this at least once, as it gives you a really good feeling for what the filter is doing. You can use the Edit . . . Undo command to revert to the unfiltered version of the file.

Once you've got a feel for the basic action of the filter, you can play with some of the more complex settings. The online Help button provides an excellent overview of the function of these controls. For example, the Get Noise Floor button lets you create a noise profile of the file.

1. Select an area of the file that contains only hiss, but no music.
2. Select the Hiss Reduction command. Press Get Noise Floor. Press Close.
3. Select the entire file, and again select Hiss Reduction. Now you can filter the whole file using the Noise Floor information. This selectively applies more or less noise filtering at different frequencies, helping to preserve more of the music.

Noise reduction is a bit of a catch-all. The name relates more to the underlying technical approach than to the type of fault it's likely to correct. Essentially, the cleaning tools that call themselves noise filters work by first creating a frequency profile of the unwanted noise in a file, then filtering out anything that has a similar frequency signature.

It's actually quite easy to get a noise profile. Just select a "silent" section of the recording. When you're recording from LP, for example, be sure to keep the lead-in and lead-out—the parts before the phonograph needle hits the start of the first track, and after it leaves the last track on its way toward the paper label in the middle. These segments generally contain all the undesirable sounds, with no music to get in the way.

Noise Reduction in Cool Edit 2000

The Noise Reduction filter deals with various kinds of background noise, including hiss, hum, and various kinds of rumbles. It also smooths out the audio waveform, eliminating a lot of the crackly sound that you get in badly worn record grooves. Overzealous noise reduction mutes the sound and makes it seem flat and lifeless. Here's how it works:

1. Select a relatively silent part of the file, such as the lead-in or lead-out of an LP, where no music is playing but all the background noise is present.
2. Select the Transform . . . Noise Reduction . . . Noise Reduction command. In the dialog box, press the Get Profile from Selection button. This will generate a hazy coloured line in the graph area, representing the noise profile. You can test your setting at this point by running the filter on the selected lead-in area.

3. Otherwise, exit the dialog and select the entire file. Select the Noise Reduction command again. Set the Noise Reduction Level slider to 5 or less. Higher settings are very likely to degrade the music. With some recordings you may be able to go higher, but start low. Press OK. Or, if you want to double-check your setting, click on the Keep Only Noise radio button, and then press OK. This will remove everything *except* what the filter is selecting. If you can make out the melody by listening to this version, the filter is set to remove quite a bit of the music. When you're done reviewing the noise, use the Edit . . . Undo command to revert to the unfiltered version of the file. Now you can return to Noise Reduction and try running the filter again.

Click removal denotes a class of tools that play seek-and-destroy with those sharp cracks and pops you hear on old vinyl recordings that have gotten badly scuffed up over the years.

The problem seems a lot simpler than it actually turns out to be. Heck, you can actually *see* these noises—those tall, thin spikes sticking out of the main body of your waveform. You can go in and manually snip them off by redrawing the wave line. So why shouldn't the computer find them for you?

In practice, this seems to be the most problematic of the noise-reduction tools. Settings that find all the cracks and pops and background crackle will definitely remove some of your music. This can be acceptable, or it can be disastrous. With badly worn LP recordings, you can easily end up introducing strange echoing or warbling effects, especially in forceful, sibilant or high-pitched passages.

Doing click removal properly will require quite a bit of patience and messing with detailed parameters, which we won't go into here. Just be sure and save your original and work on a smaller sample file until you've got a setting that gives results you can live with.

Noise Reduction in DARTPro 98

The nicest thing about DARTPro 98 is that you can preview your filter settings as you make them, providing your computer is fast enough! My Pentium III 450 managed to keep up most of the time, but the preview sound tended to break up with the more complicated filters.

When it works, however, live preview lets you twiddle each setting back and forth and instantly assess the degree of improvement—or degradation—in the sound. Here's how this works:

1. Open a WAV file, preferably something really noisy, like a recording from an old LP. Right-click and set Resolution (i.e. zoom level) to 1000. This lets you see enough of the music to get a general feel for the major features.
2. Hold Ctrl and click and drag the pointer to select a few adjacent phrases (clumps) in the waveform. Choose Restore . . . DeClick from the menu or press F2.
3. Ignore the controls in the dialog box for a moment and just press the Test button. Another box pops up, similar to the first. You'll note that there are three major controls at the top—*Smoothing*, *Postfiltering*, and *Outlier Detection*—and two main buttons near the bottom—Play Source and Play Result. Before doing anything else, click the Range: drop-down list and select the last option, Block. This sets your selected block as the area to preview.
4. Okay . . . click the Play Source button, then after a moment the Play Result button. You should be able to hear a clear difference.
5. Press Play Result, then try altering the settings at the top, either by moving the sliders from side to side or by selecting settings in the drop-down boxes other than the default "normal."

Smoothing takes out crackle and harshness by literally smoothing out the music waveform. At the default setting or below, the curve is mildly smoothed, retaining the clarity of the music. Higher settings make the music sound dull or muffled.

Postfiltering takes out more pervasive noise, such as tape hiss, and also counteracts the less desirable side effects of smoothing. Excessively high settings distort the music, adding an unpleasant echoing quality.

Outlier Detection tries to detect isolated cracks and pops. There are two settings that help adjust the detection to the specific recording you're trying to fix.

The main slider setting decides the height of the spikes to seek out. Reducing the setting makes detection more sensitive to smaller pops, helping to reduce constant low-level crackle. Turning the level up lets more noise through. The *Maximum length of detection alarms* setting is even more important, determining how narrow a spike (i.e. how many spikes per second) to go after. With noisy records, I found the default setting of 50 much too high; try a setting of 5 or 10. Too high a setting makes the music sound fuzzy in forceful passages.

Conclusion

Okay . . . hopefully that all made sense. If not, don't worry—it comes clear very quickly with a little practice. Fire up Sound Forge XP or Cool Edit 2000, load a WAV file (use a copy, just to be safe!), and hack away. You'll be surprised how you can modify the sound, yet with just a bit of care, achieve really professional-sounding results.

If you're using Cool Edit 2000 with the Studio Add-In, or some more advanced editor, you can even try multitrack editing, which we haven't talked about in this chapter, but which is really easier, once you get the hang of it. Using multiple tracks, you can preview all your mixes and splices and change them around, before finally committing the result to a new WAV file.

There's lots more to know about editing, but this gives you a starting point. Now let's move on to *storage*—the software and hardware you need in order to properly preserve your musical treasures.

5

Storing It

The last major problem with digital music is storing it. In this chapter we'll look at a number of software and hardware tools that help with this task:

- Audio Compression software
- CD-R Hardware
- CD-R Software
- Related Software Tools

ULTIMATELY, UNLESS YOU RESTRICT YOURSELF entirely to streaming "Internet radio" listening, you'll need to store the music you download. Hard-drive capacity is rapidly expanding, but even the largest of today's hard drives is going to fill up pretty quickly when you start downloading 5-, 10- or 20-megabyte audio tracks on a regular basis. What's more, until we all move into networked homes, we're likely to want to listen to music somewhere other than at the computer. So, eventually, you'll need to package up the music you've recorded or downloaded. There are two aspects to this: software and hardware.

The first aspect of music storage is the software. The software technology has already been discussed extensively in Chapter 1— audio compression. Since music files are so large, compressing them can really help you economize on storage. If you've downloaded files in compressed form, no problem—they're not going to get much smaller. However, if you record your own audio from CD, LP, or tape, or from live performance, for that matter, you may find yourself needing to compress it. Hence the first half of this chapter deals with audio compression software and techniques.

The second aspect of music storage is the hardware—the physical devices that you can use to hold those gigabytes of audio data. There are several types of high-capacity disk drives that you could use, but each has fairly major disadvantages. But along with MP3 compression, it was the arrival of cheap CD-recordable (CD-R) drives that really touched off the digital music revolution, and these devices remain the most efficient and economical choice. They let you store large quantities of data, are inexpensive, and can be recorded in either a format that will play on virtually any personal computer or audio CD player.

The second half of this chapter will give you all the know-how necessary to reliably create your own CD-R discs, and then keep track of them as your collection grows.

Compressed Audio Encoders

As explained in Chapter 1, there are several technologies available for compressing audio data. The best-known is MP3, but others are certainly worth considering, depending on your own needs. Even if you choose MP3, there's a choice of software products for doing the actual encoding. Each has its own advantages and disadvantages.

Since MP3 has become the de facto standard, it's certainly the type of compression to start with. As you become more experienced, you may find you prefer other formats for specific purposes.

As was noted in Chapter 1, the developers of MP3 technology, Fraunhofer Institut and Thomson Multimedia, require a royalty payment for software that creates MP3 files. Thus you wouldn't expect to find MP3 encoders being given away for free. In fact, there are free encoders that essentially "slip under the radar," and (so far, at least) haven't been worth pursuing. However, fully licensed encoding software doesn't have to be expensive, either, so there's no reason to skimp.

Fraunhofer

Fraunhofer's own encoder is available as a stand-alone program under the name l3enc.exe. This runs from within an MS-DOS Prompt command-line session, and hence is anything but user-friendly. However, it was widely (if illegally) distributed on the Internet, and became the standard by which all encoders would be judged.

Today, various Windows programs incorporate the Fraunhofer encoder technology, and pay a legitimate royalty for the privilege. Almost any good audio editing package, for example, will include the ability to read from and save to MP3 format. This may be built in to the software as standard equipment or available as an optional add-on.

For example, the two popular low-cost sound editors discussed in Chapter 4 both provide MP3 capability, albeit in different ways. Sound Forge XP 4.5, from Sonic Foundry, offers an MP3 Plug-In as a US$19.95 upgrade. Cool Edit 2000, from Syntrillium, includes MP3 capability in the base product, painlessly priced at US$69. With either of these, you can simply select Save . . . As, then pick MP3 as the file type.

Recall that software publishers can either license the Fraunhofer/Thomson patents and develop their own encoder, or license the actual Fraunhofer/Thomson software and incorporate it in their product. The latter is preferred, since the Fraunhofer/Thomson software is still widely considered to do the best job, encoding with the least loss in audio quality. Look for the Fraunhofer logo or copyright message; in many cases, as with Cool Edit 2000, the publisher will boast up front that they've got this prized encoder "under the hood."

Jukeboxes

A simpler and less expensive approach is to grab one of the two popular jukebox programs. These all-in-one products, discussed previously in Chapter 3, act as music players, CD rippers, *and* MP3 encoders. They have their annoyances, but they're also the quickest way to acquire a full digital audio toolkit.

RealJukebox Plus lets you rip tracks from audio CD, then encode them in either MP3 or Real's own proprietary RealAudio format.

Annoyingly, RealAudio always comes up as the default format, even though there's no earthly reason why anyone (other than streaming-content providers) would ever want to use it. Not only is it less well supported, RealAudio is limited to the relatively low bitrate of 96 kbps, and thus gives lower quality than most users would prefer. (Anyone serious about creating streaming content should use the company's complete RealProducer G2 Authoring Kit rather than RealJukebox.)

However, once you manually select MP3 as the destination format, things go very smoothly. You can select the full range of bitrates from 32 kbps, in mono, up to 320 kbps. You can also enable or disable variable bitrate encoding, although in my tests this seemed to have no effect on the output.

Encoding is extremely fast, requiring only about a fifth of the real-time duration of the track. Sound quality seems quite good, nonetheless.

MP3 Compression in RealJukebox Plus

Creating MP3 files in RealJukebox isn't overly difficult, but there are a few tricks to be aware of.

1. Select the Options . . . Preferences menu command. Click on the Encoding Options tab in the dialog box, and ensure that the Secure Files box is *not* checked (contrary to the boldface recommendation shown next to it). Securing your files may make copyright owners happy, but it won't create a standard MP3 file. Instead, you'll get a file in the unique .RMX format that can't be played in anything but your own personal copy of RealJukebox—and not even there, if you happen to lose your personal-security information

(which RealJukebox does prompt you to carefully back up). Disabling the check box will present you with a huge legal disclaimer. Just accept this and go on with your life.

2. Select a WAV file in the RealJukebox Library window. (This can be tricky. If you get stuck, select All Tracks under Master Library in the tree view at the left, then drag a WAV file from Windows Explorer onto the RealJukebox window.) Select File . . . Save As, or right-click on the file and select Save Track As. . . .

3. Set your desired options. Regardless of your settings under Preferences, the default will be to save as a RealAudio file. Select MP3 from the drop-down list, then select the desired bitrate (if in doubt, use 128 as a starting point).

4. *Note:* if you have the "Erase the current track" option checked down below, under Additional Options, your original WAV file will be deleted when the encoding is finished. It's much safer to do this yourself, *after* you've double-checked that you're happy with the compressed file. On the other hand, once you've got some experience with RealJukebox, you may want to enable this setting in order to free up hard-drive space as quickly as possible.

MusicMatch Jukebox has an even simpler approach to creating compressed files. It's generally pleasanter to use than RealJukebox, as well, with no advertising to clutter up its display, and a rather more usable Library organizer. (It still can't handle music stored on CD-R, however. You can add songs from CD-R to the Library listing, but try to play one with the CD-R put away and all you get is the unhelpful message "Song file is missing.")

MusicMatch 5 uses the latest version of the Fraunhofer encoder, considered to be just about the best available. It does constant or variable bitrates.

On top of this, MusicMatch Jukebox can also compress in Windows Media WMA format.

Creating MP3 files
with MusicMatch Jukebox 5

In MusicMatch Jukebox, MP3 files are a breeze to create.

1. Select the Options . . . File . . . Convert command.
2. In the left side of the dialog box, select the original WAV file(s) you want to convert.
3. At the bottom of the dialog box, select the compression type from the Destination Data Type drop-down list. You can select either MP3 CBR (constant bitrate) or MP3 VBR (variable bitrate), or Windows Media WMA. The label on the adjacent slider changes depending on this setting, showing the actual bitrate in CBR or WMA mode, and a percentage compression ratio in VBR mode. A 50 percent VBR setting will produce a file almost identical in size to the 128 CBR setting.
4. You don't get the opportunity to choose new names for your resulting MP3 files, but you can select a new folder to hold them, using the tree view in the top-right area of the conversion dialog box. Press Start when you're ready.

Again, encoding is very fast, yet sound quality is surprisingly good. MusicMatch Jukebox seemed to do a better job with a badly beaten-up originals. High-pitched crackle was slightly emphasized compared to the WAV recording, but there were no other oddities, and the overall sound was good.

When it comes to encoding CD audio, MusicMatch Jukebox and RealJukebox seem evenly matched. But for encoding poor-quality originals, MusicMatch seems to have a slight edge. For most practical purposes, however, you won't hear much difference.

BladeEnc

If you really want to get by on the minimum-cash outlay, there are in fact "free" MP3 encoders floating around on the Internet. These include mpegEncoder, by SoloH (www.euronet.nl/~soloh/mpegEnc/) and Blade (www.bladeenc.mp3.no). Although these are based on publicly available program samples from ISO (see Chapter 1), they probably do violate the patent rights of the companies that developed the technology. SoloH apparently received notice to this effect, and his Web site states that further work on his encoder has been terminated. Oddly, as of February 2000, BladeEnc continued to thrive. Possibly the patent holders had concluded that trying to stamp out such efforts was likely to do more harm than good. Or possibly they just hadn't gotten around to lowering the boom.

In either case, these free encoders are worth mentioning for historical reasons. Ironically, their availability was an important factor in making MP3 the standard that it has become, thereby making the patents worth protecting. Looking ahead into the future, if the limelight shifts to newer formats such as AAC or WMA, it's entirely possible that MP3 might once more revert to underground status, no longer worth fighting over.

The avowed "hobby project" of Tord Jansson, a professional game programmer, BladeEnc in particular has gained a reputation as one of the fastest and highest-quality encoders around. Although it's a text-based, command-line program, BladeEnc is written in true 32-bit Windows code. If you don't like typing text commands, there are many *shell* programs that let you control the BladeEnc encoder using all the amenities of Windows, such as dragging and dropping files to be converted. You'll find a good selection of these shells on the Blade home page.

Shell. A piece of software that "wraps around" another, usually in order to provide a friendlier way of controlling it. For example, Windows was originally a shell that substituted visual commands for the less obvious text commands of the old MS-DOS operating system.

The most significant limitation of BladeEnc is that it currently does not support variable bitrate (VBR) encoding. As noted earlier, VBR can save a significant amount of file space, while retaining sound quality equivalent to the higher MP3 bitrates.

Interestingly, BladeEnc itself is distributed under the terms of the *GNU* Lesser General Public License (LGPL), widely used within the programming community to allow creators to retain control of their products while allowing those products to circulate freely and without charge. The relevance of this movement on the whole online music scene will be discussed in more detail in Chapter 6.

GNU. Self-referential acronym for Gnu's Not Unix, the starting point for what is now the Free Software Foundation Inc. (www.fsf.org), an organization dedicated to the promotion of *copyleft*, a scheme that allows programmers to distribute software free of charge, confident that it will remain free, and without fear that it might later be appropriated for profit by someone else.

Encoding with MKW

About the nicest way of using the BladeEnc encoder is via mkw Audio Compression Tool. (See also lossless encoding, page 198). mkwACT is a free program by Michael K. Weise, available from Michael's home site at home.att.net/~mkw/mkwact.html.

When you first start up mkwACT, you'll see a small window, showing four lines of text that explain just about everything you need to know about operating the program.

1. First, do a little set-up. Select the Options . . . MPEG Options command. A dialog box appears, allowing you to set your desired bitrate, from 160 to 320 kbps. There are two other options that control the quality of the

output, but you shouldn't need to change their default settings.

2. Press and hold the Ctrl key, then use the mouse to drag the WAV files to be compressed from a Windows Explorer window onto the mkwACT window. That's it! You'll see a bar showing the progress of the operation. You can click the Pause check box to pause encoding at any time.

mkwACT seems to work very nicely in the background, so you can start encoding a whole bunch of files then go on using the computer for other things. It's not as fast as RealJukebox Plus or MusicMatch Jukebox, but creates very high-quality MP3 files and is much easier to use.

Ultimately, if all this concerns or confuses you, by all means stick with a commercial encoder that has all licence fees paid up to date. These products are easy to use, well supported, and not particularly expensive. Alternatively, you can use Microsoft's Windows Media format, for which Microsoft imposes no royalty fees. In fact, the mere availability of Windows Media is likely to keep prices down on all encoders, even if all free MP3 encoders could be forced out of existence.

Windows Media Encoder

At the start of 2000, the Windows Media format was one of the least well known. That's very likely to change, fast. The technology provides excellent sound quality at very small size, and, perhaps most compelling of all, is available for free to users and developers.

Let's look at two different ways of creating WMA files: Music-Match Jukebox and Microsoft's own Windows Media Encoder. You can get the latter from Microsoft's Windows Media Web page, at http://www.microsoft.com/windows/windowsmedia/EN/default.asp, under Downloads. (Other products that support WMA encoding include the CD rippers Audiograbber, CDCopy, and Easy CD-DA Extractor.)

MusicMatch Jukebox encodes to WMA exactly the same way it encodes to MP3 (see page 188). Just select WMA in the Destination Data Type drop-down list. The slider control lets you select bitrates from 5 kbps to 160 kbps; however, the lowest actual encoding rate is 32 kbps, and the 160 kbps setting seemed to frequently (but not always!) give files encoded at 96 kbps. Sound, at any bitrate, is re-markably good. Low bitrates exhibit some obvious loss in the high-frequency sparkle, but retain excellent depth and detail otherwise.

WMA encoding is quite fast at any bitrate, about 30 seconds for an average three-and-a-half-minute song.

Compared to MusicMatch Jukebox, Microsoft's Windows Media Encoder is crude and awkward, but at least it does encode at the bitrate it says it's going to. To set the output file name, you have to select the Encode . . . Properties command, then choose the Output tab in the dialog box. Check the box that says "To a local ASF file" and enter a file name. Then select File . . . Input File to specify the WAV file you want to convert. Files end up with the ASF extension, although they seem to work with any software that expects WMA.

Unfortunately, there's no way to queue up multiple files, and you have to manually change the output file name every time. What's more, the program crashes if your file names are too long!

Obviously, WMA encoding still isn't as well established as MP3. But over time it seems likely to become a very significant part of the audio landscape.

Lossy Compression

At first listen, a well-compressed MP3 or WMA file may sound al-most indistinguishable from the original CD track. But if you listen closely, and especially if you can arrange some back-and-forth com-parisons between compressed and uncompressed tracks, you'll start to become aware of significant differences. Try it on your stereo sys-tem, as opposed to your computer, and the difference will become even more apparent.

Testing Audio Quality

You'll have to skip ahead a bit to try this, or, better yet, wait until you've mastered some of the required procedures and then come back and do the following test.

1. Copy (rip) several tracks from your CD collection (see Chapter 2). Pick different kinds of music—rock, classical, pop vocals—with different mixtures of high and low notes.
2. Use the software of your choice to compress these tracks to MP3 (or other) format. You can even try making multiple versions of each track, with different amounts of compression.
3. Use WinAmp or MKW to uncompress these tracks back to WAV files.
4. Record both the original WAV files and the versions you created in step 3 to a CD-R audio disc (see page 209 for information on CD recordable software). Place different versions of the same tracks adjacent to one another, but be sure to remember which is which. (If you can get a friend to shuffle the order you can do a "blind" test.)
5. Play this disc on your stereo system. You can flip between versions of each track and listen for obvious differences.

You can do an even closer comparison if you have two CD players, or a CD player and a DVD player, hooked into your stereo. You can place the original audio CD in the DVD player (most won't handle CD-R discs!) and your compressed/uncompressed version on the CD player. Play both versions simultaneously, and use your amplifier to switch between them.

Even once you begin to notice the differences, you may find it difficult to pin them down. However, it's worth understanding what's kept and what's lost in the compression process.

With tape, the limitations on audio quality are fairly obvious: a loss of high frequencies and introduction of high-pitched background hiss. A good cassette recorder can capture sounds only up to about 16 kHz—considerably short of the 22 kHz that CDs can handle. At the same time, irregularities in the metallic recording medium of the tape create a distinctive hissing sound.

This is why most tape decks include preprocessing technology from Dolby Laboratories Inc., specifically designed to eliminate hiss and extend the range of useful frequencies. Also, better tape decks and higher-quality tape will capture more of the high frequency, giving you a sharper, clearer recording.

As with tape, digital compression tends to lop off a lot of the high frequencies, above about 16 kHz. These sounds aren't all that clearly audible to the average ear, but they contribute a lot to a general feeling of "brightness" and "clarity" in the recording. So MP3 files will sound a bit duller and less lively than the original CD audio. You can see this very clearly by comparing Figures 5.1 and 5.2. The graphs show the amount of each sound frequency that's present in the file, with high frequencies at the right. The abrupt drop-off in the graph of the MP3 file in Figure 5.2 shows that high frequencies present in the original WAV are entirely missing in the compressed version.

Lossy digital compression also has more subtle effects throughout the frequency spectrum. Notice that none of the compressed frequency charts really matches the original closely at any point from left to right. Compression can introduce a whole world of *artifacts*, based on a complex interaction between the specific encoder used and the make-up of the sound file itself.

Artifact. Generically, something made by human activity. Referring to sound, it denotes unwanted side effects of processing—identifiable noise, distortion, or other effects.

For example, some encoders seem to have particular trouble compressing low-quality recordings. It seems that the presence of lots of hiss and crackle in the audio fools the logic of the software, and the

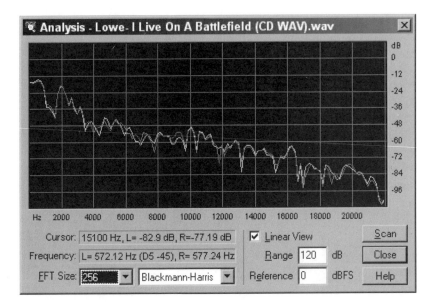

Figure 5.1 Sound frequencies contained in original WAV track

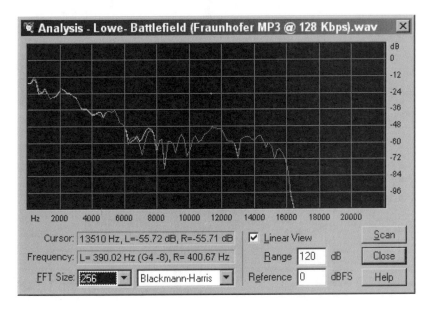

Figure 5.2 Sound frequencies contained in MP3 at 128 kbps bitrate

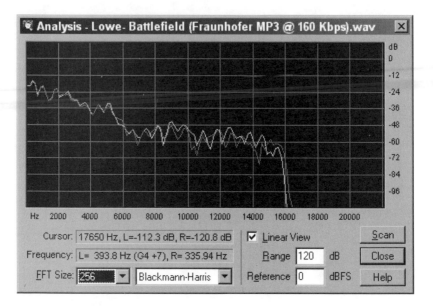

Figure 5.3 Sound frequencies contained in MP3 at 160 kbps bitrate

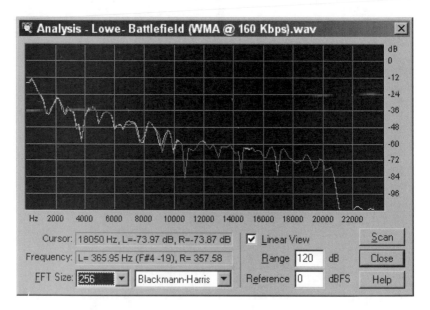

Figure 5.4 Sound frequencies contained in WMA at 160 kbps bitrate

resulting compressed track may end up sounding garbled, with an odd warbling quality to it.

One strange effect noted by devoted music fans is that even when the compressed version exhibits no obvious degradation in sound quality, it will be in some vague sense less enjoyable than the original. This seems to be a very real effect, based not on grossly audible faults such as loss of crisp high notes or introduction of noise, but on loss of nuance and ambience in the music.

A good parallel was recently demonstrated by Sony, which is currently introducing its new Super Audio CD (SACD) next-generation music CD system in Canada. In carefully conducted eyes-closed listening tests, using top-notch stereo gear, a good CD recording of a church choir sounded great, but still like a recording. An SACD recording sounded like *being there*.

Obviously, the nuances that our brain interprets as room ambience were being reproduced much more accurately. We may not perceive these subtle effects as sound, but at a gut level we are acutely aware of them. Some of this is within your control. Check the graphs again. You can see that the original CD-audio track contains a significant amount of frequency information even above 20 kHz. Most of us can't distinguish frequencies this high as discrete sounds, but we do sense them as ambience.

At 96 kbps things get much worse: the frequency curve is sliced clean away above about 12 kHz. This is going to sound muffled and lacking in clarity—not much better than a telephone conversation. But when the track is compressed at a bitrate of 160 kbps in Figure 5.3, the drop-off moves up dramatically—to about 16 kHz. That's more like audio tape. This version should retain all the most obvious sounds, losing only a little bit of clarity and some ambience.

Going to 320 kbps doesn't improve the frequency content much. This does make sense, if you recall that the MP3 codec is optimized for 128 kbps—we're simply pushing it beyond its intended use.

But look what happens with WMA! The response curve in Figure 5.4 actually extends way out *past* 22 kHz, even though the bitrate is still just 160 kbps. This lends some credence to Microsoft's claims that WMA is twice as good as MP3. However, there is a trade-off.

Although the original curve is on a slightly different scale (chosen by the Cool Edit Pro, in this case), you can see that the entire WMA curve is subtly different from the original. It would appear that Microsoft has opted to distribute its losses across the frequency spectrum. Nonetheless, these graphs do show a clear advantage for WMA.

So what does all this add up to? First, that good encoding does matter. Even if you're not a fanatical audiophile, you will hear the difference—or *feel* it. It will colour your emotional response to the music, and emotional response is, after all, why we're listening to music in the first place. Second, that it's very definitely worthwhile encoding MP3 at 160 kbps, but that there's less benefit in going to higher bitrates. And third, that next-generation compression technologies such as WMA *do* offer considerably better sound quality for a given volume of data. The absence of consumer-level AAC encoders makes it difficult to say how this format compares, but all indications are that it is similar in performance to WMA. So, as PC users gradually become more conscious of audio quality, we'll undoubtedly see these new formats gaining in popularity.

Lossless Compression

The most futuristic formats of all are those that use lossless compression. Unlike the lossy techniques we've been focusing on, these formats discard nothing. An audio track that has been compressed in this way and then uncompressed will be absolutely identical to the original.

The downside is that the level of compression is dramatically reduced. While MP3 files can be as small as one-fifth or one-tenth of the original CD-quality track, the best that lossless compression can promise are files two-thirds to one-half the size of the original.

Nonetheless, lossless compression schemes are gaining ground on the Internet, propelled by users who have both a passion for uncompromising sound quality and access to a high-speed Internet connection, such as ADSL or cable.

The two most popular lossless formats are WaveZip, from Gadget Labs (www.gadgetlabs.com), and Shorten, from SoftSound Ltd. (www.softsound.com).

Although the WaveZip compressor is the slicker, more professional-looking product, it seems to be getting less support among Internet enthusiasts, for whatever reason, than Shorten. Specific Usenet newsgroups already exist for the express purpose of passing around audio material as Shorten SHN files. You'll find many SHN files in alt.binaries.sounds.misc, and the group alt.binaries.sounds.gdead. highspeed is entirely devoted to SHN postings of live recordings by the Grateful Dead. There are also networks of fans passing SHN files in other ways, including ftp.

Deadheads are amongst the most avid audiophiles on the Net, many having spent thousands of dollars on portable taping equipment with which to capture their beloved band's wildly improvisational performances over the 35-odd years since its formation. "The Dead" were probably the first band to explicitly allow taping of their concerts by fans, and the subsequent noncommercial trading of these recordings. Amazingly, this utopian "business model" is now catching on with much more mainstream performers.

Aside from the much larger size of lossless files, there's another key difference compared to the lossy formats: they can't be streamed. With these lossless formats, if you don't have every single bit of the compressed file, you can't uncompress it. This is not only a drawback when it comes to Internet Radio applications, it also imposes an all-or-nothing urgency to downloads. With files this big, it's easy to grab tens of megabytes of data, only to find it worthless because the last few bytes are missing.

Still, as Internet connections and storage space get cheaper and more capacious, lossless compression is bound to gain in popularity. Also, lossless compression promises to be extremely useful for serious production work, where huge amounts of audio data must be stored but no loss in quality can be tolerated.

If you'd like to check it out, you can download evaluation versions of both WaveZip and Shorten from their respective Web sites.

WaveZip works for only 15 days, and then costs US$49.95 to register. The evaluation version of Shorten is free for noncommercial use (which may be why it's become more popular), but for US$29.95 the licensed version adds some convenient features, such as the ability to encode multiple files in batches, and to create self-extracting files that can be passed to users who don't have the Shorten software. The freeware mkwACT program mentioned earlier in this chapter also includes the ability to compress and uncompress in Shorten format.

Going Back: Converting MP3 to WAV

Eventually, you will need to uncompress your MP3, WMA, or other compressed files, converting them once more into WAV format. The likeliest reason is in order to record them onto audio CDs.

> Remember, there's a permanent loss in sound quality when a file is originally *compressed*. There's no loss involved in *un*compressing, but the original loss incurred in compression is retained. Bottom line, use the original WAV recording for any processing you need to do, and compress *last*. (This doesn't apply to the lossless formats such as Shorten and WaveZip, but these are still comparatively rare.)

Of course, the compressed version will often be all you have. If you've obtained music over the Internet, chances are it's been compressed in MP3 format to reduce upload/download times. You can enjoy such MP3 files directly, using your computer or a portable MP3 player, but if you want to edit the music, or store it onto an audio CD that you can play anywhere, you'll need to uncompress it back to WAV files.

There are several ways to uncompress an MP3 file, depending on what software you want to use.

One is to play them through WinAmp, setting the output to a disk file. This isn't exactly convenient, but it is reliable and the software is both free and widely available. There are two advantages to using WinAmp in this way. One is that it can apply any Equalizer settings to the output, allowing you to do some quick-and-dirty processing on the music, say, to boost the bass. Another advantage is that if you've installed extra codecs, such as the Liquid Audio playback plug-in, you'll be able to convert these types of files to WAV as well. Since you're essentially just "playing" the music to disk, anything that plays will save as a file.

On the test system, it only took about 30 seconds to convert a 5-to-8-minute compressed file. The main drawback is that it's awkward to switch WinAmp into its play-to-disk mode.

Uncompressing Files with WinAmp 2.5

Like any audio player, WinAmp must uncompress a compressed file in order to play it. If you want to keep the uncompressed version in WAV format, you can tell WinAmp to "play" the file to your hard disk instead of to your speakers. Whatever you would have heard normally ends up stored in a file.

1. If you wish to apply Equalizer settings to your output, press the EQ button. The WinAmp Equalizer will open up. Set the sliders as desired. For example, Figure 5.2 shows a set-up that's roughly equivalent to the "loudness" button found on most home stereo amplifiers, boosting bass notes that would otherwise tend to be lost when you're playing the music at a quiet volume level. Be sure the On button in the top-left part of the Equalizer is lit, showing that the Equalizer is enabled.
2. Right-click anywhere on the WinAmp player, or left-click on the little sine wave icon in the top-left corner of the WinAmp player, then select Options . . . Preferences from the pop-up menu. Or simply press Ctrl+P.

Figure 5.5 Boosting "loudness" using the WinAmp equalizer

3. In the tree view at the left, select Plug-ins . . . Output.
   Then in the list at the right, select Nullsoft Disk Writer
   Plug-in. (There'll be some version information on the
   same line, but don't worry about this; "Disk Writer Plug-
   in" is the important designation. It will probably be the
   second item in the list)

4. Press the Configure button at the bottom of the Preferences window. Another window will pop open, allowing
   you to select the folder in which your uncompressed files
   will be stored. Click on the folder you want, then click
   OK.

5. Select a file to play, exactly as you would normally. Either
   drag it onto the WinAmp player, or press L and select it
   from the file Open dialog. You probably won't have to do
   anything else, but if the player doesn't start up, you can

press the Play button. You won't hear anything, but you should see any visuals that you have enabled in the WinAmp player, and your hard-drive light will come on and stay on.

6. When all your conversions are finished, don't forget to open the Preferences window again and select Nullsoft waveOut plug-in under Output . . . Plug-ins, or you'll end up making a bunch of unwanted WAV data next time you try to listen to some music. Also, if you want to check the Equalizer effect on your output file, be sure to turn the Equalizer button in WinAmp *off*, or you'll be listening with *double* settings, the ones in the file and the ones still active in WinAmp itself.

Setting the WinAmp Equalizer is something that takes a little practice. If your home stereo has an equalizer, you may already be familiar with the basics. Otherwise, experiment with the settings when WinAmp is in its normal playback mode. What you hear is what you'll get when saving a file to disk.

You can also use either RealJukebox Plus or MusicMatch Jukebox. The process in either program is very similar to encoding to MP3. Select a compressed file to start with, and then select WAV as the destination format.

Remember that WAV files can get very big. If you're uncompressing a lot of tightly packed MP3 files, be sure you have enough hard drive space to hold the results!

The utility I personally favour for MP3 to WAV conversion is mkwACT, for two main reasons. First, it's extremely convenient, working either via drag-and-drop, if the mkwACT window is open, or from the pop-up menu displayed by Windows when you right-click on one or more MP3 files. Second, it's completely goof-proof. mkwACT offers no options or settings to mess up. So when you un-compress an MP3 file, you know you're going to get exactly the same sound in the resulting WAV file.

Uncompressing files with mkwACT

With mkwACT installed on your system, you have two easy ways to decompress MP3 files.

1. Start mkwACT. Select MP3 files in Windows Explorer and drag them onto the mkwACT window. WAV files with the same names will be created in the MP3 file folder; or
2. Select one or more MP3 files in Windows Explorer and right-click on them. In the pop-up menu, select "decode to wav." The results are the same either way.

Note: if you select Options . . . File Options in mkwACT and check the box to "Delete MPEG files after decoding to WAV," the original MP3 files will be deleted. To avoid losing files inadvertently, ensure that this option is unchecked.

CD Recordable Hardware

So much for compression. But whether you're compressing your music or storing it in WAV form, it's still going to take up a fair bit of room. Eventually you'll need to get it off the hard drive, and that inevitably means saving it on a recordable CD.

CD-R. Short for Compact Disc Recordable. These are one-time recordable optical discs that store either 650 MB

of data, in a form readable on virtually any desktop computer, or 74 minutes of audio, readable in any audio CD
player (including the CD-ROM drive in your PC or Mac).

CD-RW. Short for Compact Disc ReWritable. A standard
for reusable optical discs that store about 500 MB of data.
These can take up to an hour to prepare (format) for first
use, but allow data to be erased, so the disc can be reused.
However, the discs may not be readable without the original software used to create them.

CD recorders are still mysterious devices, poorly understood and
temperamental. Most new computers are still not automatically
equipped with a CD-R drive, and few computer users actually know
how to use one properly. It's not that these devices are particularly
difficult to use, most of the time, but they do take a bit more know-
how than just dragging and dropping files on a floppy or Zip disk.
You need special software to *burn* a CD-R disc, and there are surprisingly many different ways of doing it.

Burn. To record a CD-R disc. The term refers to the fact
that the laser head etches pits into the disc in order to
store the data.

Ever have trouble removing a CD from its case? Try pressing
down on the star-shaped clip in the middle. And remember
that CD-R discs are far more fragile than commercially pressed
CDs, especially before they've been recorded. So be gentle!

CD-R Hardware

A CD-R burner is the sort of device that you'll only notice when it
fails. When they work, all makes of CD-R drives are more or less
alike. What make of hard drive do you have in your computer?

Chances are that even if you picked it out yourself when you bought the system, you can't remember now.

There are several major features that distinguish CD-R drives:

1. Data Interface. CD-R drives can connect to your computer in one of several ways. The most common is the IDE (Integrated Drive Electronics) interface used by most PC hard drives and CD-ROM drives. This is the simplest solution for most PC owners. Virtually all PCs have an IDE connector on their motherboard. Up to four disk drives connect to this via flat multi-wire "ribbon" cables.

The other main type of connection to consider is SCSI (Small Computer Systems Interface), originally popularized by the Macintosh and lately found on some higher-priced PC motherboards. In theory, SCSI is a higher-performance connection, but in practice most of us needn't worry about the difference.

The chief material advantage of connecting a CD-R burner using a SCSI connector is that this connection will place less demand on your computer's main processor. For someone burning a lot (and I mean a *lot*) of discs, this could be a consideration. It might mean that the computer can be used for other things, with less risk of interfering with the recording process.

This might be worth thinking about if you're a pro or semi-pro musician, or a recording studio, or a software developer—anyone burning demo or commercial discs in large quantities. Otherwise, you'll see little difference.

Recently, external CD-R drives have been appearing that use the USB (Universal Serial Bus) connector. These are certainly easy to plug in, although the internal IDE type is likely to be more reliable. The one type of interface to avoid is the parallel port. You still see a few drives around that use this, but it's an awkward and unreliable approach.

2. Speed. As you'd expect, newer CD-R drives are faster than older ones. To appreciate what this means, you have to be able to interpret the threefold speed rating used by manufacturers. Drive speed is measured for recording CD-R discs, recording CD-RW discs, and reading CD-ROM discs.

Speed for CD-R drives, as for CD-ROM drives, is measured in units of "X," where 1X ("one-eks") is defined as 300 revolutions per minute, the fixed speed of an audio CD player, which allows data to be read off the disc just fast enough to be played in realtime. Computer data usually isn't used in realtime, and if it is, can be stored temporarily on the hard drive. Therefore CD-ROM drives can be much faster than audio CD players. A 6X CD-ROM drive would spin six times faster than an audio CD player.

CD-R recording speeds hit 8X late in 1999. An 8X drive can record a 74-minute audio CD in one-eighth of its playback time, or about 9.5 minutes. Older 4X drives take 18.5 minutes, which is a long time to wait. A new generation of 12X drives should arrive some time during 2000.

CD-RW speeds are still only about 4X. However, the entire CD-RW technology is peculiar enough that most users never bother with it. (Discs tend to be incompatible with different systems, and the blanks are still quite a bit more expensive than CD-R blanks.)

CD-ROM read speed is becoming more important now that it's beginning to rival the speed of conventional CD-ROM drives. A CD-R drive that can read at 24X or faster can serve as a total replacement for your CD-ROM drive, meaning one less component in your system.

3. Quality. This is a very difficult thing to judge, yet very important when it comes to CD-R drives. Poor-quality drives will be less compatible with varying grades of CD-R blanks. They'll be more likely to produce *coasters*, and, worse, may even produce subtly less-defined recordings that will either show up as errors over time or turn out to be unreadable in some CD-ROM drives. About the only thing you can do is read published reviews, and go with well-established brand names. The CD-R drive is not yet a commodity item, so don't buy the cheapest one in the store!

Coaster. A nice, shiny table protector to put under your cold drink; about the only use a CD-R disc can be put to if the burn is unsuccessful.

Frank's Pick: Plextor PlexWriter 8/4/32

Plextor Corp., a subsidiary of Shinao Kenshi Corp. of Japan, builds what they like to think of as the Ferrari of CD-R drives. The $400 PlexWriter 8/4/32 is its first CD-R drive to use the IDE interface rather than SCSI, which means it can at last offer Plextor's high-quality construction and extra software capabilities at much less than Ferrari pricing.

Coincidentally, the PlexWriter 8/4/32 is also the fastest-drive Plextor has ever made. The drive's name is its speed rating: 8X CD-R burn, 4X CD-RW burn, and 32X CD-ROM read. The last of these three specs means that this can be a total replacement for your CD-ROM drive. For CD-R recording, 8X means you can burn a brimful 74-minute audio CD in a mere ten minutes. It's still not like shooting a bunch of files to a Zip disk, but it's also not so long that you plan your day around it.

One of the crucial questions with 8X drives is whether they really have time to blast data pits emphatically enough into the CD-R blank. The quality of the blank media can vary quite a bit, and the fear is that you'll either a) end up burning a lot of coasters very quickly, or b) end up paying a painful premium for certified genuine "8X" CD-R blanks. But in testing the PlexWriter 8/4/32 with the cheapest CD-R blanks I could find, it performed admirably, never losing a single data bit.

The software bundle is excellent, including not just Easy CD Creator, the best recording software, but several neat programs of

Plextor's own devising, such as a disc-copy utility and a tricky little driver that lets you view an audio CD as if it were a data CD-ROM, and rip tracks to your PC by dragging and dropping in Windows.

The PlexWriter also comes through with an entirely unexpected advantage: it's by far the quietest drive I've used since the days of 2X CD-ROMs. Only a very badly off-balance disc will cause it to produce any of the usual 32X thrumming sound; most of the time, it's almost inaudible.

There are a number of other excellent brand names in CD-R, including Hewlett-Packard, Yamaha, and Sony. However, Plextor is unique in specializing exclusively in CD-ROM and CD-R products, and the tight focus certainly seems to pay off.

CD Recordable Software

There are quite a few software products on the market that let you burn CD-R discs. However, after trying a handful, I found that the choices get whittled away rather quickly. Most of the products have a specialized orientation that makes them unsuitable for general use by regular folks. And most seem to have enough peculiarities that you get the feeling they're not quite ready for prime time.

Easy CD Creator

Ultimately, the most commonly available product turns out to be by far the best—Easy CD Creator 4 Deluxe Edition, US$99, from Adaptec Inc.

Easy CD Creator is far from perfect. It could be easier to use, and some new features just plain didn't work in version 4. However, it is by far the most reliable and usable product available. And Adaptec seems to have a strong commitment to continuous improvement; a major upgrade was scheduled for the first half of 2000, which promised to fix some of the known problems and improve many features.

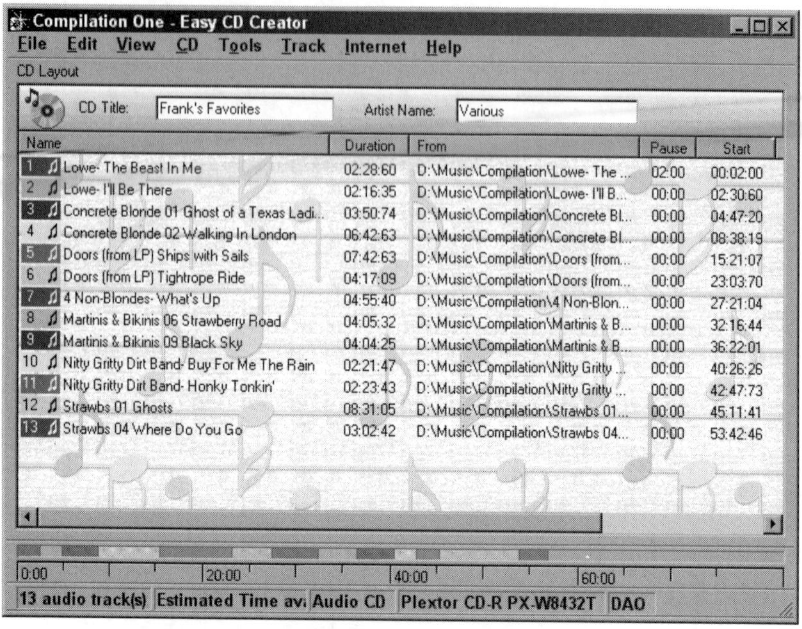

Figure 5.6 Creating an audio CD in Easy CD Creator 4

In its favor, Easy CD Creator 4 certainly provides lots of capabilities for the money. Aside from burning CD-R and CD-RW discs, it can record audio from CD or analog sources, do at least a fairly simple noise reduction on old material, copy CDs, and even print *jewel case* inserts or sticky CD labels.

Jewel Case. The flat plastic case that CD-ROMs and audio CDs come packaged in.

The basic process of recording CD-R discs with Easy CD Creator is fairly straightforward—once you get it set up. Unfortunately, however, there are a lot of incomprehensible options to set along the way.

Let's start with making data CDs. Here are some of the settings you need to be aware of. The first two are set using File . . . CD Layout Properties dialog. The third is set in the Advanced section of the Create CD . . . dialog.

1. **File System.** The format used to store files on the disc. Choices are ISO9660 and Joliet. The former is the original standard, but you probably want the latter. Joliet is a mildly modified version of the basic ISO9660 format, the chief difference being that it allows you to use file names up to 64 characters in length, and containing spaces. (The DOS-standard 8.3 file name is also recorded, allowing the disc to be read on older systems.)

   Note that 64-character file names allow you to store most MP3 files using the nice, long, descriptive names you've undoubtedly given them. Most but not all, since Windows allows 256 characters. Easy CD Creator will warn you when file names are too long, and pop up a dialog that lets you shorten them.

2. **Mode.** There are two choices, CD-ROM, or CD-ROM XA. The former is basically the usual CD-ROM layout, with a single spiral track written from the centre of the disc outward. CD-ROM XA is the format used by *multisession* discs, which can be added to repeatedly—in multiple recording sessions—until they are full.

Multisession. Refers to the ability of a CD-R drive to record data to a disc in multiple sessions. For example, you might record 30MB of data on Monday, then 120MB on Tuesday and 400MB on Friday. After the third recording session, you might decide you won't need to store anything else on that disc. The software can then close the disc so data can no longer be written to it.

Although the CD-ROM XA format is an accepted standard, it is less compatible, and is worth avoiding if possible. It's certainly fine for making temporary working discs for your own use. If you do record in CD-ROM XA mode, you should select the "Automatically import previous session" option, which allows all the files you've written to appear as part of the last session. This makes reading them slightly less troublesome.

3. Disc-at-Once or Track-at-Once. This deter-
mines how the laser burns the data track. Select Track-at-
Once for multisession discs; you can either close the disc,
preventing further burns, or leave it open for more sessions. For most storage, however, Disc-at-Once is the safest
and most compatible choice. It writes the entire disc in one
long burn, without turning off the laser. This gives the
closest emulation of a factory-made CD-ROM disc.

You don't actually have to use Disc-at-Once, but it will
ensure the best possible compatibility. A good approach is
to accumulate 650 MB of files on your hard drive, then
burn the whole works at once. Unfortunately, you will tend
to end up with several groups of 650 MB accumulating at
one time, according to theme. This puts a strain on your
storage space, unless you have a good-sized hard drive—
say, 20 GB or larger.

Beyond these tricky choices, there are several simpler ones. You
can set the Write Speed, which you'll need to reduce from its maximum only if you're particularly concerned about the ability of your
CD-R blanks to handle it properly. You can also select Test Only or
Test and Create CD options. Test Only sends data to the CD-R drive
but tells it not to actually turn on the laser. This lets you do a dry run,
ensuring that everything is working right without wasting a blank
disc. Test and Create automatically carries on if the test is successful
and actually burns the disc.

Don't get fingerprints, gunk, or scratches on your discs, especially
before they've been recorded. Although many users treat CDs
with total disregard, the amount of data lost to scuff marks and
greasy buildup is quite measurable. Losing data when reading a
disc is bad enough, but the system will typically keep trying until
it gets enough to piece together the complete file or audio track.
Losing data when *writing* a CD-R can result in burning coasters.

To create a disc, select File . . . New CD Layout . . . Data CD, then drag the files you want to record from the top-right pane of the Easy CD Creator window into the CD Layout window at the bottom-left. Alternatively, you can hide the top two panes by unchecking the View . . . Show Windows Explorer option, then just drag files in from an actual Explorer window on your Windows desktop.

Watch the thermometer bar at the bottom of the Easy CD Creator window; when it reads just below 650 MB, you're ready to burn. Select File . . . Create CD . . . and click OK.

Making an audio CD is basically the same process, except that you can only drag audio CD tracks, WAV files, or MP3 files into the layout. Easy CD Creator will automatically convert MP3 files to WAV before burning them.

If you try to play your freshly burned CD-R audio discs in your brand-new DVD video player, you'll be in for a nasty shock. Virtually all DVD players are incompatible with CD-R discs, and will claim the disc is blank. A few high-end DVD players incorporate a second laser specifically in order to read CD-R discs. You have to either splurge for one of these, or resign yourself to having two disc players in your home entertainment system for a while longer.

Other Software

Of the other CD-R software I tried, only one other package really needs to be mentioned here. Nero Burning ROM, despite the silly name, is a serious contender when it comes to CD-R burning, and perhaps even friendlier to use than Easy CD Creator. Nero is available as a downloadable demo from its publisher, Ahead Software Gmbh (www.ahead.de). Unlocking the full features requires a US$49 registration.

You create discs in roughly the same way as Easy CD Creator, by dragging and dropping files. Nero makes it easier to set up the disc properties, however, offering them all in a single tabbed dialog.

In extensive testing, Nero was both faster and slightly less reliable than the ultraconservative Easy CD Creator. The latter has a disconcerting habit of copying all the files before burning them to CD-R. However, this helps ensure that they stream off your hard drive smoothly. Nero omits this annoyingly time-consuming step, but this seems to lead to a much higher chance of burning a dud disc.

Nonetheless, depending on how well it works on your particular hardware, Nero is very definitely worth a look. Assuming the product continues to improve, it could be a serious challenger to Easy CD Creator.

How CD-Rs fail

You only get one chance with a CD-R, so bad recordings are a major concern. If you get a data error when you try to read the disc, you can't just reformat and try again, as with a floppy disk; you have to chuck the disc in the trash and try again. Do this too often and it can start to get expensive.

The leading cause of botched CD-R recordings is *buffer underrun*. Data is recorded to the CD-R in a continuous stream. The drive includes a memory buffer that acts as a temporary reservoir of data; if this reservoir runs dry at any point, the drive is going to be at a loss as to what to record, and is likely to make an error.

The way to avoid buffer underrun is to make sure that your music data is ready and waiting, easily accessible, and that nothing else within the computer is likely to hamper it as it goes on its way. In practical terms, this means two things:

1. Put your data on a fast disc. Any hard drive should do, but if you record from a CD or Zip disc directly to a CD-R, you're running a much higher risk. It's worth defragmenting your drive at regular intervals, using a product such as Norton Utilities 2000.

2. Don't do anything else on your computer while the recording is in progress. Shut down all your software, with particular

care to close behind-the-scenes utility software that may be active all the time.

Good examples of software that may be running all the time, but hidden, would include antivirus software or indexing software (such as the annoying indexing program installed by Microsoft Office). Tracking these down can take some skill, but you'll find a few hints in the box: Closing Down Excess Software.

This stuff may never interfere with a burn, but it won't hurt to ditch it. I found that these types of utilities almost inevitably do more harm than good, especially antivirus software, which most users probably only need to run once a day or once a week.

As computers get faster and CD-R burners more efficient, this will be less of an issue. For example, recent CD-R drives incorporate increasing amounts of buffer memory. With 2 to 4 MB of data held in reserve within the drive itself, the laser is much less likely to run short at any time as it writes to the disc.

Closing Down Excess Software

If you haven't tried to explore the innards of Windows, you may not be aware how many little pieces of software load themselves up without telling you. The following is a very cursory overview of the only reliable method of eradicating them.

1. Look in the Tray area (the little indentation) at one end of the Windows taskbar for tiny program icons. Left- or right-clicking on of these usually gives you the option of shutting down the program they relate to.
2. Press Ctrl-Alt-Del. This will display a listing of all programs that are currently loaded and running. "Mystery programs" can be shut down using the End Task option. Use this with caution; save all your files first, and then

keep an eye out to see if anything essential stops working, or if Windows crashes. (Explorer and Systray are two programs you *shouldn't* shut down. There may be others on your system. Shutting down the wrong one may crash your computer, but is very unlikely to do damage to your stored data.)

3. Click on Start, go to the Programs menu, and look in the StartUp sub-menu. There should be nothing in there. If you find a bunch of things listed, you can temporarily move them to another branch of the Start menu and again, see if anything vital stops working next time you reboot.

4. After checking the StartUp sub-menu and/or pressing Ctrl-Alt-Del, you can try to eliminate programs that insist on running by simply uninstalling them. Most applications have an Uninstall option in their own Start sub-menu. You can also use the Add-Remove Programs applet from the Windows Control Panel.

5. If you're willing and able to dig into the guts of your computer, use the System Configuration Utility msconfig.exe that comes with Windows 98. You can run it by selecting the Run command from the Start menu, then typing in msconfig and pressing OK. Selecting the Startup tab from the main window shows a list of what's set to run automatically when Windows starts up. You can try unchecking any or all of these items. If something fails when you reboot, you can re-enable the program by running msconfig.exe again and putting back the appropriate check mark.

Turning off everything you see in the System Configuration Utility window isn't likely to harm your system, but it may make some important services stop working. You can usually tell what each item in the list refers to by looking at the full program path at the right. You shouldn't uncheck ScanRegistry, TaskMonitor, or SystemTray; these are all located in the Windows folder, and are in fact standard Windows components.

Warning: this book can't teach you how to be a Windows wizard. If you're not comfortable messing with this stuff, you should probably leave it alone. If do you find that you are burning bad CD-R discs, get a knowledgeable friend to have a look.

Another thing to do is make sure your computer is actually running properly to start with. Obviously, this is desirable for more than just recording music, but music is currently one of the more demanding applications, and it's likely to stress your computer to its limits.

Here's a checklist:

- Make sure you've got all the most recent *driver* software for all your hardware devices. You'll find drivers on the hardware manufacturer's Web site. Check once as soon as you install a new piece of hardware; chances are, the driver has been revised since the hardware left the factory. Bookmark each updates page and check back again every month or so. Very important: Make sure you have the latest Adaptec ASPI driver, which is used by virtually all CD-R drivers. You can get a utility called aspichk.exe from the Adaptec Web site, to check the version number of the ASPI driver on your system.

Driver. A small piece of software that's responsible for communication between a piece of hardware, such as a printer, scanner, or disk drive, and the computer's operating system. The beauty of drivers is that they allow everything to be standardized. For example, any CD-recording software should be able to talk to any CD-R drive, provided you've got the appropriate driver installed.

- Remove "dead drivers" from Windows. This is a tricky process (see "Removing Dead Drivers from Windows"), but can make a dramatic difference to the stability of your system.
- Run diagnostic software, such as the Norton Utilities 2000, on a regular basis. Let it clean out some of the deadwood from your Windows Registry.

Registry. A pair of database files, stored in your C:\Windows folder, that contain all the information that defines your specific Windows set-up, including what hardware and software are installed. Damage to the Registry is the most prevalent cause of disastrous system crashes in Windows. Back up your Registry files about once a week.

Removing Dead Drivers from Windows

Windows 95/98 does a reasonable job of housekeeping itself, but the failures accumulate, like cobwebs in the corners. Eventually, the built-up problems can choke the system to the point that it becomes unstable and crash-prone. You may experience mysterious failures that you attribute to evil plotting in Redmond, WA, or bad karma, or fluctuating electrical power in your house.

In fact, you can clear up a lot of these problems by the following simple procedure. It can seem scary, but there's nothing in it that the average user can't handle. (Of course, there's *always* a possibility of things going wrong! But this procedure is one of the safer ones you can try.)

1. Select Shut Down from the Start Menu, and then Restart.
2. Just before the screen says Starting Windows, press the F8 key. Choose Safe Mode from the menu. (The timing of when to press F8 is tricky, and may take a time or two before you get it right.)
3. Right-click on My Computer and select Properties. Then click the Device Manager tab at the top of the dialog.
4. Double-click on each of the headings to expand it. Look down the list of devices for exact duplicates.
5. When you find a duplicated entry, delete *both* copies and restart the system. When the Windows desktop appears, you should see a message something like "new hardware detected." Windows should now reinstall a single copy of the device you deleted.
6. Repeat as many times as necessary until there are no more duplicates in the Device Manager list.

You can delete all the duplicated entries in a single run, but Windows has been known to get confused when trying to reinstall multiple devices at one time. The above procedure is tedious but relatively safe. It can have an absolutely miraculous effect on your computer's reliability. As before, however, remember: if you have doubts about your ability to get through this, ask a more knowledgeable friend.

Another good way of manufacturing trouble for yourself is to use the cheapest media, in the cheapest CD-R drive, at the highest recording speed. This may not produce discs immediately identifiable as coasters, but it can have nasty consequences down the road. The reason is that, while CD-ROM and CD-R discs are recorded digitally, we live in an analog world, and digital data is only as good as its weakest bit.

Even factory-made CD-ROM discs are never truly flawless, but CD-R discs are worse. I've seen cheap discs come out of the box with scratches or even cracks in them. Brand names are your only guide, and even then, watch for the specific product name. Some manufacturers have lower-quality brands, which may be little better than no-name products.

One thing *not* to watch for, however, is disc colour. Although the colour of the recording medium has a lot of mystique surrounding it, all experts seem to agree that the type of dye used is really unimportant, as long as the standard of quality control is good. You'll see light and dark blue discs, light and dark green, and gold. These colours are produced by the interaction between the colour of dye embedded in the plastic and the colour of the metallic recording layer. As long as the manufacturer went to the right amount of trouble, any colour you get is fine.

Tracking Your Collection

As your stack of music CDs grows—both in compressed data or standard audio format—you'll wonder how to keep track of individual items. All CD-Rs look pretty much alike. But which one had that live concert from June 1995? Somebody has just posted a rare recording on Usenet—but didn't you already download it six months ago?

There are several types of software than can help:

- **Renaming and tagging.** Give your music files descriptive, logical names, and use their internal ID3 tags to describe them.
- **Cataloguing.** Create and maintain a database that tells you what you've got, and where.
- **Labelling.** Create sticky labels and card inserts for your CDs and plastic jewel-case boxes.

The most important thing with all data management, not just music, is to *be consistent*. Always follow the same pattern for naming your files and folders, always create CD-Rs and labels with roughly the same layout. This will make it a lot easier to track your collection, in this new world of music, where everything doesn't arrive prelabelled and elegantly packaged.

Labeling Your Files

MP3 files are labelled in two ways: a conventional file name, and an internal text *tag*. The former is visible to all computer software; the latter shows up in an increasing number of MP3-aware applications.

Tag. When speaking of MP3, this refers to a small block of text that's included within the file. ID3 is the name of the current specification, which allows you inclusion of such information as the name of the performer, name of the track, name of the album it came from, the year of the recording, and the musical genre, chosen from a long list of standard designations.

The simplest way to name your files is in Windows Explorer. Select a file and press F2, or left-click a second time (slowly), then type the name. Easy enough, just be sure to pick a consistent pattern for your names. For example, *don't* name one bunch of files "Symphony 5—Beethoven," and then name another "Beethoven—Symphony 7." This will ultimately make for much more difficult file management. Cataloguing utilities, for example, are better at finding files when you have a rough idea what the file name looks like.

If you find you're downloading a lot of music, a batch-renaming utility can be invaluable. The best of the bunch is THE Rename, by Hervé Thouzard (www.multimania.com/hervet/index.shtml). This little freeware gem lets you rename folders full of files according to various powerful specifications.

For example, you can instantly remove spaces, or just inadvertent double spaces. You can capitalize all the words in each name. You can add text to the start or end of each name, or add counters, numbering your files from, say, 001 to 999. You can even search and replace parts of the names, as you might in a word processor. And,

THE Rename includes a complete Undo, so you can always revert the entire batch of files to their previous names.

In months of demanding use, I've yet to find anything that THE Rename *can't* do. If you're willing to delve into its little mini-scripting language, you can create your own complex rename commands, extracting specific chunks of the original name and recombining them with new text, counters, or whatever you like.

There are other naming utilities available on the Internet, but THE Rename seems both the most powerful and the simplest to use. It's a good tool to have around, just for everyday file management.

As of version 1.7, released early in 2000, THE Rename was just starting to take notice of MP3 tags. For now, you'll need another utility to deal with these effectively.

If you want to see an example of an MP3 tag, play a track in WinAmp and press Alt+3 or right-click and select View File Info. You'll see that there are fields that can contain the track Title, the Artist it was performed by, the Album it was released on, the Year, and the Genre (chosen from a long list of possibilities).

You can actually type in new ID3 tag information right in the WinAmp File Info dialog. However, renaming even a dozen files this way would be tedious in the extreme. A better bet is to use a separate tagger. These are still not as well evolved as they might be, but about the best I've run across is ID3 Master, a freeware utility by programmer MicheliN (id3master.mute.cz). ID3 Master cooks the process down to three steps, represented by tabs at the top of the window. Step 1: Select the MP3 files to process. Step 2: Set up the exact naming operation, which can include entering specific text in one field for all files (such as the performer name), using parts of the file name to fill in fields, or pulling tag entries from a previously prepared text file. Step 3: Execute your changes.

Although it's not 100 percent bug free, ID3 Master is very functional and complete, and worth the time it takes to learn all its features and peculiarities. Hopefully its author will continue to evolve this nice little program.

Labeling Your Discs

The most obvious difference between a CD-R you make yourself and one you buy from a retailer is that the latter includes a colourful insert card or booklet in the front of the plastic jewel case the disc is stored in.

It turns out that this difference is far from trivial. Once you've burned your first dozen discs or so, you're going to find that they can be very difficult to tell apart. What you need is a quick, easy way of printing descriptive labels. You'll want to make up the occasional artistic masterpiece too, for favourite discs, or gift-giving, or just to impress your friends. But you can't be spending an hour labelling every disc you burn; there has to be a more efficient solution.

In fact, there are quite a few CD labelling products out there but, amazingly, none of them actually handle this seemingly trivial task as well as they ought to.

Good label-printing software should have several features:

- Obviously, it should be able to create a label layout. Actually, it should create three separate layouts: one for a round sticky label that goes on the CD itself; another for the booklet that fits in the front of the jewel case; and a third for the insert card that fits inside the back of the case (underneath the piece that actually holds the CD). It should store these in one file, but offer to print them one at a time.
- It should be able to read a list of tracks from an audio CD, and a list of files and folders from a data CD, and automatically incorporate it in the layout. Audio CDs should be checked both against Escient's CDDB Internet database and your own CD list, compiled by whatever CD-player software you use.
- Finally, it should let you customize the layout, adding your own graphic embellishments or modifying the text to suit your own filing system. This implies some reasonable text formatting, such as bulleted lists, italics, and columns or tables.

Should you place sticky labels on your CD-R discs? Expert opinion is evenly divided. A label protects the delicate data layer on top of the disc, but can put the disc off-balance if it's even slightly off-center. My own suggestion is not to bother with most discs—just mark them with a soft felt-tip pen. You can make labels for a few "presentation" discs, but the cost of the blank labels adds a lot to the total expense. One thing's for sure: if you do put a sticky label on a CD-R, never, *never* try to peel it off, even if the label claims to be peelable. The data layer is very easily damaged, and once it's nicked you can kiss your data goodbye.

There are currently four main choices in CD labelling software. Amazingly, none of them fulfills all of these simple conditions:

1. **SureThing CD Labeler.** A US$39.95 program from MicroVision Development Inc. (www.surething.com), SureThing is probably the best stand-alone product. It has a slick feel to it, and lets you create booklets, inserts, and CD labels. You can format text with considerable control, positioning to top or bottom, inserting tabs to line up columns, and even adding various decorative bullets to set off points in a list.

   Graphic placement is quite powerful. You can manually set the scale, retain object proportions or not, as desired, and even set one colour to be transparent, allowing your page background to show through.

   Unfortunately, SureThing can't automatically center an image on the layout, and won't automatically read and insert a disc directory listing. That's a significant inconvenience, especially with full CD-R discs that hold a *lot* of files and really need cataloguing, but ultimately you can always type in the folder or track names yourself.

   SureThing is a fun product to use and a very good choice for making highly decorative labels. However,

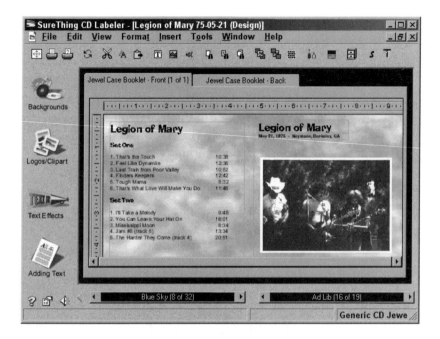

Figure 5.7 Creating a jewel case booklet in SureThing CD Labeler

it's somewhat inefficient for labelling data discs in bulk quantities.

Instead of tediously copying file names by hand into a jewel-case layout, use a little free utility called FileGrab, published by PC Magazine, and available at hotfiles.zdnet.com. When you select and drag files from a Windows Explorer window to the FileGrab window, only the names are actually copied. In the FileGrab window, you can then select and copy the names to the Windows clipboard. They are then available to be pasted wherever you're editing text, usually via the standard Windows shortcut Ctrl+V.

2. cdrLabel. A US$15 shareware program by Earle F. Philhower III (www.ziplabel.com), cdrLabel is almost the exact opposite of SureThing—it will suit those who don't want to mess with fancy formatting, but would like to quickly produce a clear, comprehensive listing of a disc's contents.

Where most other labellers just can't seem to read your discs, cdrLabel not only reads file and folder listings, it automatically lays them out in up to seven columns. However, you don't get a lot of other formatting options, and lists are printed with unsightly ruling lines between lines of text, pretty much destroying any chance of artistic layout. Also, while cdrLabel will read track numbers and times (very important!) from an audio CD, it doesn't query CDDB or your local CD Player database, so you'll have to type in track names manually.

cdrLabel does have some basic graphic options. You can easily place a background image, for example, and add title text.

Overall, cdrLabel is a powerful, efficient product, the best choice for pumping out labels in a hurry.

For printing jewel-case inserts and booklets, plain paper works very well. However, a good flat-bed paper cutter is an excellent investment, making it easy to get nice clean cuts around the edges of the printed area. Of course, when it comes to round, sticky disc labels, you'll just have to shell out for custom label blanks.

3. Easy CD Creator. With version 4, Adaptec moved the formerly integrated label-printing features of Easy CD Creator into a separate program, albeit still included as part of the US$99 package. Jewel Case Creator looks slick but is cursed with some infuriating omissions.

Problems include the inability to import a graphic without stretching it out of shape; inability to read a list of tracks from a CD without jumbling it into a single mass of text; and lack of text-format controls, such as tabs and bullets (for lists). Also, for reasons unknown, the program reliably crashes if you try to print to a Hewlett-Packard LaserJet III.

Despite these annoyances, Jewel Case Creator is capable of producing attractive labels, if you're willing to fiddle a bit. You can customize the background pattern and add your own graphics. Printing options are flexible, allowing you to create just the pieces you require—disc label, booklet, or insert.

Adaptec has promised a major update to the Easy CD Creator package, and we can only hope that it will bring out the full potential of this promising but as yet incomplete utility.

4. Neato MediaFACE. This product is available as a free download from NEATO LLC (www.neato.com), and included with Neato labelling kits. It's a nice-looking program, but hits you right off with the hideous necessity of choosing a template file from a list made up entirely of baffling entries like USAUDJ_B.NTT and USZIPJ_B.NTT. You'll have to check the Readme file to pick the one you need.

Even then, templates provides only a blank rectangle of the appropriate dimensions, leaving everything else up to you. You can place graphics and resize them while maintaining their correct proportions, but you can't specify a size. You can supposedly include folder and audio CD contents, but in practice these features don't work.

One nice feature is the inclusion of a CD Envelope template (USCDENV.NTT). This makes a sleeve that will hold a single CD very compactly; just fold the tabs and paste. Neato's Web page also lets you download prepared label templates for a number of common programs, including CorelDraw, Adobe Illustrator, Adobe PhotoShop, and Microsoft Word. These are nicely set up, although they still lack detail.

Overall, MediaFACE isn't *totally* terrible at what it does, but it needs to evolve quite a bit to become truly convenient.

As you can see, there's currently no one program that will solve all labelling problems. Of course, as a last resort, you can work with a generic piece of layout software. Good choices include CorelDraw and Corel PhotoPaint, Adobe Illustrator and PhotoShop, and Jasc Paint Shop Pro. Take a bit of time at the start to create a template with the correct dimensions—or download the templates available on the Neato Web site and embellish to suit yourself.

Lastly, you may wonder what kind of printer works best for labelling. In fact, the best bet is a modestly priced inkjet.

I ran various types of label forms through both an Epson Stylus Color 660 and a Lexmark Z51. Both gave excellent results, with no jams or smearing on special label stock, and with very crisp print quality even on standard bond photocopy paper. The Lexmark is more solid physically and more friendly to use, and includes a USB connection, which can be very handy if you have more than one printer to hook up (or a Creative Nomad player hogging your parallel port!). The Epson handles wider paper and goes up to higher resolution, giving it an edge on photographic reproduction.

More important, both printers offer a reasonably straight-through paper path, which means less trouble with stiff, multilayer stock such as labels. And neither unit sells for more than a few hundred dollars, which is certainly important to your budget. If you decide to spend more money, you'll probably be paying mainly for faster throughput. Where you will want to watch price is on consumables, chiefly ink. Plan your printouts carefully and double-check print previews to avoid wasting money on flawed prints.

Laser printers should also work, but in this case they're at a disadvantage, offering only black print, and typically using a more tortuous paper path through their internal rollers. The cost of each printed page is lower, but if that starts to matter, you're burning way too many discs!

Finding Your Discs

No matter how nicely you name your files and label your discs, it's still difficult to keep track of them after a while. A perennial problem is checking whether you've already downloaded something. You don't want to browse your entire shelf of CD-R discs every time you're not sure!

The best solution is a disc-cataloging utility. The best I've found is WhereIsIt, a US$30 shareware program by Robert Galle (www. whereisit-soft.com).

WhereIsIt resembles Windows Explorer. It shows a tree view at the left and a file list at the right. However, the tree view shows not folders, as in Explorer, but Catalogs that you create. Once a disc is added to a Catalog, you can use WhereIsIt to browse its contents, even when the disc isn't physically present.

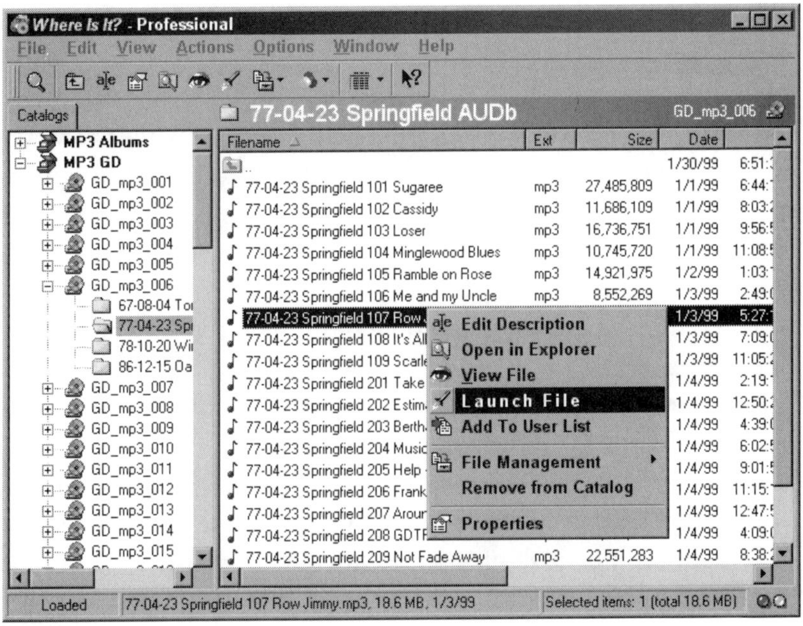

Figure 5.8 Tracking your music collection in WhereIsIt

You can't open the files, of course, without supplying the disc they're stored on. But you *can* check their name, file size, creation date, and other information. In the case of MP3 files, WhereIsIt will even show you the bitrate, sample rate (typically 44.1 kHz), and duration of the track in minutes and seconds.

Most important, WhereIsIt will let you search all your Catalog files for files matching any of these criteria. This makes it a snap to check all the tracks by a certain performer, for example.

When you've burned a CD-R, you select the catalogue you want to add it to, then press Ctrl+A and select the drive letter of your CD-R or CD-ROM drive from a series of buttons. WhereIsIt takes a minute or two to read all the information it needs. You can catalogue other types of disks too, and your hard drive as well.

With increasing amounts of data to keep track of, it's going to be difficult to survive without something like WhereIsIt. Used regularly, it can save you a lot of confusion and frustration.

Conclusion

With that, we come to the end of the line. If you've worked through the material in the last five chapters, you should know just about everything you need to understand digital music, to find it online, and to play it on your PC, on digital players or on a conventional CD player.

You'll have a basic understanding of music recording, both from analog sources such as LPs and by copying digital recordings from audio CDs. And you will have at least tasted some of the endless possibilities of editing your own digital recordings.

Finally, in this chapter, we've looked at the very practical matter of physically storing and cataloging your growing music collection.

The next, and final, chapter is different from the others—not hands-on, but concerned with more philosophical matters—like staying out of jail. We'll look at the current state of legal knowledge regarding music online, and speculate a bit about the future: what's going to happen next in this remarkable field.

6

Commercializing It

In previous chapters we've seen how to deal with digitized music. This chapter deals with several remaining questions, including the legality of this processing and posting music, and the efforts to create an ordered economic structure from the current amateur-driven anarchy. Topics include:

Legalities
- What's legal and what isn't
- The problems of piracy and counterfeiting

Possible Solutions
- Blank-media levies: who pays, and for what?
- Using technology to make online music secure

The Future
- Alternative views on intellectual property
- The economic potential of online music

You and Your Rights

WHEN YOU START USING your PC as a music-editing and recording studio, it is only reasonable to give some thought to copyrights. Most of us would like to stay on the right side of the law, not just for fear of being caught and punished, but simply for our own peace of mind. What's more, nobody who loves music enough to copy it is going to want to rip off the creators of that music—again, not just because of a selfish fear that the sources might dry up, but also because we feel that it's *wrong* to steal.

Unfortunately, the debate over piracy is characterized by inflammatory rhetoric and vague assumptions, with very little hard fact.

What's Legal

Copyright law is a mysterious area of knowledge, even compared to other areas of law. At least one basic question, however, has apparently been answered: that is, whether consumers have a right to make copies, for their own use, of recorded material they have purchased. The good news is that Part VIII of the Canadian Copyright Act, which came into force in March 1998, specifically legalized the practice of "private copying," defined as "the copying of sound recordings of musical works onto audio recording media for the private use of the person who makes the copy." (The bad news, dealt with later in this chapter, is that the same amendment authorized a cash levy on blank recording media.)

The U.S. Situation

Our Canadian approach to copyright is strongly influenced by moves south of the border, but does not parallel them exactly.

The whole issue of home taping originally came to a head in 1981 due to a United States court decision regarding the Sony Betamax VCR. The Home Recording Rights Coalition (HRRC) was formed to spearhead the fight to allow the fledgling home-VCR industry to exist at all, after a decision by the U.S. Court of Appeals for the Ninth Circuit threatened to wipe it out. Although VCRs obviously are sold today, the legal fight in the U.S. has not ended in a clear victory for either side.

"I think avoiding establishing any precedent has been the name of the game for both sides," remarks Bob Schwartz, a lawyer with McDermott, Will and Emery in Washington, D.C., and adviser to the HRRC, in Washington, D.C. "Manufacturers did not want to be embroiled in litigation that would result in an uncertain court decision." The result, in the music world at least, was a sort of détente—a mutual agreement that the recording industry would not make an issue of personal-use "time-shift" taping, and take action only regarding "copies of copies"—in other words, distribution of taped material beyond the original taper. The U.S. Audio Home Recording Act (AHRA) of 1992 further stipulated that a 3 percent levy would be paid on the net price of blank tapes by importers or manufacturers, and a further 2 percent would be paid by manufacturers of recorders. Some of these revenues get distributed to creators' organizations, but the larger share goes to music publishers.

It's interesting that in its ruling in favour of Sony, the U.S. Supreme Court noted that home "time-shift" taping did not reduce the market for the original work—in this case, TV shows or movies—and merely extended the users' ability to enjoy programs as they were originally intended to by the broadcaster. These tests may be useful to bear in mind as we move forward with audio and Internet copying. (In fact, a similar observation was made by the Ninth Circuit Panel when it recently held that the Diamond Rio portable MP3 player is a legal device.)

The Emedia Professional Web site has a superb summary of the U.S. situation, written by Robert A. Starrett in 1998, at www.emediapro.com/EM1998/starrett2.html.

In Canada, the chief group representing the music industry is the Canadian Recording Industry Association (CRIA). The CRIA Web site (www.cria.ca) offers a lot of useful information on the whole topic of copyright infringement, neatly summarizing the industry point of view. Particularly interesting are the site's official definitions of the terms *piracy*, *bootlegging* and *counterfeiting*.

> **Piracy.** The CRIA Web site states that "Piracy is the general term that refers to the unauthorized and therefore unlawful reproduction or copying of sound recordings and distribution of unlawfully made copies of sound recordings on a commercial scale."

The definition of piracy is largely a useful one, except for the unexpected reference to "commercial" distribution. Most consumers would probably assume the term "piracy" includes (or perhaps is limited to) private, non-commercial copying. Elsewhere, the CRIA site states simply that "Piracy is the unauthorized duplication of existing legitimate sound recordings," which seems more useful, but then goes on to speak of "pirated products," obviously assuming these are being offered for sale.

> **Bootlegging.** According to the CRIA Web site, this is "the unauthorized recording of either an artist's live concert (usually known as an "underground" recording) or of a live performance broadcast on radio or television."

The CRIA definition of bootlegging seems intuitively correct, as does the flat assertion that such recording is an infringement. Unfortunately, it is not always clear when live recordings are "unauthorized." As noted earlier, many bands today actively encourage concert taping. In some cases, the performers may be at odds with their own record label over this practice, so the recordings may be officially "unauthorized" even though openly sanctioned by the musicians themselves.

> **Counterfeiting.** According to CRIA, "Counterfeiting is the unauthorized duplication not only of the sound

recording but also of the graphics, including original artwork, logo, trademark and packaging of legitimate recordings." This is the equivalent of cheap knock-offs of designer jeans: a facsimile of the original product, produced in volume and intended for sale.

The least controversial or contradictory of the three terms is counterfeiting, which most of us probably assume to mean exactly what CRIA states. This, at least, is a practice that almost no one would rise to defend. With profit as a motive, counterfeiters are clearly just opportunistic profiteers. On the other hand, they're also the easiest target of enforcement, since their activities would necessarily be structured like any other business, with accounting, warehousing and distribution all concentrated in specific locations.

The legalities of copyright infringement are particularly slippery in that they're governed by civil law, where rulings can often seem arbitrary. (Recall that a civil court found O.J. Simpson financially liable for an act that a criminal court unequivocally said he was "not guilty" of.) If you make a copy of a copyrighted recording, it's not up to the police to come knocking on your door. Instead, tracking you down and extracting financial satisfaction is the responsibility of the copyright holder.

Copyright holders, no matter how huge and affluent they may be, do have limited means, and many calls upon their attention. That's one reason that infringement proceedings tend to focus on the most egregious offenders—people who are actively distributing huge quantities of material. Such cases are likely to be easier to win, and they bring larger, or at least less insignificant, rewards.

This last point is important. If you're found to have infringed a copyright, you don't go to jail. You're simply liable for damages. In the case of intellectual property, those damages can be difficult to measure.

"When you copy someone else's work without their permission, you take a calculated risk," warns David Jones, computer science professor at McMaster University in Hamilton, Ontario, and president of Electronic Frontier Canada. However, he adds that a lawsuit can only recover damages. "It's all about money," he notes. "It makes no economic sense to spend tens of thousands of dollars to silence a seventeen-year-old kid who isn't costing you any money. . . ." In fact, the complaint in the Betamax VCR case initially included a retailer and a consumer as defendants, but they were dropped owing to a strong PR backlash.

> **Intellectual Property.** Creative works that are owned, just like physical property, and with all the same ramifications as far as theft, trespassing, sale, rental and so on. In a wider sense, "intellectual property" is also the philosophy that suggests such works *can* be owned in this way, a concept that probably dates back no further than the early 1600s, when the first patent law was enacted.

In October, 1999, the Canadian Copyright Board handed down a landmark decision, intended to set the framework for translating copyright law to the Internet. Based on a surprisingly canny analysis of how the Internet actually works, the decision makes several very important points that will help shape the debate over intellectual property online.

Very loosely and non-legally, the key points are:

1. Internet transmissions are "communications" in the same sense as radio or TV broadcasting, regardless of how you scramble or delay the data. This is a key point, as it establishes that the same standards of copyright can be applied to digitized versions of copyrighted works as to versions transmitted by more traditional media. In particular, it had apparently been argued that compression and decompression meant that something other that a musical work was being transmitted. The decision says the intermediate steps don't matter, as long as the end result is "reconstitution on the end user's hardware of all that is required to view, play or store the work." This may seem obvious, but it lays vital groundwork.

2. Merely having a copyrighted work on a server does not constitute infringing communication of that work. The infringement happens only when someone downloads and uses the material, whether that occurs immediately or much later.

3. In particular, Internet Service Providers and other Internet intermediaries are *not* liable for copyrighted material posted using their facilities. The person who originally posted the material *is* liable, even if it isn't downloaded immediately.

4. Creating "passive links" to copyrighted works does not constitute infringement. However, "embedded hyperlinks" that activate themselves without intervention from the user *do*.

5. For the purpose of copyright, "communications" occur at the site of the *server* from which the work is transmitted. This is crucial; for infringement to be actionable in Canada, the server must be in Canada. Similarly, material activated by a hyperlink is communicated from the server that's being linked *to*. Amazingly, this suggests that Canadians can post infringing material with impunity, as long as they use a server located outside our borders. Needless to say, the point is likely to be disputed.

6. In general (subject to interpretation that I won't attempt to unscramble), "public" communications are any that reach more than one individual. Thus you could probably e-mail a music file to one friend, but not to three at once. Postings to Usenet are specifically identified as being "public."

What all this means, basically, is that Law has come to the Electronic Frontier. The Internet is no longer a no man's land or technological haven for copyright infringement. The legal machinery is in place and ready to grind offenders up in its gears. But as stated earlier, what use will be made of this machinery is entirely up to the copyright holders.

How Big is the Problem?

In most public debate on MP3 and music online, there's an implicit assumption that "piracy is rampant" on the Internet. But is this true? If so, to what extent?

It's certainly true that you can find considerable amounts of copyright music floating around on the Net. But exactly *how* much? The International Federation of the Phonographic Industry (IFPI) Web site reports that "at any one time there are in excess of one million infringing files in MP3 format available over the Internet, but the problem is evolving and is still growing rapidly." IFPI does admit that "it is difficult to measure the number of infringing tracks downloaded each year." (If the music is just sitting on a server, it's not doing much damage.) However, IFPI cites a Forrester Research report stating that at the beginning of 1999 there were more than 3 million infringing MP3 files being downloaded every day.

These are remarkable numbers—so remarkable that they're difficult to take entirely at face value. If these gargantuan estimates are correct, one may ask why there hasn't been a more massive impact on industry revenues, which in fact seem to be very stable (as we will see later in this chapter).

David Jones advises skepticism. "Any number they could give you is unverifiable," he cautions. As for financial damage, he adds: "Even if there were X-number of pirated copies out there, it is not clear how much they hurt the industry."

On the Canadian scene, the CRIA Web site is reasonably clear regarding commercial sales of unlicensed recordings, but vague on the subject of individual and Internet-based copying. CRIA states: "In 1997, the total retail value of all legitimate sound recording sales [in Canada] exceeded $1.3 billion CDN. Based on industry statistics and international comparisons CRIA estimates that sales of pirated sound recordings drains an additional $30 million CDN." However, the last figure relates not so much to individual "piracy" as to large-scale counterfeiting (mostly offshore imports) of commercial recordings for retail sale.

A further page on the CRIA site discusses "Internet piracy" but offers no concrete numbers, beyond stating that "unauthorized use of sound recordings on the Internet is a growing problem which has implications worldwide. Hundreds of thousands of unauthorized copies of sound recordings are available on music files that utilize a compression process known as MP3, which allows down loading and hence further unauthorized copying."

Elsewhere on the site are overall industry market statistics compiled by CRIA. These show total Canadian revenues for 1999 at about three-quarters of a billion dollars, almost exactly the same as in 1998. As you might expect, cassette sales are waning, down by just over 30 percent in both dollar and unit terms. But CD sales, more than ten times larger, were up over 1998 by 1 percent in units, 2 percent in dollars.

These figures do seem to depict a stagnant business. But how much growth should one expect in what must surely be a mature and well-saturated market? With everybody already buying about as much music as they can afford, growth in units might be expected to parallel population growth, and growth in dollars to parallel inflation rates. More rapid growth *could* take place by stealing revenue from other forms of entertainment, but with music up against such booming products as DVD movies or electronic games, this seems unlikely.

Flat numbers might explain the industry's emphasis on combatting piracy, as there may simply be few other avenues open to it for significantly increasing its revenues. At the same time, there's little indication that the business is being decimated by the onset of MP3. If anything, revenues seem to have been on a gently improving trend throughout 1999, exactly the period when MP3 began to rear its ugly head.

Of course, none of this proves that Internet piracy isn't a big problem, nor provides any guarantee that it won't rapidly become a big problem. The music industry is quite right to fear that we're now just seeing the thin end of the wedge. There's no doubt that, as more people acquire fast Internet connections, passing digital recordings will become easier, and could become commonplace.

And yet, it's tempting to suspect that there's some sort of equilibrium involved. *If* piracy caused legitimate CD sales to plummet, there'd be no new releases, and nobody would have anything to pirate. Long before such a catastrophic point, it seems likely that things would equalize in some way. For example, CD pricing might be forced down. If CDs sold for $10—which may well be possible, with reduced promotions and Internet-based distribution—then nobody would bother to pirate them.

What Should CDs Cost?

Most of us have lengthy CD wish lists, indicating that we simply can't afford to buy all the music we'd like to hear. But is it reasonable to hope for prices to come down, even with Internet technology helping to shave distribution costs?

As with many such questions, the answers are vague and unsatisfying. Retailers claim that they pay $13 to $15 per disc, wholesale, and actually lose money on top-ten albums, loss-leaders that may sell for as little as $12 or $13. Musicians typically get much less than $1 per disc sold. Manufacturing the CD, case, and booklet accounts for another $1 to $2. The remaining $10 includes costs such as shipping, promotion, and miscellaneous overheads. This includes the cost of *uncertainty*; only about one album in ten makes money, and it has to bear the cost of the remaining nine.

There's no doubt that some of these costs could be greatly reduced, but it's very difficult to say by how much. Selling via the Internet will allow shipping costs to be greatly reduced or eliminated entirely in the case of downloadable purchases. Promotion *could* be reduced, perhaps, but as long as heavily advertised acts continue to make the most money, it's not going to happen.

The music industry, meanwhile, tends to look through the other end of the telescope, justifying pricing based not on costs, but on the more nebulous concept of *value*. "CDs give you endless pleasure and almost never wear out," runs the argument. "Surely $20 isn't too high a price to pay?"

Our expectations as far as recording quality also tend to stay ahead of the available technology, especially if the music industry plays its cards right in collaborating with the consumer electronics industry. Currently there are two higher-quality CD standards ready to roll out. If the industry can ever agree on one of them, by the time everyone can easily download all those old Beatles albums off the Net, they *could* be champing at the bit to get new improved commercial versions instead—versions that would again be much too big to move electronically, and possibly copy-protected as well.

The Music Industry

The music industry actually has a schizoid approach to music online, attempting to reconcile two conflicting desires:

1. To hold the technology back and control it.
2. To promote the technology and profit from it.

The recording industry is positively eager to use the Internet as a way of reaching consumers, but worries that consumers will use the Net as a way of bypassing its own efforts and devaluing its intellectual property holdings.

To some extent, the industry's fears are self-fulfilling. Philosophical turmoil prevents viable products from reaching the market. Consumers, in the absence of clear choices from the industry, evolve their own solutions—like adopting MP3 as a de facto standard, after several digital recording technologies were allowed to die for lack of industry support.

In fact, consumers have shown a canny resistance to crippled or half-hearted product initiatives. Both Digital Compact Cassette (DCC) and Digital Audio Tape (DAT) lacked the industry commitment to succeed, and DAT in particular came weighted down with copy-management technology that put off the very audiophiles who would otherwise have been early adopters. A more recent case is that of *Divx*, a version of the DVD video disc that required submission-of-payment information by modem every time the disc was played. Divx failed miserably, mainly owing to lack of buy-in (outright hostility, actually) from technologically hip consumers.

> **Divx.** A short-lived variant on the DVD video disc, literally developed by lawyers (a Los Angeles legal firm). Divx discs played digital-quality movies just like DVD discs, but sold for a much lower price, comparable to that of renting a movie. The catch was that they would play for only 48 hours, after which they would play only after connecting to a central sales center and incurring a charge against the customer's account. Divx discs required special Divx players, that worked exactly like DVD players, but were equipped with a modem to allow for the billing process.

The tumultuous evolution of music online is being driven by an explosive mingling of two very different markets: personal computers and consumer electronics. The latter is driven by single-purpose, self-limiting devices. A CD player just plays CDs, nothing else. A cassette deck plays and records, but gives little control over the process. A personal computer, on the other hand, offers total control over all data. Once it's on a PC, text, music, or video is controlled by the user, who can edit it, compress, transmit and duplicate it, almost without restriction. Some operations are easier than others, but the point is that they are possible; both the tools (software and peripherals) and the expertise are within the reach of any individual.

Rough Justice

In response to cries from the music industry, the Canadian government's Judgment of Solomon has been to legalize home recording and simultaneously introduce a system of monetary "levies" payable to the industry. In December 1999, the copyright board set up a tariff covering "private copying levies" on blank audio-recording media, to be paid by manufacturers and importers, as follows:

- 60.8¢ on CD-R Audio, CD-RW Audio and MiniDisc
- 5.2¢ on CD-R and CD-RW
- 23.3¢ on audio cassette tapes of 40 minutes or longer

The recording industry's position is that some proportion of the total blank media sold is used to pirate their copyrighted music, so they should have a right to collect compensation. The Copyright Board estimated that the levy would collect $9 million in the course of 2000.

Flaws in the logic aren't slow to suggest themselves. For one thing, note the enormous distinction between "CD-R Audio" and straight "CD-R" discs. These are virtually identical media, although the "Audio" discs are electronically marked for use in home audio recorders. These expensive and limited devices have been understandably slow to catch on, and the Copyright Board decision isn't likely to improve their market position.

The levy on data CD-R discs, while seemingly very low, is the most controversial. Even though the per-disc amount is small, it will be paid not just by any (presumed) music copiers, but also by all legitimate data processing users, including software publishers, large commercial institutions, and small businesses. These organizations have zero interest in music, let alone the illicit copying thereof, yet will in aggregate pay the largest part of the levy.

In fact, using recording media sales projections for 2000 included in the copyright board's own Fact Sheet (www.cb-cda.gc.ca/fact-e.html), the expected amounts can easily be estimated, and are shown in Table 6-1.

Table 6-1

Media	Units (M)	Total Levy ($M)
Cassette	18.5	$4.3
MiniDisc, CD-R/RW Audio	0.5	$0.3
CD-R	88	$4.6

"I think that the levy on blank media will have a negative impact on digital creators," predicts David Jones. "It also hurts Canadian creators relative to American ones." Nor is Jones a big fan of the levy as a whole. "It's a technique this lobby group has used to get a government handout," is his analysis.

Levy revenues will be distributed by the specially formed Canadian Private Copying Collective (CPCC), acting as a front end for several major artists' and publishers' organizations, including the Society of Composers, Authors and Music Publishers of Canada (SOCAN).

It's worth noting that in the CPCC's press release the day the blank-media levy was announced, Brian Chater, special consultant for the organization, stated: "CPCC members are quite disappointed with the rates the [copyright] board has approved, because in our view they represent much less than the value of the music being copied. The rights owners will continue to argue in the future that authors, music publishers, performers and producers should receive the same amount, whether a private copy of their work is being made or a pre-recorded copy is being purchased."

From the consumer point of view, there are two ways to look at these levies, neither entirely satisfying. On the one hand, the Canadian levy, unlike the one in the U.S., does accompany an official sanction for home recording, so it can be seen as reasonably benign. A few cents per disc is not an unreasonable fee to pay for the extra right to copy the music to suit one's own convenience. The U.S. agreement includes "immunity from suit," rather than a clear statement of rights.

Unfortunately, for reasons that are certain to escape the average consumer, the levy wasn't imposed in this way, as an extra payment attached to the copyrighted material in question. Applying the levy in an entirely separate market—blank media—makes an otherwise reasonable payment seem unreasonable, and exacts payment from innocent and uninterested parties who will derive no benefit from the right to copy music—however freely!

A less tolerant view is that the levy is simply another tax to benefit our supposedly endangered cultural industries, and probably an improperly constituted tax, at that. This is the position taken by Howard Knopf, an Ottawa-based lawyer with the firm of Shapiro,

Cohen who has represented the Independent Canadian Recording Media Coalition (ICRMC), which is attempting to fight the levy decision. Interestingly, Knopf notes that in 1993 a similar levy was thrown out by the Australian government on much this basis.

For now, while no one is exactly happy with the decision, no one party seems unhappier than any other. If the amounts of the levies aren't raised, as the CPCC seems to wish, the situation may well settle down to a status quo. On the other hand, legitimate users of digital media will undoubtedly keep trying to have that portion of the levy reduced or rescinded.

More Acronyms: DRM and SDMI

Media levies are a financial solution to the issue of copyright management. Ultimately, however, the music industry is aiming to create a more ironclad technological solution. Digital Rights Management (DRM) is the blanket term applied to this endeavour. The idea is to prevent the music from "leaking out" at any point from the publisher's server to the consumer's player. Only authorized activities are possible at every stage. Only those who have paid may listen or download; only those who own the music may store it or transfer it to other devices. Nobody can make copies, unless specifically permitted to do so by the copyright holder.

A modest immediate goal is to watermark, or digitally imprint every recording in such a way that it can be tracked back to its origin. For example, when you purchase a track for download, it could be imprinted with your credit card information. If the track is found circulating on the Net, you are immediately identified as the culprit.

Technically, the idea behind watermarks is to embed extra information in the audio signal itself, which users can't hear and which can't be obliterated without seriously degrading the overall sound quality. One problem is that such a watermark will necessarily be characterized as "noise" from a musical point of view, and making it entirely inaudible is tricky. What's more, the value of watermarks when it comes to mass market music could be limited. If you post a CD rip of the Beatles White Album, there's never going to be much doubt that it's an infringement, but your name won't be on it. Unless watermarks are applied simultaneously to all forms of recording, they could act as a disincentive to those media that are marked, for example, inhibiting online sales, in favour of CDs.

The music industry's Manhattan Project of intellectual property protection is the Secure Digital Music Initiative (SDMI). This isn't a single technology, but a forum for discussion, ultimately aimed at producing a set of technical guidelines for securing music. The idea is to create a complete new generation of devices that can play all existing, unsecure music formats—including MP3—in addition to a new wave of secure SDMI-compliant content. The only restriction on these new devices will be that they'll refuse to play illegal copies of SDMI-compliant recordings.

This seems a sensible approach, but there are problems. If the SDMI implementation on new CDs is restricted to watermarking, it really doesn't do much to improve their security. As noted above, it's already pretty clear which music is copyrighted, and by whom. Unless the watermark is specific to the purchaser—something that's possible with online downloads, but more difficult with pre-manufactured CDs—it changes little. On the other hand, if new CDs were issued in some sort of protected format, consumers would have to buy new CD players just to play them—obviously not likely to be a popular idea. So far, it seems that plans for securing the audio CD are limited to watermarking.

On the computer, or on new generations of portable devices, the problem is more easily handled in software. For example, security can be upgraded over time. The device's SDMI software receives a "signal" when new technology is available, and insists that the user get the upgrade (probably by Internet download) in order to play any content that uses the new protection.

Seemingly aware of possible concerns, SDMI documents repeatedly made statements such as: "The SDMI specification is focused on enabling consumers to get convenient access to the music that they enjoy." In fact, it's plain that SDMI provides no *direct* benefit to consumers, but rather prevents access to some music that they might well "enjoy" (regardless of whether it happens to infringe on somebody's copyrights). There is an *indirect* benefit, however, and it could be very substantial. Once a secure music format is established, the music industry would be in a position to innovate in the area of delivery and licensing. Things such as single-play, or one-week-play licences would be possible. Consumers would benefit by having more purchase options to choose from.

On the other hand, as the failure of Divx reminds us, consumers have a remarkable dislike for purchasing "rights" that fall short of what is at least perceived as complete ownership. Licensing is a concept that appeals to lawyers, but ownership is a deeply ingrained concept that we learn in earliest childhood.

There's also a looming question as to whether the sort of protection envisioned by SDMI is even theoretically possible. In a world where teenage hackers seem more industrious, more clever, and vastly more numerous than the legitimate software developers, how long can any such system remain secure?

Finally, there's the problem of market viability. If a significant proportion of independent musicians opt to take their chances and distribute their music in unsecure formats, consumers could be faced with a choice between purchasing virtually unrestricted ownership, on the one hand, or much more obviously limited rights on the other. The music industry could put massive promotional resources behind their approach, but they'd risk losing a significant chunk of business.

SDMI raises particularly difficult issues for the desktop PC. Will we see a new generation of CD-R burners that refuse to copy "protected" recordings, or CD-ROM drives that refuse to play recordings that they deem to be illegal? Do we envision a Windows operating system that plays an active part in overseeing all our activities and makes decisions about whether to allow them, eventually maybe even deciding when to report us to some outside authority? Probably not. There are just too many people who are accustomed to tinkering with the hardware and software.

Ultimately, somewhere deep within any secure program, there's a little bit of code that asks "Is it okay to play this?" Any hacker worth his or her salt should be able to ensure that the answer always comes up "Yes!" Once created, such hacked software would tend to speedily proliferate on the Internet. Of course, the industry lives in hope that a technical solution can be found, but experience to date clearly suggests otherwise.

Even if all efforts at technological protection are doomed to failure, should we be surprised? This has already proved true of print. Nobody has yet found a way of creating a "secure" photocopier. (Perhaps you're reading a photocopy or an electronic scan of this book!) Creative content eventually must be seen and heard by the legitimate user. If the only way that people could enjoy the Mona Lisa was to take it home with them overnight, eventually one of them would figure out how to photograph it, and go into business selling prints.

In the long run, it's very difficult to predict the role that will be played by SDMI. The viability of the scheme will partly depend on how transparent it becomes. For example, the RCA Lyra portable music player encrypts every file you want to play. This is a major annoyance; if all portable players try to do the same, it could easily spell the end of this entire class of devices. And no matter how carefully it's mapped out, the SDMI architecture could create even more serious impediments to the future evolution of new types of devices.

Ironically, given what we can learn from history, such "heroic" measures may turn out to be quite unnecessary. The movie industry fought tooth and nail against the introduction of the VCR, and lost, only to win vast profits in the long run. Today, it's viable to make movies based solely on their potential tape-rental revenues. Although there clearly is lots of home-taping, piracy, and mass counterfeiting of VHS movies, the movie business as a whole has prospered.

You might argue that it could be doing even better, but consider that people only have so much to spend. As David Jones points out, the music industry itself gives away huge numbers of demo tracks. They must feel that this helps their bottom line, rather than undermining it.

What Happens Next?

Everything we've looked at so far relates to the current situation, as of early 2000. But this is just the beginning of the beginning. Music online is only the first harbinger of a sweeping revolution. It's often been referred to as *convergence*—the coming-together of consumer electronics, communications, computing, and entertainment.

Giving the phenomenon a name, however, hardly captures the scope of the transformation that's about to take place. If you think things have been moving fast in the world of computing, "you ain't heard nothing yet." (You may recall that this phrase once signalled another sort of convergence.)

In the last part of this last chapter, I'd like to pass on a few speculations that came up in the course of writing this book.

Intellectual Property Revisited

Since we've been looking at copyrights and legalities, let's start by considering the future of intellectual property as a whole. If you thought that the moves being made to protect digital music seemed almost insanely byzantine, you're not alone. A strong movement has arisen that seeks to abolish the concept of "intellectual property" entirely, or at least modify it almost beyond recognition.

It's an undeniable fact that what we call "intellectual property" is very different from any other kind of property. Unlike physical property, which pretty much stays where you put it, intellectual property *tends* to 'leak out.' Once you are exposed to an idea, or image, or piece of music, it becomes an inseparable part of you. What's more, unlike physical property, which can't be in two places at once, intellectual property is infinitely divisible. It behaves like the loaves and the fishes of the Bible—you can go on handing it out indefinitely and never run short.

This realization puts the "theft" of intellectual property in a very different light. The chief harm done by theft of physical property is that the rightful owner is deprived of it. If I take your bicycle, not only do I have it, but also *you don't*. However, if I "steal" your music, I've got it *and* you've still got it. I may be depriving you of your expected revenues, of course, so the whole problem becomes rather tangled.

Another complication is the issue of fair use—what is sometimes referred to as "the right of the commons" when it comes to physical real estate. Some things simply cry out to be community property. If there's only one road from A to B, I probably don't have the right to build a wall across it, even if that wall lies entirely on "my" land. If I buy the Mona Lisa, I almost certainly don't have the right to use it for kindling in my fireplace.

> **Fair Use.** A legal principle that allows use of copyrighted material without the owner's permission, for certain specific purposes—most notably, as part of criticism or debate of the material. For example, a magazine article might quote material from this book for the purpose of reviewing it. The term "fair use" is often used loosely (and rather incorrectly) to mean any acceptable use of copyrighted material.

There's a specific parallel when it comes to music. While nobody begrudges the music industry a fair profit, too much of the music that's being "protected" is unavailable in any legal way. If a copyright holder hasn't reissued a particular album in 20 years, most fans would feel not only morally justified but extremely fortunate to acquire a "bootleg" copy.

The Internet holds the promise of cheaper music publishing, so perhaps this problem will evaporate as copyright holders find that it increasingly makes good economic sense to put their "back catalogues" back in circulation. However, when copyright law is inevitably re-examined, it would be nice if some sort of use-it-or-lose-it provision was included, specifying that some rights will lapse if the material isn't made commercially available over a reasonable interval.

Advocates of what's been sardonically dubbed *copyleft* take the more drastic view that our entire concept of intellectual property is seriously warped, and particularly ill adapted to the new digital reality. They point out that the very idea of intellectual property dates back only a few hundred years, and that most great works of art and literature were created entirely without copyright or other protection. (You can find lots of fascinating material on this subject by starting from Carter Butts' Page Against Intellectual Property, www.andrew.cmu.edu/~ctb/anarchy/intelprop.html.) or from the FSF page at www.fsf.org.

> **Copyleft.** A term originating with programmer Richard Stallman and the Free Software Foundation (FSF), describing the approach it promotes for distribution of software. Copyleft grants the right to use, copy or change a piece of software, and mandates that when the user passes the software along, they must grant the same rights to others. The copyleft license is a necessary protection; without it, software simply released for free (into the public domain) can be made into proprietary software and ultimately sold for profit.

They also assert that intellectual property law has always been mainly for the protection of large enterprises, not individual creators. The music industry did a lot to bolster this view late in 1999, by sneaking through an astounding bit of legislation in the U.S. that allows them to treat all sound recordings as "works for hire"—meaning that, by default, the record company, rather than the artist, owns the work. Although big-name musicians can certainly negotiate a better deal, this kind of "intellectual property" seems to run along remarkably feudal lines, with the music industry becoming a sort of entrenched landed gentry.

Whether one buys into all these debates or not, it's clear that alternative approaches to intellectual property can work. An excellent example is the rising jamband phenomenon. While most commercial bands timidly offer a few sample tracks for download, many bands or musicians give away huge volumes of music, yet manage to prosper financially.

Jambands place an emphasis on live performance. The originators of the approach, the prototypical hippie-era phenomenon, the Grateful Dead, played up to 200 concerts a year and became one of the top-grossing acts in the world while never having an album or single in the Top Ten. Other bands eventually picked up on this success and cloned the methodology. For example, when the band Phish played three days straight for New Year's 2000, complete recordings were available on the Internet within just a few days—with the band's blessing. Arlo Guthrie's Web site provides a bulletin-board area where fans can trade and track down favourite live recordings.

These performers do retain copyright control, but relax restrictions on some kinds of copying. They've found that this lets them forge a tight bond with their fans and eliminate many potential problems. For example, ticket scalping is almost totally eradicated by selling direct by mail or via the Internet. Piracy is actively resisted by fans who value the ability to trade live recordings, willingly pay for any and all commercial recordings as quickly as they are released, and diligently police Internet sites to help prevent unauthorized copying.

This certainly isn't the only possible model, but the fact that it works so well by any traditional business measure suggests a number of things: first, that in future, live performance may be reemphasized, since it retains its uniqueness and can never become a commodity; second, that the music business can materially benefit by fostering a cooperative, rather than antagonistic, relationship with music fans; and third, that the future of music may not lie in the Top Ten. Although the big international superstars get all the attention, the music business as a whole is increasingly about "niche" performers, whose fans make up for their smaller numbers by their stronger loyalty.

There's certainly too much ferment going on within the music world to fully describe here. The key point is that there's more than one way to make money on music. As music begins to flow over the Internet, we'll undoubtedly see entirely new business models emerging.

The Business of Music

So what's going to happen to the music industry as we know it today? Unquestionably, it will adapt and prosper. Old ways of doing things are already being reexamined, and new ways evolved.

As Andrea Fleming, vice president of corporate marketing with Liquid Audio points out, the big record companies still have a major role to play in promoting and marketing performers. Also, she adds,

"They're kind of a bank." The label serves as a source of venture capital, funding the development of new talent. They can give musicians cash in advance—not just eating money, but vital development money. These functions won't go away just because music is marketed electronically.

Today all record companies are exploiting the World Wide Web as a promotional vehicle. They operate sites on behalf of their individual performers, run online promotions, and distribute music samples. As the listening public spends more time online, the music industry places more of its own emphasis there as well.

Online retailing will continue to evolve, although perhaps not at breakneck speed. The IFPI Web site cites "independent forecasts" predicting that online album sales will be more than US$5 billion in 2005. However, the bulk of this business is expected to consist of CDs ordered over the Internet and delivered physically.

Although it's theoretically possible to distribute all music—in fact, virtually all entertainment—over the Internet, in practice it just doesn't seem likely that we humans will abandon the age-old thrill of the marketplace—the chance to rub shoulders with the rest of our community, to fondle products before we make them our own, to haggle with the shopkeepers.

What's been happening in book retailing may serve as a foretaste of what's to come in music retailing. While the online outlet Amazon.com has become one of the most influential (if not the most profitable) booksellers in the world, real-world retailers such as Indigo, Chapters, and Barnes & Noble have been doing equally well in their bricks-and-mortar outlets. But the bookstore has changed as a result. Today it offers a better selection, a more pleasant shopping environment, and various value-added services—such as coffee and doughnuts. (Amazon.com may be convenient, but you still have to get your own coffee!)

Music retailers are sure to consider this model as online album sales continue to grow. Retail outlets may play more live music, have wider aisles and more listening stations. Rather than trying to hustle consumers in and hustle them out, they will probably become "shopping destinations" where you'll want to linger a while.

One key difference between music and books is that music can be "printed" on-demand, while you wait. For example, Liquid Audio is testing music-delivery kiosks on a limited basis in Korea, using CD-burning systems based on standard Windows NT PCs. A central server in the store contains all the tracks in the current Liquid Audio library, and discs take 15 or 20 minutes to deliver. That's just enough time to sit and have a coffee, and maybe make a few impulse buys.

Overall, the music-buying experience will likely undergo a dramatic improvement. Those who want selection, especially of obscure and hard-to-find items, will certainly get it online. Those who prefer to shop in person for more mainstream material will find the retail environment becoming increasingly pleasant. Entertainment retailing will actually become more entertaining.

The Best is Yet to Come!

One final point: while this book has dealt with the specific issue of music online, music is only a harbinger of bigger things to come, a microcosm that lets us preview the changes that will soon overtake every facet of the entertainment media.

For example, video online is starting to happen even as this book is going to print. All the confusion and upheaval we're seeing with music is being replicated on an even larger scale. Enthusiasts were uploading and downloading complete copies of *Star Wars: The Phantom Menace* on the Internet even before the movie appeared on videotape. Streaming technologies such as Real and Windows Media were incorporating increasing amounts of video in their content. Renegade video broadcasters were in court, and legitimate video-on-demand projects were forging rapidly ahead.

But music is going to be remembered as where this revolution started, and MP3 as the technological spark that touched off the conflagration.

It's a very exciting time. So warm up your hard drives and your modems, music fans—the best is yet to come.

Appendix

A Music Online Internet Directory

Software Sources

ACD Systems
www.acdsystems.com
ACDSee
Graphics viewer
Excellent tool for viewing, retouching, and printing graphic images. Very handy for preparing CD cover art. Demo version for download, full registration costs C$75.

Adaptec
www.adaptec.com
Easy CD Creator
CD-R recorder
Still the best way of creating data and audio CDs on your PC. Corporate site includes product information, technical support, downloadable updates, and much more. Also operate CD-R Central (www.cdrcentral.com), a friendly information site for users of the software.

Ahead Software gmbh
www.ahead.de/
Nero Burning ROM
CD-R recorder
One of the better CD-R burning programs. Easy to use but with complete control over disc layout. Site includes lots of information on the product, allows purchasing online.

Audiograbber
www.audiograbber.com-us.net/
Audiograbber
CD ripper
Friendly software for extracting CD audio to data files. Site includes good product info, download of limited demo version, and registration to unlock full features. There's also an interesting list of links, compiling the sites that visitors to the Audiograbber site have come from.

BladeEnc
bladeenc.mp3.no/
BladeEnc
MP3 encoder
The best freeware MP3 encoder, available both as a stand alone command-line program and a DLL module that plugs in to many other software products. Site operated by software creator Tord Jansson, includes product FAQs, complete manual, plus some interesting discussions and very good links to other MP3 software.

CDex
www.cdex.n3.net/
CDex
CD ripper
Well-known ripper. Lean and simple site operated by software author Albert Faber, with FAQ and some interesting MP3 software-related links.

CeQuadrat
www.cequadrat.com
WinOnCD
CD-R recorder
Software offers precise control over tracks, extra features for storing images, MP3 files. Site is attractive, makes heavy use of Flash graphics (if appropriate browser plug-in is detected).

Computall Services
www.ncf.carleton.ca/~aa571
CDDA32
CD ripper
Bare-bones presentation, but with lots of product information, FAQs, and technical background documents.

CoolPlayer
coolplayer.8m.com
Cool Player
MP3 player

Slick and tiny player, slick and tiny site. Just a couple of pages plus an extensive message board for users to exchange information.

DARTECH Inc.
www.dartech.com
Dart Pro32
Audio noise-reduction
Powerful but somewhat cumbersome noise-reduction software. Demo version available for download. Small site, but slick and well organized.

Destiny Software Productions Inc.
www.radiodestiny.com
Destiny
Audio player
Vancouver-based company (www.destiny-software.com) promoting its own music format for streaming audio. Destiny Media Player software plays MP3, WAV and MID files, as well as streaming MP3 and audio CDs. Also provides connection to the RadioDestiny Network of streaming stations. Developer tools available for adding Destiny content to Web sites. Site includes directory of active broadcasters, background info.

Direct Logic Systems
www.directlogic.com
CoverPro
CD-cover creator
Software assumes you're starting with a bitmapped image such as a GIF or JPG file. Demo version does 15 printouts, registration costs US$9.95. Site is straightforward, includes screen images.

Exact Audio Copy
www.exactaudiocopy.de
Exact Audio Copy (EAC)
CD ripper

Still the most highly regarded CD ripper, with easy interface, detailed configurability, and excellent error correction. And still free. Site operated by programmer Andre Wiethoff has plain but clear and effective layout. Lots of technical info, good links to even more.

Forte Inc.
www.forteinc.com
Agent
Usenet newsreader
The most powerful and reliable Usenet software to date. Free Agent version is free, missing several features. One-month demo version of full Agent software also available, registration costs US$29. Drab, minimalist site offers product information and downloads, but very little else. Rarely updated.

FreeAmp
www.freeamp.org
MP3 player
Home page for the FreeAmp project, a collaborative effort supporting a completely free MP3 player based on the Open Source model, which allows sharing of the program code. FreeAmp currently runs on Windows 95, 98, and NT, as well as Linux. Also available: the Obsequieum MP3 Jukebox for Linux, which lets many users play music from a single network server. Sponsored by EMusic.com.

Gadget Labs Inc.
www.gadgetlabs.com
WaveZIP
WAV compressor
Lossless compression for WAV audio files. Downloadable demo, US$49.95 registration fee. Site is plain and simple, but includes screen shots and complete product info.

GameSpy Network
www.radiospy.com
RadioSpy
Streaming audio search
Free software provides a single control centre that searches for and connects to SHOUTcast, Windows Media, and RealAudio streaming servers. Registration removes ad banners for US$20. Elaborate site includes streaming links, album reviews, and industry news.

GlobalSCAPE Inc.
www.globalscape.com
CuteFTP
File transfer
One of the leading tools for uploading and downloading files to and from ftp sites on the Internet. Includes MP3 search. Free version for download, registration costs US$39.95.

Golden Hawk Technology
www.goldenhawk.com
CD recorder
Powerful but inscrutable CD-R burning software. Allows total control over data placement, but requires some study to master. Downloadable demo, US$49 registration. Straightforward site includes complete product info and FAQ.

Green Point Software UK Ltd.
www.gpsoftuk.com
CD Box Labeler
CD label creator
Idiosyncratic but very complete and powerful CD-label and jewel-case creator. Free download, US$24.95 registration. Site is simple, with product info and download pages.

Headlight Software
www.getright.com
GetRight
Download manager

Tool for controlling Internet downloads. Resumes interrupted downloads, allows automatic downloading at off-peak times, shuts down computer when download is complete, etc. Free demo version, register for US$20.

High Criteria Inc.
www.highcriteria.com
Total Recorder
Streaming content capture
Allows recording of live audio from sound card, or capturing of streaming content from software that may not otherwise allow saving. Demo version available for download, records only 40 seconds. Registration C$17.95. Toronto-based company.

Innovative Quality Software
www.iqsoft.com
SAWPlus32, SAW32Lite
Audio editor (pro)
Powerful, expensive (US$900) audio editing software. Attractive site, good product info, some good links to other audio-related product sites.

K-Jöfol
kjofol.org
K-Jöfol
Audio player
Clever, free audio player, originally intended mainly to play Yamaha VQF-format files, but now expanded to be comparable to other MP3 players. Simple site, but a few interesting links.

L.A.M.E.
www.sulaco.org/mp3/
LAME
MP3 encoder
Home site of programmers maintaining a free MP3 encoder, based on the ISO sample source code. Interesting links

and info about the drive to create a patent-free audio compression format. (LAME stands for Lame Ain't an MP3 Encoder.)

Liquid Audio Inc.
www.liquidaudio.com
Liquid Player
Audio player
Home site for Liquid Audio song distribution system. Allows free download of Liquid Player software, includes lots of content links for music available in Liquid's streaming format.

Mediascience Inc.
www.sonique.com
Sonique
Audio player
Owned by Lycos, operators of the well-known portal site www.lycos.com, Sonique is a popular, full-featured audio player, with support for plug-ins, skins, etc. Plays MP3, WAV, MOD, and Windows Media WMA content, as well as audio CDs. Spiffy-looking site includes links to music content, downloads of software and plug-ins, etc.

MicroPlanet Inc.
www.microplanet.com
Gravity
Newsreader
An interesting product for browsing Usenet newsgroups. Simple site offers good product info with lots of screen images.

Microsoft Corp.
www.microsoft.com/windows/windows media
Windows Media Player
Audio player
Start page for Microsoft's entire Windows Media initiative. Massive site

includes download of Windows Media Player, plus extensive background material, and links for developers and content providers.

MicroVision Development Inc.
www.mvd.com
SureThing CD Labeler
CD-label creator
One of the best tools for creating CD labels and jewel case inserts. Trial copy available for free download, or register for US$39.95. Lots of product info available on site.

mkwACT
home.att.net/~mkw/mkwact.html
mkwACT
Audio compressor
Plain and simple personal home page operated by programmer Michael K. Weise offers free download of small, useful tool that handles compression and decompression between WAV and MP3 (lossy) or Shorten (lossless) formats. A few interesting personal links, including info on favourite bands.

MO Software
www.neuesvon.de/mo/
CD-Cover, CD-Booklet
CD-label creator
Attractive software for creating CD insert booklets. Site is small and uncomplicated, though split between German and English.

MODPlug Central
www.modplug.com
MODPlug
Home site for the best MOD player, MODPlug, by Olivier Lapicque. Allows free download of the software, includes extensive background resources and links on the entire MOD phenomenon.

Newsletter available. Broadcasts MOD music (in MP3 form) via its own online radio station.

MusicMatch Inc.
www.musicmatch.com
MusicMatch Jukebox
Audio player, compressor, ripper
Home page for full-featured combination player, compressor, ripper, audio manager. Download demo for free, register for US$29.99. Site includes links to music-content sites.

Napster Inc.
www.napster.com
Napster
MP3 exchange
Tiny free program allows users to exchange MP3 files with each other, directly between their own computers. Site is very small, includes basic product info, little else.

NEATO LLC
www.neato.com
MediaFACE
CD-label creator
Slick graphical program for creating CD-case inserts and labels. The software is free, in the expectation that users will buy NEATO stationary packs. Similar kits also available for most other storage media, including cassette tapes, Zip disks, and videotapes. Nicely colour-coordinated site includes attractive product information and purchasing pages, but little else.

Net-Toys
net-toys.8k.com
POWER-POST 2000
Usenet binary uploader
SUCK THE BEST
Usenet newsreader

POWER-POST 2000 is the best program so far for uploading huge binary files, including music files, to Usenet newsgroups. Files dragged into the program window are queued for uploading and automatically split into appropriately sized message parts. SUCK THE BEST is a new newsgroup reader, still in relatively early stages. All software is free. Minimal site operated by software creator Chris Morse, includes links to large Usenet providers, as well as FAQ files for several major newsgroups.

Nico Mak Computing Inc.
www.winzip.com
WinZip
File compressor
The most popular tool for combining and compressing files into a single archive (ZIP file). Indispensable if you're downloading software or other large files. Demo version for download, registration costs US$29.

Notify CD Player
www.artech.se/~mlt/
Notify CD Player
CD player
Clever, tiny, free CD player, loads in Tray area of Windows Taskbar. Pops up to give complete control over CD play. Bare-bones site includes screen images of the software, minimal background info.

Nullsoft Inc.
www.winamp.com
WinAmp
Audio player
The most popular, and still the all-round best Windows audio player. Handles most formats, including MP3, WAV, Windows Media WMA, and even Liquid Audio LQT or Yamaha VQF,

with widely available plug-ins. Free download. Also tunes in to SHOUTcast streaming content. Site is extensive, with lots of product info and downloads of software and accessories, as well as extensive content links.

OPTICOM
www.opticom.de
mp3 Producer
Audio compressor
OPTICOM bills itself as a spinoff of MP3 developer Fraunhofer Institut, and was the first to sell a commercial MP3 encoder. mp3 Producer is still considered one of the fastest and highest-quality compressors available. Site is elegant, with product and technology background, plus links to a few major MP3 audio sites.

Pacific Tech Imaging
www.cosmicwave.com
JewlLinr
CD-label creator
Supplier of perforated stationery for CD, DVD, Zip, Jaz, and cassette insert cards. JewlLinr software available for download.

Padus Inc.
www.padus.inc
DiscJuggler
CD-R recorder
Powerful professional CD-R mastering and duplication software. Clear, attractive site with product info and company background.

Pay & Play Software
www.payplaysoftware.com
Ultimate Label Printer Pro
CD-label creator
Fairly powerful label and jewel-box insert creator. Download shareware demo

or register by credit card. Rather ugly site includes minimal product info, no links.

Poikosoft
www.poikosoft.com
Easky CD-DA Extractor
CD ripper
Quite good at pulling digital audio off CDs. Includes MP3 encoding, and supports third-party MP3 encoders such as Fraunhofer and BladeEnc. Spartan page includes minimal product info and downloads.

Power Technology
www.power-t.com
DFX
Audio playback enhancer
Slick plug-in for WinAmp, RealPlayer, and RealJukebox, adding adjustable ambience effects. Download demo, registration costs US$19.95. Power also offers professional effects plug-ins for use with audio-editing software. Straightforward site layout leads to separate domains for each product category, with complete product info.

Qdesign 2.0
www.qdesign.com
MVP
Audio player
Home page for Vancouver-based audio software developer. Key products include MVP player/encoder for MP3 audio and QuickTime movies, running on both Windows and Macintosh. QDesign is one of very few companies to create not only its own MP3 encoder, but also its own alternative compression scheme. Comprehensive company site includes links to more specific sites, such as www.mvpsite.com for the MVP player itself.

Quinnware.com
www.quinnware.com
Quintessential CD
CD player
One of the most elegant audio CD players for Windows. Spiffy user interface, accepts alternate skins. Download for free, register for US$10. Futuristic-looking site, with good links for add-ons and other sites of interest.

Radiate
www.gozilla.com
Go!Zilla
Download manager
Tool for controlling Internet downloads. Resumes interrupted downloads, allows multiple simultaneous downloads on fast connection. Software is free but runs advertising banners until registered for US$24.95.

RarSoft
www.rarsoft.com
WinRAR
Compression and archiving tool often used on the Internet to pass very large files, especially if they need to be split into smaller pieces. Demo version for download, full registration costs US$35.

RealNetworks Inc.
www.realnetworks.com, www.real.com
RealPlayer
Streaming audio player
RealJukebox
Audio player, encoder
Large company site includes background information on products and services, news, technical information. Complete info and access to developer products such as RealProducer, for creating RealAudio streaming content. Consumer-oriented www.real.com is the place to get

RealPlayer or RealJukebox software, also includes extensive music content links. Attractive layout, lots of information.

S&H Computer Systems
www.newsrover.com
News Rover
Usenet newsreader
A clever Usenet client, but confusing and still rough around the edges. Demo version available for download. Site is drab but functional, with extensive product information and technical help.

SoftSound Ltd.
www.softsound.com
Shorten
Audio compressor
Currently the most popular lossless compression technology on the Internet. Compresses by 30 to 50%, as opposed to 1000% or higher rates offered by lossy technologies such as MP3, but retains perfect fidelity to original sound. Free evaluation software available for download. Very basic site includes product screenshots, company background, and technical info, but little else.

Sonic Foundry Inc.
www.sonicfoundry.com
Sound Forge
Audio editor
Excellent range of professional sound, editing tools, including Sound Forge audio editor and ACID PRO loop editor. Also offers inexpensive consumer editor Sound Forge XP. Large, attractive site includes extensive product info, FAQs, tutorials, and download of demo versions.

Steinberg Soft- and Hardware GmbH
www.steinberg.net,
www.ca.steinberg.net
CubaseVST, WaveLab
Audio Editor
Clean!
Noise-reduction
Offers a complete range of professional audio tools, including CubaseVST and WaveLab audio editors. Also consumer-priced Clean! noise-reduction and Get It On CD recording and CD burning software. Canadian site is under construction, with product information links leading back to the main site, and online purchasing not yet operational. Main company site is elegantly laid out, with lots of product information, updates, and company news.

Stomp Inc.
www.stompinc.com/
CD Stomper Pro
CD-label creator
Good product info. The system uses SureThing labelling software, and the site includes a link to let you purchase this online.

Streambox.com Inc.
www.streambox.com
Streambox Ripper
Audio conversion
Software rips audio CDs and converts RealAudio, MP3, or WAV audio formats to WAV, MP3, or Windows Media WMA files. Free demo version allows ten working sessions. Portal site offers extensive music-content links, search engine, discussion forums, etc.

Syntrillium Software Corp.
www.Syntrillium.com
Cool Edit
Audio editor
Offers widely accepted Cool Edit Pro professional software as well as bargain-priced Cool Edit 2000 consumer version. Demo software available for

download. Somewhat cluttered site includes excellent product information, technical help, FAQs, etc.

THE Rename
www.multimania.com/hervet
THE Rename
File renamer
The best way of renaming large numbers of files. Searches and replaces, inserts counters, adds date information, etc. Simple personal site offers product info and free download. Much of the content is in French.

WhereIsIt
www.whereisit-soft.com
Disk catalogue
Absolutely indispensable cataloguing program, creates a database of all files on local or removable disks. Free demo version available for download, registration to full version US$30.

Xing Technology Corp.
www.xingtech.com
AudioCatalyst
CD ripper
A friendly all-round tool for CD ripping and MP3 compression. Xing is one of few companies to make its own MP3 software compressor. Streamlined, good-looking site offers good product info, demo downloads, and audio news.

Xnews
xnews.3dnews.net
Xnews
Usenet newsreader
Excellent freeware newsreader, offers simple, logical operation, straightforward simultaneous access to multiple servers. Some configuration is difficult, however. One-page site

operated by software creator Luu Tran is plain and basic, offering only minimal product info and downloads of software and documentation.

Yamaha Corp.
www.yamaha-xg.com/english/xg/SoundVQ
SoundVQ
Audio player
Main page for Yamaha's software supporting the TwinVQ (VQF file) audio format. Simple, rarely updated site includes software download and basic FAQ info.

ZipLabel.com
www.ziplabel.com
cdrLabel
CD-label creator
One of the better tools for creating jewel-case inserts. Reads CD directories and prints track and folder names in multi-column format. Free demo available for download, registration costs US$15.

Companies & Organizations

Canadian Independent Record Production Association (CIRPA)
www.cirpa.ca
Home site for Toronto-based trade organization representing independent music production. Lots of excellent background information on the Canadian music business. Music-industry directory sections do not seem to be working, unfortunately.

Canadian Musical Reproduction Rights Agency (CMRRA)
www.cmrra.ca
Non-profit agency that handles licensing of reproduction rights for copyrighted music.

Canadian Private Copying Collective (CPCC)
www.cpcc.ca
The organization that administers collection and distribution of the levy on blank audio-recording media. Good-looking site includes good background on the levy, plus links to other organizations.

Canadian Recording Industry Association (CRIA)
www.cria.ca
Simple but attractive and usable site containing indispensable background on the Canadian music business, including details of anti-piracy programs, listings of gold- and platinum-certified albums, national sales statistics, and quite a bit more.

Copyright Board Canada
www.cb-cda.gc.ca
Official site of the Copyright Board, the regulatory body that administers copyrights in Canada. A plain-vanilla site, but mandatory reading for anyone trying to understand the legalities of online music distribution and piracy.

Fraunhofer-Gesellschaft
http://www.fhg.de/english
Main English-language page for the Fraunhofer organization. Massive, elaborate site includes background on all Fraunhofer research activities.

Home Recording Rights Coalition (HRRC)
www.hrrc.org

Home site of the group created originally to fight for the legality of home videotaping. Now an excellent starting point for learning about the ongoing conflict between copyright and consumers' rights, although very US-centric. Includes a timeline of major copyright decisions and events.

Moving Picture Experts Group (MPEG)
drogo.cselt.stet.it/mpeg/
Information page summarizing the activities of the MPEG working group of the International Organization for Standardization (1S0). Includes massive technical background on MP3 and other audio and video related standards. The MPEG-1 FAQ may be of particular interest, as it provides an excellent overview of MP3 audio technology.

MP3 Licensing (Fraunhofer, Thomson)
www.mp3licensing.com
Information on licensing terms for MP3 (MPEG Layer-3) encoding technology. Under construction, only a placeholder page.

Music Industries Association of Canada (MIAC)
www.miac.net/home.html
Trade association representing Canadian manufacturers, wholesalers, distributors, and retailers of musical instruments and accessories, keyboards, sound-reinforcement products, and published music. Simple site of interest mainly to MIAC members, but includes interesting links to partner organizations.

Secure Digital Music Initiative
www.sdmi.org
Drab but information-packed site,

includes background papers and links explaining the emerging standard for secure (i.e. piracy-proof) electronic music distribution.

Society of Composers, Authors and Music Publishers of Canada (SOCAN)
www.socan.ca
Basic site includes information on licensing, performing rights, and other issues relevant to working musicians.

Songwriters Association of Canada
http://www.songwriters.ca/
Plain site includes who's-who listings, upcoming events, and information bulletins.

Portals and Vendors

All-Music Guide
www.allmusic.com
Database
Absolutely the best place to get background information, discographies and album 'liner notes' on any musician. Search by artist, album, song title, style, or record label. Displays listing of LP/CD releases for each artist. Album info usually includes cover art, historical information, musician and production credits, song titles, and songwriter credits. Also includes an extensive series of background articles on topics such as bootleg recordings, Motown, and Women in Rock.

Canadian Hip Hop Online
www.hiphopca.cihost.com
Portal
Excellent, very comprehensive site for hip-hop lovers. Includes artist lists, photos, club listings, radio, show times, and more.

Canadian Music Online
www.ualberta.ca/~adavies/
Directory
A great site, lists hundreds of Canadian artists, distributors, record labels, magazines, associations, venues, and much more. Privately operated in Edmonton by Aaron Davies.

Canadian Musician
www.canadianmusician.com
Magazine
Web site supporting the eponymous print magazine, published by Norris-Whitney Communications Inc. Obviously aimed at working musicians, also contains masses of information useful to listeners, such as complete set of alphabetized links to Canadian musicians' own Web sites.

Canehdian Music
www.canehdian.com/
Portal
Large, comprehensive site includes Canadian music news, reviews, artist links, extensive links to record labels, concert guide, and more. MP3 and CD purchase links jump to MP3.com and Amazon.com, respectively.

CBC Entertainment
infoculture.cbc.ca/musop.phtml
News
Lively site with particular emphasis on jazz, world music, and opera. A good place to browse if you're *not* as interested in the Top-40 artists. Feature stories typically include audio and video clips (Real). Events calendar allows searching by date, type of performance, or name of artist, tends to include obscure and eclectic events but not mainstream events.

CD Plus.com Inc.
www.cdplus.com
CD e-tailer
One of Canada's earliest online vendors of audio CDs, videotapes and DVDs. Pricing par or slightly below major urban retailers. Album info typically includes cover art, track list, liner notes, artist bio, and sound clips (Windows Media). However, text info is completely unformatted and difficult to read, often filling the entire browser window without a single paragraph division. Selection seems slightly below par, with albums off the beaten track somewhat less likely to be found than on other Canadian CD vendor sites.

Shipping is via Parcel Post and by far the slowest of any Canadian site. CD Plus suggests allowing "1–3 weeks" for delivery, where most others deliver in 1–3 *days*. Shipping costs are not correspondingly lower, starting at $3.50 for 1-2 discs. However, purchases can be picked up at numerous CD Plus locations across Canada. Another interesting feature is the CD Plus Exchange, which claims to be "the largest and most inexpensive source for used compact discs."

CDDB Inc.
www.cddb.com
Directory
The definitive database of commercial audio CDs. Doesn't provide background notes or pretty pictures, but this is the place to go to find track lists, especially for albums you can't track down anywhere else. The CDDB service is used automatically by a lot of music software, to look up track names. Site is nicely designed but quite simple. Includes links for music player software.

Chapters Online Inc.
www.chapters.ca/Music
CD e-tailer
Designed with a comfortable feel comparable to Chapters bookstores, this site offers excellent album information on mainstream titles, including cover art, track listings, detailed notes, and sound samples (Real). Pricing on common titles can be excellent, especially with Chapter 1 Club membership, which provides at least 10% discount on all purchases for a flat fee of $15 annually. As with other sites, pricing on more unusual imports can vary widely, and may compare very unfavourably to the cost of buying from a U.S.-based site.

Despite the bookstore tie-in, selection of music CDs seems excellent, comparable to that on Canadian CD e-tail sites. Default shipping within Canada is via Canada Post Xpresspost, a slightly faster, and higher-priced, option than those offered by other Canadian sites, at $4 per order, plus $1 per item within the order. Shipping is free on orders over $50.

Cheap Thrills
www.cheapthrills.ca
CD e-tailer
Specializing in jazz, avant-garde, experimental, and blues music, but also carrying rock, soul, international, and classical music. Originally Montreal's first used-record store. Prices are about equal to major urban record stores. Listings include little detail. Shipping is $4.50 for first CD, $0.50 for each additional.

Compact Disc Depot
www.chatsubo.com/cddepot/
CD e-tailer
Specializing in the Celtic music of Atlantic Canada, selling new and used CDs, cassettes, and vinyl. Album listings

show price in Canadian and American dollars, but provide no other info. Located in Sydney, Nova Scotia. Orders are shipped first-class air, with insurance prepaid on orders over $100.

EMedia Professional
www.emediapro.com
Magazine
Web site based on print publication aimed at professionals involved in publishing, archiving, and distributing digital content. Lots of news and information about audio CD, CD-R, DVD, and related technologies.

EMusic.com Inc.
www.emusic.com
CD e-tailer
Downloadable music for sale. Lively site features a growing catalogue of unique offerings, at prices notably lower than audio CDs, even after U.S. currency exchange is factored in. Most items can be sampled in either MP3 or Real format, and most "albums" may be purchased by individual tracks.

HMV Canada Inc.
www.hmv.com
CD e-tailer
Striking black, white, and shocking-pink layout enhances complete shopping site. Album info usually includes cover art, track listing, liner notes, artist bio, and sound clips (Real). Selection seems excellent overall, and pricing is roughly on a par with major urban stores, although prices on some obscure imports can be quite attractive.

At $3 for 1–3 items, shipping cost is similar to other Canadian sites, with free shipping offered on orders of four items or more. Carrier is Canada Post Xpedited service. Faster services are available at higher, but still reasonable, cost.

HMV has been active in organizing online promotions and Webcasts from the site.

Indie Canada
www.indiecanada.com
Portal
Slick, commercial page promoting Canadian independent musicians. Includes search, downloadable clips, streaming audio (low-bitrate MP3), concert listings, and CD purchase. Musicians pay $200 to $350 annually to be listed on the site. Operated by Punch Media (www.punchmedia.com).

Internet Underground Music Archive (IUMA)
www.iuma.com
Portal
Nifty-looking site features downloadable tracks by unknown acts. Broadcasts streaming content in Windows Media format.

Jam! Showbiz
www.canoe.com/Jam
Portal
Part of the Canoe portal site, Jam! Showbiz offers music and movie news, reviews, interviews, and feature stories, plus concert listings and an encyclopedia of Canadian pop music.

Juno Beat 2000
www.juno-awards.ca
Portal
Exhaustive background information about the Canadian Juno music awards. Includes artist features and links, news, audio and video clips (in RealAudio and Windows Media format), information about past winners, and more. Also

includes links to the Canadian Academy of Recording Arts and Sciences (CARAS), which handles the event.

Kick in the Head
www.kickinthehead.com
Directory
Unique independent music guide operated by Jeffrey Haas, allows Canadian bands to sign up the site and create their own listings, also includes added listings for major bands. Users can browse by province and territory or search by name. Includes links to music news on other sites.

Launch.com
www.launch.com
Streaming
Excellent streaming-audio site, with unique rating approach that lets you tailor the broadcast to your own musical tastes. Excellent sound quality via Windows Media technology.

Listen.com
listen.com
Downloadable music
Directory of free downloadable music tracks legally available on the Web with permission of the copyright holders, categorized and searchable. Pick a track and your browser is redirected to the actual source site for the download. Includes a beginner's guide to online music.

Mars Subway
www.monkey-boy.com/cmusic/
Directory
Massive alphabetical listing of links to Canadian music artist Web sites. Also includes list of related sites, such as associations, concert venues, and radio stations. Based in Vancouver and operated privately by David Hathaway, with

space provided by The Electric Mail Company (www.electric.net).

MP3.ca: Canada's Online Music Label
www.mp3.ca
Portal
Attempting to become a gathering place for Canadian independent bands, MP3.ca is gradually building up the content to go with its commercial aspirations and its memorable Web address. However, as late as spring 2000, many basic parts of the site, such as links to MP3 player software, were still completely blank, and the concert search returned only a database error message.

The site allows musicians to sign up for free to have a listing and to provide music tracks for download. MP3.ca promises to pay $1,000 to the most-downloaded band every six months. It also promises a 50% royalty on CD sales and paid downloads, although these facilities have yet to be implemented.

The MP3.ca we've seen so far seems largely just a placeholder, existing mostly in order to stake out the priceless address. Still, the site is worth a look to check out the strange mix of artists who have already set up their own pages there.

MP3.com
www.mp3.com
Downloadable music
Offers downloadable and streaming MP3 music in most musical genres, either high- or low-quality. New Beam-It service allows users to play CDs over the Net. Includes excellent links to most of the best music-related software.

Music and Audio Connection
www.musicandaudio.com
Portal
Large collection of music resources,

including links to artists, retailers, companies, associations and educational institutions, events calendar, and more. Open, airy layout, with content covering both U.S. and Canada.

Music by Mail Canada
www.musicbymailcanada.com
Directory
Supreme directory of all mail-order sources for purchasing Canadian music, in or out of Canada, accessible on the Internet or more traditionally by phone or fax. Includes tips on shipping and shopping, extensive links to other Canadian organizations and sites. Patriotic but rather garish red-and-white layout. Privately operated by Rob McIntyre.

New Worlds
www.newworldcds.com/
CD e-tailer
Canadian artists on Canadian labels. Specializing in discontinued out-of-print and hard-to-find titles. Shipping is via Small Packet mail, $2.95 for first disc or $1.95 shipped flat without the jewel case. Based in Grimsby, Ontario.

Official Web site of Canadian Music
www.canmusic.com/
Directory
Massive directory with bags of information on events, awards, venues. Alphabetic lists of musicians and organizations. Ugly layout, but lots of info.

RioPort.com
www.rioport.com
Portal
Offers considerable number of free music tracks for download, as well as RioPort Audio Manager software.

Sam the Record Man
www.samscd.com
CD e-tailer
Big, flashy, interesting shopping location. Album cover art, track lists, and sound clips (Real) for most albums, although detailed reviews are included only for recent or particularly important albums. Prices are generally excellent, often considerably lower than normal retail levels. However, prices on more specialized import albums can be dramatically higher than buying the same albums from U.S. e-tail sites, so comparison shopping is advisable. Shipping is reasonably priced, at $3 for 1–2 items. When last checked, shipping was free on orders over $25; however, this was billed as a limited-time promotion, so be sure to check current terms before ordering. Shipping is via Canada Post Xpresspost, which guarantees delivery to Canadian addresses within two business days.

SHOUTcast
www.shoutcast.com
Streaming
Monumental directory of stations broadcasting in streaming MP3 format. Search by genre or keyword. Station listings show type of content, current and maximum number of listeners and bitrate. Simply click to connect. Elegant black-and-gold layout.

Streaming Media
www.streamingmedia.com
News
Operated by First Conferences Inc. in San Francisco, California, this site seems to have originated as a support for Streaming Media conferences, but has expanded into a worthwhile destination in its own right. Pleasant layout includes

an excellent industry directory, feature articles, news, and more. The site also allows you to subscribe to an e-mail newsletter and an e-mail discussion list. Video clips (both Real and Windows Media formats) show highlights of past Streaming Media conferences.

Ticketmaster Canada Ltd.
www.ticketmaster.ca
Events
Buying tickets online is a big improvement. This site lets you search events by location, dates and performer, then buy tickets instantly. You still have to pick them up at a physical location, but you can tell right away what kind of seats you're getting.

Ultimate Band List
www.ubl.com
Portal
Multifaceted compendium of downloadable music, feature articles, and an incredibly detailed list of bands, with biographies, Web links, tour dates, downloadable content, and CD purchasing (with audio samples).

VQF.com
www.vqf.com
Portal
Comprehensive, privately operated site offering support for Yamaha VQF compressed-audio format. Includes software archive with VQF players, technical information, and comparisons of VQF to MP3, and links to related sites. Attractive layout, lots of good information; definitely the place to start if you're interested in VQF technology.

WinFiles
www.winfiles.cnet.com
Software archive

The best place to search for all Windows shareware and freeware. Displays available products in a very convenient card-file format showing all important information at a glance. Audio players and editors page is at winfiles.cnet.com/apps/98/sound-mpeg.html. Originally a private site operated by Steve Jenkins, now owned by CNET Inc.

World Records Ltd.
www.worldrecords.com/
Portal
Large site operated by independent Vancouver-based record label, includes search engine, lots of links, CD sales. Worldwide electronic booking service for bands.

FAQs & Info

Note: many of the sites listed in this section are maintained by private individuals in their spare time, and hence may change, stagnate, relocate, or vanish entirely. Usually, you can work around invalid addresses by tracing links from other related sites, which will usually lead you either to the desired site's new location, if there is one, or to other sites that offer similar information.

Against Intellectual Property
www.andrew.cmu.edu/~ctb/anarchy/intelprop.html
Law
Excellent single-page collection of links, providing quick access to background on the evolving anti-copyright movement. An excellent starting point for many hours' reading.

Bands that Allow Taping
www.enteract.com/~wagner/btat/
Recording
Unofficial but well-supported list of
bands that allow or even encourage taping and trading of their live performances
by fans. Note that in some cases the
band's desire may be at odds with that of
their own record label, so caution is ad-
vised. Also available at the Resources for
Tape Traders site (see below).

**Canadian Internet Law Resource Page
(CILRP)**
aix1.uottawa.ca/~geist/cilrp1.html
Law
Voluminous information resource
aimed chiefly at legal professionals.
Contains articles, links, and recent
news. Compiled and maintained by
Michael Geist, professor at the Univer-
sity of Ottawa Law School, and
Internet-law columnist for *The Globe
and Mail.*

CD-Info Company Inc.
www.cd-info.com
CD-R
Interesting, though somewhat older,
collection of technical articles, aimed
mainly at the CD duplicating industry.

CD-Recordable FAQ
www.fadden.com/cdrfaq/
CD-R
Maintained by Andy McFadden, this is
the Bible of all information pertaining
to CD-R, including technical
background on the technology, tips on
burning, troubleshooting information,
known issues with specific hardware and
software, and a whole lot more. You can
also download a complete HTML version of the FAQ.

KissThisGuy.com
www.kissthisguy.com
Trivia
Entertaining archive of commonly mis-
heard lyrics, sometimes referred to as
mondegreens. The site's name is an example, a misreading of Jimi Hendrix's
"'Scuse me while I *kiss the sky.*"

MIDI is the Language of Gods
www.borg.com/~jglatt/
MIDI
Excellent beginners' guide to MIDI technology. Includes tutorials, downloadable
software, technical backgrounders, and a
long list of company-links.

**Official FAQ for
alt.binaries.sounds.mp3**
www.mp3-faq.org
Usenet
Absolutely indispensable guide to the
main MP3 newsgroup on Usenet, also
includes answers to virtually all basic
questions concerning recording,
playback and storage of music files, plus
links to many other valuable references.

Resources for Tape Traders
www.resourcesfortapers.com
Recording
Maintained by Jeff Tiedrich, this massive
site either contains or has links to just
about every piece of knowledge required
to make and trade live band recordings.

Canadian & Regional

Canadian Music Centre
www.ffa.ucalgary.ca/cmc/
Scores, parts, and recordings by over
500 Canadian composers. Supports

orchestral, choral, opera, and electro-acoustic works. Includes CD listing, alphabetical list of scores, etc. Part of a network of Music Information Centres in 30 countries.

Cape Breton Music Online
cbmusic.com
Big, comprehensive site offering news, artist listings, and sound clips (Real), plus good resource links for everything to do with traditional Cape Breton music.

Music Alliance Project (MAP)
www.interlog.com/~mapsters/
Association
Ontario-based group provides education, resources, info, and advocacy for the culturally diverse music industry. Events, links, and online registration and feedback.

North by Northeast Music Festival and Conference (NXNE)
www.virtualnoise.com/nxne/
Press releases, marketing information, band registration, and band listings for Toronto-based festival and conference, operated by VirtualNoise Corp.

Nova Scotia Choral Federation
www.chebucto.ns.ca/Culture/NSCF/ns cf-home.html
Plain site provides newsletter, upcoming events, lots of information and resources.

Okanagan Music Online
www.communityinternet.com/music/
Interesting overview of music in the Okanagan area of British Columbia. Lists bands and venues.

Ontario Country Music Association (OCMA)
www.members.tripod.com/~OCMA/ index.html
Events list, links, awards listing, history.

Saskatchewan Original Music Association. (SOMA)
www.freeyellow.com/members2/ somanet/index.html
Specializing in developing and expanding all forms of music in Saskatchewan and beyond. Simple site provides membership, classifieds, and links.

The Jam
www.thejam.com
Specializing in musicians from Vancouver. Site contains music online to hear and buy, reviews and concert listings. Listing of who's playing in local clubs.

Toronto Blues Society
www.torontobluessociety.com
Spiffy black-and-blue site includes news, radio listings, events calendar, links.

Vancouver Recital Society
www.vanrecital.com/main.cfm
Information about recital season, Vancouver Chamber Music Festival. Press releases.

Victoria Jazz Society
www.vicjazz.bc.ca/
Classy site includes events calendar, links to other jazz-related organizations, and Web pages.

Usenet Newsgroups

The following is by no means an exhaustive list of newsgroups pertaining to music, and new groups are constantly being added. For example, binary groups relating specifically to the group The Doors appeared during the writing of this book. Don't forget to check for new groups every week or two.

To find all the content on a particular topic, consider the keywords that groups might include, and use the search function in your Usenet software. For example, "binaries" and "sounds" are good terms for narrowing a search.

On the other hand, beware of groups with similar names. Often, one alternative is preferred over the others, and you'll find that there's little or no activity in some of the groups.

MP3 Music: General

MP3 files are posted to a number of binaries groups in the alt. (alternative) classification. The largest of these is simply the ".mp3" group. This is supported by a number of more specialized groups.

alt.binaries.sounds.mp3
alt.binaries.sounds.misc
alt.binaries.sounds.mp3.beatles
alt.binaries.sounds.mp3.blues
alt.binaries.sounds.mp3.brazilian
alt.binaries.sounds.mp3.chinese
alt.binaries.sounds.mp3.christian
alt.binaries.sounds.mp3.classic-rock
alt.binaries.sounds.mp3.comedy
alt.binaries.sounds.mp3.country
alt.binaries.sounds.mp3.dance
alt.binaries.sounds.mp3.french
alt.binaries.sounds.mp3.heavy-metal
alt.binaries.sounds.mp3.jazz
alt.binaries.sounds.mp3.rap-hiphop
alt.binaries.sounds.mp3.reggae
alt.binaries.sounds.mp3.rock
alt.binaries.sounds.mp3.soundtracks
alt.binaries.sounds.mp3.bootlegs

The following groups don't quite fit the '.mp3' naming convention, possibly be-cause they were originally intended for pictures and other non-musical content.

alt.binaries.gdead
alt.binaries.gdead.reposts
alt.binaries.gdead.highspeed
alt.binaries.gdead.highspeed.reposts
alt.binaries.phish
alt.binaries.sounds.radio.oldtime
alt.binaries.music.the-doors

MID and MOD Music

As with MP3, the main groups for post-ing MID and MOD files are supported by more specialized groups oriented toward particular musical genres.

alt.binaries.sounds.midi
alt.binaries.sounds.mods
alt.binaries.sounds.midi.classical
alt.binaries.sounds.midi.jazz
alt.binaries.sounds.midi.originals
alt.binaries.sounds.midi.rock
alt.binaries.sounds.mods.techno

Discussion

There are many discussion groups that relate to music, of which the following lists are a mere sampling. If you don't see the one you're looking for, search the complete groups list in your Usenet reader using the name of the performer, or just parts of the name.

The groups in the first list are discus-sion groups that relate to specific bina-ries groups, and are distinguished by the ".d" suffix.

alt.binaries.sounds.d
alt.binaries.sounds.mp3.d
alt.binaries.sounds.mp3.requests
alt.binaries.sounds.78rpm-era.d
alt.binaries.gdead.d
alt.binaries.sounds.midi.d
alt.binaries.sounds.mods.d

The next list is a selection of discussion groups relating to specific music genres and artists. There are many more, some of which will be identifiable only to fans. Be sure to search occasionally on your favourite artists' names to see if new groups have appeared.

alt.music
alt.music.alanis.morissette
alt.music.barenaked-ladies
alt.music.beethoven
alt.music.bela-fleck
alt.music.blue-rodeo
alt.music.blues
alt.music.bruce-cockburn
alt.music.canada
alt.music.ct-dummies
alt.music.dance
alt.music.holly-cole
alt.music.lilith-fair
alt.music.lor-mckennitt
alt.music.lyrics
alt.music.midi
alt.music.moxy-fruvous
alt.music.neil-young
alt.music.s-mclachlan
alt.music.soul
alt.music.southern-rock
alt.music.tragically-hip
alt.fan.muchmusic

The final list includes a mere sampling of the many music-related groups in the "rec" (recreational) classification. To see them all, browse down the full list of groups in your Usenet reader to the "rec.music. . . ." series.

rec.arts.music
rec.music.artists.bruce-hornsby
rec.music.artists.emmylou-harris
rec.music.artists.kiss
rec.music.artists.little-feat
rec.music.artists.paul-mccartney
rec.music.artists.springsteen
rec.music.artists.wallflowers

rec.music.barbershop
rec.music.beatles
rec.music.celtic

rec.music.classical
rec.music.collecting.cd
rec.music.collecting.vinyl
rec.music.Dylan
rec.music.folk
rec.music.gdead
rec.music.hip-hop
rec.music.opera
rec.music.phish
rec.music.ragtime
rec.music.reggae
rec.music.theory

rec.music.makers.bagpipe
rec.music.makers.bass
rec.music.makers.chamber-music
rec.music.makers.guitar
rec.music.makers.jazz
rec.music.makers.piano

Technical Advice

Finally, don't overlook Usenet as a tech-support resource. You can often get an answer to a configuration question quicker by posting it to the appropriate Usenet group than by calling the manufacturer's support line. The following list contains some of the groups that pertain to audio and multimedia, most of which are found in the comp. (computing) classification.

comp.multimedia
comp.music.midi
comp.music.misc

comp.windows.misc
comp.windows.setup.win95

comp.sys.ibm.pc.soundcard.misc
comp.sys.ibm.pc.soundcard.music
comp.sys.ibm.pc.soundcard.tech
alt.comp.periphs.soundcard.sblive

Index

AAC, 29-20, 66, 144, 189
Accessories, 112-13,
132-38
ACDSee, 17
ACD Systems, 17
Adaptec Inc., 28, 105, 168,
171, 209, 217, 226, 227
Addresses, 45, 51, 48-49,
76-77, 78
Adobe Acrobat, 53, 55, 90
Adobe Illustrator, 227
Adobe PDF, 37
Adobe PhotoShop, 145, 227
ADSL [defn], 33
Advanced Audio Coding. See
AAC
aEGiS cORP, 127
Agent, 42, 82, 84, 86-87,
88-89, 90, 91, 94-95
Ahead Software Gmbh, 28,
213
Aldridge, Michael, 65, 66
Algorithm [defn], 17
Altec-Lansing, 117
Amazon.com, 59, 253
Ambience, 13
Amplifiers, 100-1, 121
Amplitude, 10, 148
Analog, 8, 9[defn],10
Antivirus software, 215
AOL, 61, 67, 123
Apple, 28,36
Artifact [defn], 194

@PET RP-U100 Receiver,
121
AudioCatalyst, 106, 107
Audiograbber, 192
Audio objects, 30
Audio quality, testing, 193
Aureal Inc., 114
Aureate Media, 46
Australian Whoopi!, 63

Bandwidth [defn], 33
Barnes & Noble, 253
Beam-It, 52, 53
Bell Labs, 32
Binaries, 10, 13, 72[defn]
downloading large, 92-95
groups [Usenet], 72-73
Bit, 10
Bitrate, 18
Blade, 189
BladeEnc, 189-91
Blank-media levy, 242-45
Book retailing, 253
Bootlegging [defn], 234
Bose, 117
Bowie, David, 60
Brandenburg, Karlheinz, 26
Browser, 42
Brujo, 137-38
Buffer, 6
Buffer underrun, 214
Bulletproof ftp, 96
Burn [defn], 205

Cakewalk, 28
Cakewalk Express Gold, 36,
115
Cambridge SoundWorks
Four-Point Surround
System, 117, 120
Canadian Copyright Act, 232
Canadian Copyright Board,
242, 243, 244
Canadian Private Copying
Collective, 244
Canadian Recording Industry
Association (CRIA),
233-34, 238
Carter Butts' Page Against In-
tellectual Property, 250-51
Cassette tapes, recording. See
Home recording
CD[s]:
bitrate, calculating, 19
care of, 212
defn, 9
development of, 9
downloading, 53-56
pricing, and piracy, 240
principle behind, 10
recording, 105-6
ripping, 105-7, 129
sampling rate, 12-13
CDCopy, 192
CDDB Inc., 106
CDnow, 59
CD Plus, 50, 51-52

CD-R [defn], 204-5
CD-R burner, 205-6
CD-R discs, 205-6, 214-15, 219-20
blank, 207, 208
cataloging, 229-30
labeling, 223-28
CD-R hardware, 204-9
cdrLabel, 225-26
CD-Recorder (Dartech), 172
CD-R software, 209-14
CD-ROM:
defn, 10
development of, 9
drives, speed, 207
recording, 105
CD-ROM XA format, 211
CD-RW:
defn, 205
speed, 207
CD Spin Doctor, 170-71
Celeron (PC), 105, 110
Chapters, 253
Circuit switching, 5
Cleaning software, 170-73
Cleaning tools, 174-80
Click removal (tools), 178
Client [defn], 42
Client-server model, 42
Clipping, 102-3, 159-60
Coasters, 207, 208[defn], 212, 219
Codec [defn], 22
Colour, discs, 220
Compact Disc DataBase (CDDB) Disc Recognition Service (DRS), 105-6, 107
Compact Disc Read-Only Memory. See CD-ROM
Compact Disc Recordable. See CD-R
Compact Disc Rewritable. See CD-RW
Compressed audio encorders, 184-204
Compression, 16-17, 144-45
free tools, 25, 28
image, 14-16
lossless, 21, 32-34, 198-200
lossy, 16-17, 21, 144, 192-98
and MP3. See MP3
new technologies, 28-37
software, 184-204
Computers, 9, 110-14, 217-20, 242, 249
Consumer electronics industry, 9, 241, 242, 249

Cool Edit, 96, 153
Cool Edit Pro, 37-38, 151, 153-54, 155, 168, 198
Cool Edit Pro 1.2, 152, 171, 173
Cool Edit 2000, 38, 101, 145-46, 148, 149, 150, 151-52, 154, 155, 156, 157, 159, 161, 162, 163, 167, 168, 177-78, 185
Cool Edit 2000 Audio Cleanup Plug-In, 171, 172
Copying, Internet-based, 233, 236-37, 238-40
Copying levies, 242-45
Copyleft, 190, 250-51
Copyright, 4, 7, 28
American approach to, 232-33, 251
Cdn. approach to, 232-37, 238-39, 242-45
and fair use, 74, 249-50
and home recording, 100, 232-33, 242
legislation. See Copyright Law
and MP3, 25-28, 56, 238, 239
and streaming music, 56
and Usenet, 73-74, 237
(See also Intellectual property; Licensing; Patents)
Copyright—Infringement: actionable, 235-36, 237
extent of problem, 238-41
Copyright Law, 98-99, 232-37, 251
Copyright—Management, solutions. See Blank-media levies; DRM; SDMI
CorelDraw, 155, 227, 228
Corel PhotoPaint, 17, 228
Counterfeiting [defn], 234-35
Creative Labs Mixer, 104
Creative Nomad, 130, 133, 136, 228
Creative Technology Ltd., 36, 114, 115, 117, 120, 132, 156
Credit cards, 47-48
Cult bands, 97
CuteFTP, 42, 96
Cutting/pasting, 164-67

D/A converter, 10
DAB, 32, 38
DAE, 105

Dartech Inc., 169, 171-73
DartPro, 32, 173
DartPro 98, 169, 171-73, 179
DAT, 140, 141, 241
DCC, 25, 140, 141, 241
Deadheads, 73-74, 92, 199
De-clickers, 143
DeClick filter, 173
Decoder [defn], 22
DeHiss filter, 173
DeHum filter, 173
Delivery—Purchases, 50-51
De-noisers, 143
Desktop audio, 4-5, 37-38, 139-42
DFX, 125
Diamond Monster Sound MX300, MX400, 114
Diamond Multimedia, 116, 134
Diamond Rio MP3 player, 233
Digital [defn], 8
Digital Audio Broadcasting. See DAB
Digital Audio Extraction See DAE
Digital Audio Tape. See DAT
Digital Compact Cassette. See DCC
Digital effects, 143
Digital Media, 64
Digital Rights Management. See DRM
Digital samples, 149
Digital signal processor. See DSP
Digital Versatile Disc. See DVD
DIMMs, 112
DirectX Plug-in [defn], 151
Disc-cataloging utility, 229
Discs. See CD(s); CD-R discs
Divx, 241-42, 242[defn], 247
DOC, 17
Dolby AC3, 29, 60
Dolby Laboratories Inc., 194
Download managers, 46, 97
Download protocols. See Transfer protocols
Download(s), 40[defn], 41, 44-45
improving, 45-46
Usenet, 71-99
Drive speeds, CD-R hardware, 207
Drivers, 217-18
DRM, 65-66, 245

DSP, 125, 143[defn]
Dual-inline memory modules. *See* DIMMs
DVD, 38, 119, 239
Easy CD Creator, 105, 170, 171, 208, 209-13, 214, 226-27
Easy CD Creator 4 Deluxe Edition, 209
Easy CD-DA Extractor, 106, 192
E-commerce. *See* E-tailing
Editing sound:
    basics, 145-46
    rules, 144-45
    software, 146, 150-57
    tasks, 157-68
Electronic Frontier Canada, 235
Electronic games, 239
Electronic retailing. *See* E-tailing
Ellison, Bob, 37, 38, 146, 154
E-mail, 6, 7, 41, 45, 48-49, 76-77, 78
Embedded hyperlink, 237
EMI [Music], 59
eMusic.com, 53-55, 127
Encoder(s):
    compressed audio, 184-204
    defn, 21
    free MP3, 189
    and licensing, 26, 28
Encoder-decoder. *See* Codec
Equalizing (EQ), 158, 161-62[defn]
Escient, 223
E-tail, e-tailing, 3-4, 48[defn]
    future of, 253
Exact Audio Copy (EAC), 106-7, 129

Fade, 158, 162-64, 163[defn]
Fair use, 74[defn], 249-50
Fan communities, 4, 97, 199, 252
FAQ [defn], 75
FileGrab, 225
File transfer protocol. *See* ftp
Flame, 77, 78[defn]
Fleming, Andrea, 57, 58, 59, 60, 252-53
Forté Agent. *See* Agent
Forté Inc., 86, 90
Foster, David, 56
Frame [defn], 167

Fraunhofer-Gesellschaft, 25, 26, 27, 28, 31, 66, 67, 184, 185
Free Agent, 90
FreeAmp, 127
Free Software Foundation, 190, 251
Freeware [defn], 28
Frequency, 10
ftp, 41, 71, 96-97, 199

Gabriel, Peter, 136
Gadget Labs LLC, 34, 198
GameSpy Industries Inc., 69
General MIDI, 35-37, 35[defn], 131-32
GetRight, 46
GIF images, 16, 17, 21, 22
Gigabyte [defn] 15
Giganews, 93
Glitch, 7
Glyph Technology, 137-38
GM. *See* General MIDI
GNU [defn], 190
Gopher, 14
Go!Zilla, 46-47, 54, 97
Grady, Rob, 61, 62, 63, 64
Grateful Dead, 73-74, 92, 199, 251
Gravity, 82-83, 91
Grimmett, John, 92
Guillemot Corp., 114, 116
Guthrie, Arlo, 252

Hackers, 247
Hard drives, 111
Harmonic analysis, 169
Hardware MP3 players, 26, 41, 132-37
Headphones, 116, 137
Headlight Software, 46
Hewlett-Packard, 137, 209
Hewlett-Packard LaserJet III, 227
Hiss reduction (tools), 175-76
HMV.com, 50-51
HMV North America, 49
Home recording, 99-100
    CD rippers, 105-7
    and copyright issues, 101, 232-33, 242
    high-quality, achieving, 101-4
    LPs/tapes, 100-1, 146
    setting record levels, 101-4
Home Recording Rights Coalition, 232

Home stereo speakers, 101, 117
Hotmail, 49, 76
HTML, 41 43[defn]

IBM, 113
ICQ, 41
IDE, 206
ID3, 221
ID3 Master, 222
Image compression, 14-16
Independent Cdn. Recording Media Coalition, 245
Indexing software, 215
Indigo, 253
Information sharing (Usenet), 71-72
Integrated Drive Electronics. *See* IDE
Intel Corp., 134
Intellectual property, 25-26
    defn, 236
    future of, 249-52
    online, 236-37
    (*See also* Copyright)
Internal modem card, 112
Intl. Electrotechnical Commission, 23
Intl. Fed. of Phonographic Industry, 238
Intl. Org. for Standardization. *See* ISO
Internet:
    copyright issues, 7, 233, 236-37, 238-40
    handsets, 41-42
    history of, 5
    moving data over. *See* Transfer protocols
    piracy on, 7-8, 234 (*See also* Copyright)
    playing music over, 6-7
    shopping on. *See* E-tailing; World Wide Web—purchases
Internet Direct, 92
Internet Explorer. *See* Windows Explorer
Internet Radio, 40, 56, 199
Internet Service Providers (ISPs), 70, 71, 93
IRC, 41
ISO, 23, 24, 27, 189

Jambands, 97, 251-52
Jansson, Tord, 189
Jasc Paint Shop Pro, 228

Jewel case, 55, 210[defn], 223, 226
Jewel Case Creator, 226-27
Jones, David, 235-36, 238, 244, 248
Jornada 430se, 137
JPG images, 16, 17, 21, 22, 23
Jukeboxes, 128-30, 185-88

Keyboards, 112-13
Kilobyte [defn] 15
K-Jöfol, 127
Klipsch LLG, 117
Klipsch ProMedia v.2-400, 119-20
Knopf, Howard, 244-45

Labelling software, 221-28
Labtec, 117
LAUNCH Media Inc., 66
LEDs, 102-3, 141, 160
Leech, 77, 78[defn]
Lesser General Public License (LGPL), 190
Licensing, patents, 25-27, 247 (See also Copyright)
Linde, Henri, 25, 26, 27, 28, 38
Link, 43-44, 44[defn]
Liquid Audio, 57-61, 135, 201, 252, 254
Liquid Audio Inc., 29, 31, 44, 45, 56, 57, 66, 254
Liquid Player, 45, 57-58
Liquid Server, 58-59
Liquid Track, 29, 57, 60
Liquifier Pro, 59
Little Feat, 59
Logitech, 113, 117
Look Communicatrions Inc., 92
Lossless compression, 21, 32-34, 33[defn], 198-200
Lossy compression, 16-17, 144, 192-98
Lotus Notes, 75
LPs, recording. See Home recording
LucasFilm, 119
Lucent Digital Radio Inc., 32
Lurker [defn], 77
Lyrics, 29

McDermott, Will and Emery, 233
McLachlan, Sarah, 49
MacMaster, Natalie, 49

Macromedia, 28
Maxi Sound series, 114
MDI, 155
MediaScience Inc., 127
Media Technologies initiative, 30
Megabyte [defn], 15
Memory. See RAM
MicheliN, 222
MICRONAS INTERMET-ALL GmbH, 26
MicroPlanet Inc., 91
Microsoft Corp., 25, 28, 30-31, 49, 56, 57, 61, 64-67, 84, 122, 191, 197
Microsoft Internet Explorer. See Windows Explorer
Microsoft Office, 215
Microsoft Research, 66
Microsoft Windows Media. See Windows Media Technologies
Microsoft Word, 227
MicroVision Development Inc., 224
MID files, 35-37, 35[defn]
MIDIland, 117
MIDI Manufacturers Association, 36
MID/MOD players, 131-32
MiniDisc products, 25
Mixing (sound), 164-67
mkwAudio Compression Tool (mkwACT), 190, 200, 203-4
MOD files, 37
Modem transfers, 45-46, 62, 93
MODPlug Player, 37, 131
Monsoon series, 117, 120-21
Moore, Gordon, 134
Moore's Law, 133, 134[defn]
Morissette, Alanis, 59-60
Movies, 24, 92, 119, 248
Moving Picture Experts Group (MPEG), 23
mpegEncoder, 189
MPEG-1, 24
MPEG-1 Layer III. See MP3
MPEG-2, 24
MPEG-4, 25, 29-30
MPEG-7, 24
MPEG-21, 24
MPEG working group, 23, 24
MP3:
    alternatives to, 28-37
    audio compression, 16-17

compared with WMA, 192-98
and copyright, 25-28, 56, 238, 239
defn, 14
and MusicMatch Jukebox 5, 188
image compression, 14-16
labeling files, 221-22
licensing plans, 26-28
lossy vs. lossless compression, 21-22, 32-34
measuring compression, 17-21
origin of, 23-25, 26, 38
and perceptual coding, 21-22
players, 26, 41, 122-27, 132-37
and streaming, 22
uncompressing to WAV, 200-4
MP3.com, 52-53
Multi-document interface. See MDI
Multipart postings, 81-82, 81[defn]
Multisession, 211, 211[defn]
Multitrack editing [defn], 151
Music-delivery kiosks, 34, 254
Music, digital:
    benefits of, 3-4, 9
    copyright issues. See Copyright
    dynamics of, 1-38
Music, digital—Playing:
    accessories, 132-38
    hardware, 110-21
    software, 121-32
Music, digital—Processing:
    cleaning up sound, 168-80
    editing tasks, 157-68
    representing sound, 147-50
    sound editing basics, 145-47
    sound editors, 150-57
    steps, 142-45
Music, digital—Storing:
    CD-R hardware, 204-9
    CD-R software, 209-14
    compressed audio encoders, 184-204
    how CD-Rs fail, 214-20
    tracking collection, 220-30
Music discussion groups, 72-73

Musical Instrument Digital Interface. *See* MIDI
MusicMatch, 28, 128, 187
MusicMatch Jukebox, 105, 106, 107, 128, 129, 130, 187, 188, 191, 192, 203
MusicMatch Jukebox 5, 188
Musicians, and free trading, 73-74, 97, 234, 251-52
My.MP3.com, 52

Nag screens, 90
Naming utilities, 222-23
Napster, 42, 98-99
Neato MediaFace, 227-28
NEC, 25
Nero Burning ROM, 213-14
Netcene, 93
netDrives, 137, 138
Netscape Communicator, 43, 84
Netscape Navigator, 42, 43
Network card, 112
Newbies [defn], 71
New Business and Intellectual Asset Management, 25
Newsgroups. *See* Usenet
Newsreaders, 82-95
News Xpress, 82, 84-85, 86, 91
NewsRover, 82-83, 90-91
Ng, Ken, 84
Ninth Circuit Panel, 232, 233
Nippon Telegraph and Telephone, 32
Noise reduction:, 168-69
  cleaning software, 170-73
  in Cool Edit 2000, 177-78
  in DARTPro 98, 179
  tools, 174-80
  types of filtering, 169-70
Non-destructive editing [defn], 152-53
Normalizing, 158-61, 158[defn]
Norton Utilities, 214, 218
Nullsoft Inc., 28, 67, 123

Old Time Radio group, 74
Open Source philosophy, 127
Outlier detection [defn], 180
Outlook Express, 42, 80, 82, 83-84, 91

PAC, 32
Passive links, 237
Patents, 25-28, 189 (*See also* Copyright)

PCM, 33
PC Magazine, 225
PC speakers, 116-21
Pentium 90, 111
Pentium 11, 105, 110
Pentium 111, 110
Perceptual Audio Coder. *See* PAC
Perceptual coding, 21-22, 26
Philips, 9
Phish, 74, 251-52
Ping rating, 69
Piracy [defn], 234
  See also Copyright
Pixels, 15
Playlist, 4, 123[defn]
Plextor Corp., 208
PlexWriter 8/4/32, 208-9
Packet switching, 5-6
PDF, 37
Players, 26, 41, 121-38, 248
Plug-in [defn], 151
Plugs (inputs/outputs), 114
Poiksoft, 106
Portable Document Format.*See* PDF
Portable music players, 26, 41, 132-37, 248
Postfiltering [defn], 180
Power Technology, 125
Prices, shopping online, 49-50
Pricing, CDs, 240 (*See also* Blank-media levy)
Printers, 228
Privacy, 45, 48-49, 76-77, 86
Private copying, 232-33, 242-43
Promotions, online, 49-50
Protocol [defn], 42 (*See also* Transfer protocols)
Pulse Code Modulation. *See* PCM

Qdesign Corporation, 28
Quick Time (Apple), 36

RadioSpy, 69-70
RAM [Random Access Memory], 111-12
RCA, 25
RCA Lyra, 130, 135, 136, 248
Reader, 42
RealAudio, 44, 186
RealJukebox, 60, 63, 105, 107, 135, 186, 188
RealJukebox Plus, 128, 129, 186-87, 203

RealMedia, 61-64
RealNetworks Inc., 6, 56, 57, 61, 62, 63-64, 128, 156, 254
RealPlayer, 60, 61-62, 125
RealPlayer Plus, 62-63
RealProducer G2 Authoring Kit, 186
RealSystem G2, 156
RealVideo, 56, 62
Recording industry:
  approach to music online, 241-42
  and blank-media levy, 242-45
  future of, 252-54
  and recording quality, 241
  revenues, 238-39, 253
Recording Industry Association of America (RIAA), 52, 98, 134
Record level, 101, 141
Registry [defn], 218
RemarQ, 93
Renaming files. *See* Naming utilities
Rio player, 134
Ripper [defn], 105
RM, 144
Roland (GS), 36
Ross, Sara, 49, 50-51
Royalties, software, 27
Routers, 6

SAMsCD.com, 50
Satellite [defn], 118
Satellite television, 25
Schwartz, Bob, 233
SCI FI.COM, 63
SCSI, 112, 206
SDMI (Secure Digital Music Initiative), 134, 135-36, 246-48
Security, 45, 47-49, 56, 65-66
Server [defn], 42
SGS Microelettronica, 26
S&H Computer Systems, 90
Shapiro, Cohen, 244-45
Shareware [defn], 90
Shell programs [defn], 189
Shinao Kenshi Corp., 208
Shipping. *See* Delivery— Purchases
SHN files, 34, 144, 199
Shorten, 34, 198-99, 200
SHOUTcast, 67-69, 124
SIMMs, 112
Sine wave [defn], 12-13

Single-line memory modules. *See* SIMMs

Skins [defn], 124

Small Computer Systems Interface. *See* SCSI

Smoothing [defn], 180

Society of Composers, Authors & Music Publishers of Canada (SOCAN), 244

SoftSound Ltd., 34, 198

Software bundles, 115

Software, excess, eradicating, 215-17

SoloH, 189

Sonic Foundry Inc., 28, 151, 154-57, 171, 185

Sonigistix, 117, 120-21

Sonique, 127

Sony, 9, 25, 132, 133, 197, 209

Sony Betamax VCR, 232-33, 336

Sound Blaster, 36

Sound Blaster Live! cards, 104, 114, 115, 156

Sound Blaster Live! Platinum, 115-16

Sound cards, 112, 114-16

Sound editors, 150-57

Sound Forge XP 4.5, 147, 148, 155, 156, 157, 166, 168, 171, 185

SoundVQ player, 32

Sound waves, 10, 147, 148-50

Spam, 45, 48[defn], 77, 78, 79-80, 87, 96

Speakers. *See* Home stereo speakers; PC speakers

Spitznagel, Jim, 138

Stallman, Richard, 251

Standards bodies, 23-24

Starrett, R.A., 233

S3 Inc., 114

STMicroelectronics, 26

Streaming, 22, 40-41, 44[defn], 56-70, 124

Streaming listening, 69-70

Sub-woofer, 118[defn], 118-19

Super Audio CD (SACD), 197

Systray, 216

SureThing CD Labeler, 224-25

Syntrillium Software Corporation, 28, 37-38, 146, 151-54, 171

System crashes, 218

Tag [defn], 221

Tape decks, 100, 141, 160, 194

Telnet, 41

Temporary Internet files, 54

That's Easy CD Creator, 168

THE Rename, 221-22

l3enc.exe, 185

Thomson Multimedia, 25, 27, 31, 38, 66, 67, 184, 185

Thomson SA, 25

Thomson Semiconducteurs, 26

Thouzard, Hervé, 221

Threads, 75-76, 76[defn]

3D sound, 117, 119, 120, 121, 143

THX certtification, 119

TIF images, 17, 33

Tiger video-on-demand server, 64

Time-shift taping, 233

Tower Records, 59

Tracking collection, 220-30

Tran, Luu, 85

Transfer protocols, 40-99

Troll, 77, 78[defn], 96

Turntables, 100

Tweeter [defn], 118

Twin VQ, 32, 66

Uncompressing files, 200-4

Underground recording, 234

Uploads, 93-95, 97

U.S. Audio Home Recording Act, 233

USB, 135, 206

U.S. Digital Millennium Copyright Act, 98-99

Usenet, 34, 41, 42, 70-95, 199, 237

Uuencoding, 80-81

Variable bitrate (VBR) encoding, 190

VCR, 232-33, 236, 248

Vortex series (sound cards), 114

VQF files, 32

VU meters, 102-3, 141, 160

Watermark, 60[defn], 245-46

WAV files, 33[defn], 34, 164-67, 200-4

Wave editing, 143

Waveform, visual rep. of, 148-50

WaveZIP, 34, 198-99, 200

Web browser, 41, 42, 43

WherIsIt, 229-30

Wiethoff, Andre, 106

Weise, Michael K., 190

WinAmp, 18, 28, 61, 67, 68, 123-27, 131, 167, 200-3, 222

Windows 98, 42, 43, 64, 85, 96, 103, 126, 151

closing down excess software, steps, 215-17

removing dead drivers, steps, 218-19

Windows Explorer, 5, 42, 43, 65, 83, 96, 122, 129, 216, 221, 225, 229

Windows Media Audio. *See* WMA

Windows Media Encoder, 191-92

Windows Media Player, 64, 66, 67, 122, 131

Windows Media Server, 65

Windows Media Technologies, 61, 64-67, 137, 254 (*See also* WMA)

Windows NT, 64, 65

Windows Sound Recorder, 148

Windows 2000, 64, 65

Windows 2000 Server, 31

WMA, 30-31, 66-67, 144, 189, 192-92, 195, 196, 197-98

Woofer [defn], 118

World Wide Web—Downloading, 41, 43-47, 53-56

World Wide Web—Purchases

alternatives, 52-53

delivery, 50-52

prices, 49-50

and privacy/security, 47-49

xDSL, 33

Xing Technology Corp., 28, 62, 106, 107

XNews, 82, 85, 91, 94

Yahoo!, 49, 59

Yamaha, 32, 36, 66, 116, 117, 121, 209